BUNNY'S LETTERS

Compiled by her daughter
Amanda Bettinson

Mrs Bunny West
Reedlands
Thorpeness
Suffolk
ENGLAND

VIA:

Acknowledgements

This book was compiled for Bunny's Grandchildren

Emily, Oliver, Laura, Cara and Max

and her Great Grandchildren

Teddy, Jemima, Arthur, Kitty and Barney.

My thanks go to family and friends who have helped in the preparations of this book. To Martyn King in Barbados, Michael Turner and my cousin Anthony Fasson for kindly allowing their fathers' letters to be published and to cousins Roderick d'Anyers Willis, Peter Barbor, and the late Tom West for their immense help and support. Also, to John Grayburn for sleuthing a copy of the 1969 edition of The Hornet, and to its publishers DC Thompson for allowing me to reproduce the relevant pages.

Most of all to my husband David and David Gillingwater for their design and technical help.

Contents

1930 - 1945

Tony

Bob

Attie

Bill

Bunny
August 1935

Preface

Helen Joan West was always known as Bunny. She never threw anything away and I felt it would be a sacrilege to burn her wonderful collection of letters spanning some 70 decades. It is important for her grandchildren and great grandchildren to know something of the era when she was very much 'a girl about town'. This book allows a view through a small porthole into life in the 30s and 40s – some are mundane but others funny, prophetic, poignant and heartbreakingly sad.

Bunny was born on Trafalgar Day, 21st October, 1916 to Gilbert (sometimes referred to as the Wicked One) and Helena (née Blair) West (sometimes referred to as wee Janie). Her mother had been married previously to Charles Barbor who died very young leaving her with two children. Bunny's brother Ronald and sister Lilias were never considered as 'half" siblings. Bunny was also called Best Aunt Bun by her niece, Buggy Bee by her great nephews in Canada, and Granny, GaGa or Gugs by her grandchildren.

It has been akin to a detective story working out how everything fitted together during the years from about 1935 till after the War, but a treasure-trove of photographs taken firstly by my grandmother from 1898, chronicling their early life in Pitlochry and Edinburgh, and then continued by Bunny over the next 80 years, helped to piece the jigsaw together.

Bunny adored her cousin Tony, Lt. Anthony Fasson RN GC, and throughout her life never once forgot him. It was a tragedy losing him so young and having read his letters it is easy to understand why Bun loved him. Her lifelong romance with Bob King started in 1937 when she was just 20. They remained in touch until the very end of their lives. It was also in Barbados that she met Atti Turner who wrote the loveliest of letters.

These letters were never written with publication in mind and, in the main, are much more akin to a weekly conversation, very much as we now would pick up the telephone and have a chat, send a quick email or text, so no word crafting has taken place. We should remember too that this was pre-war and some words are now inappropriate or politically incorrect. I have therefore changed just a few words and phrases.

I hope that what comes through in all this, is Bunny's truly indomitable spirit and, as her father said, pluck. Having lost the three people she loved most, Tony then both parents, with war time spirit she just carried on. She never ever criticised any of her children, was adored by everyone young and old and, just like her grandmother, remained young at heart until she died at 91.

Amanda Bettinson   2023

AGE OF STEEL.

Drawing by Francis Anthony Blair Fasson (FABF)
November 1932

Bunny's early childhood was spent at The White House, Mettingham, Bungay, Suffolk the house and farms having been left to her father, Gilbert West, by his Aunt Laura (née Parrington) Tallent. They moved to Darent Hulme in Shoreham, Kent in about 1926 and then to The Mare Cottage, Bovingdon, from where they would drive to Reedlands, Thorpeness, built by Gilbert as their holiday retreat.

The Blair sisters, my Grandmother Helena and her sister Lilias, married into the West and Fasson families. Bunny's cousins James, Anthony and Sheena Fasson had, from a very early age, many holidays together at the Grandparental home in Pitlochry, Scotland. Bunny adored them all but with Tony especially she had a very close relationship.

Early 1920 Jim, Tony and Sheena

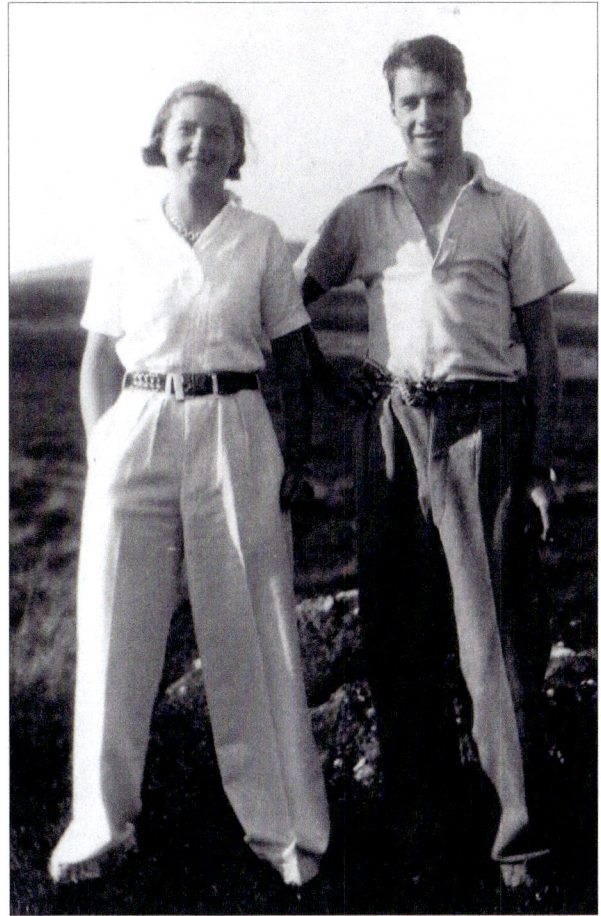

1933 With Tony on the moor, Pitlochry, wearing his trousers

The 1930's was a decade struggling to recover from the Wall Street Crash in 1929, the American Great Depression and the rise of Adolf Hitler's Nazi Germany. It was also the decade that started passenger flights, single sideband radio, the start of early television and the film industry producing films with both sound and colour. King George V was on the throne in England and Ramsey McDonald was the Labour Prime Minister (1931-35)

During August 1934 Mrs Wallis Simpson joined the then Prince of Wales on holiday in France (having met in early 1931) and in November she was introduced to Queen Mary at Buckingham Palace. King George V refused to meet her. The British press did not publicise the romance although it was covered widely in the foreign press. It wasn't until December 1936 that the story broke in the British papers.

Jubilee Day on 6th May 1935 figures in the photograph album and three months before her 19th birthday, in July 1935, Bunny was Tony Fasson's guest on HMS Curaçoa at the Royal Naval Review at Portsmouth.

The 1935 Jubilee Naval Review with the Royal Yacht Victoria and Albert in the foreground

No. 1 Flying Training School, Royal Air Force, Novair, Ross

Telephone Leuchars 16 [*RAF Leuchars – just north of St Andrews*]

Letter not dated but post mark looks to be 9 October 1935 addressed to Rathmore House, Hoddesdon, Herts (where Brother Ronald and Yvonne lived, having just married on 13th July 1935)

Bunny, my sweet,

A thousand thanks for your long letter, I liked it. Before I forget, I have just bought a grand little black Cocker, out of a Crufts winner! So, your kind offer cannot be used. It was very funny I bought him from an old friend. And not knowing her address sent the cheque by a rather roundabout way, she got windy, as I had got it very cheap, and wrote to say she would give me a bitch in exchange for old time's sake etc. I was furious as I read her letters in the wrong order; they all arrived by the same post from Leuchars. So wrote a stinker back, then a letter from her, saying cheque received everything OK crossed mine. All very awkward, however a phone call put things right again!

Life up here is paradise! It is a very compact little camp. One edge of the aerodrome being Invergordon Forth. Jolly to do a forced landing on! I have got on fairly well so far, 8 ½ hours dual with my solo test tomorrow. If I get it, I will have gone solo well inside the average of 12 hours. But I don't hope too much!

Stanley Baldwin was Conservative Prime Minister (1935-37) and had the difficult task of managing the abdication of Edward VIII. Mussolini invades Ethiopia. Persia becomes Iran. Heinrich Himmler starts a breeding program to produce an Aryan super race. First Gallop Poll to predict election outcomes. George Gershwin's Porgy and Bess premiered. Alan Lane at Penguin reintroduces the paperback.

No, we still wear Naval Uniform and keep the Navy very much to the fore. Because the RAF are incredibly mixed! My instructor is actually a Pilot Sergeant, a DFC and rather better bred I should say than a lot of the officers!

They ran a rugger side down at Leuchars and are very keen. So three of us fly down at weekends, 180 miles in 1hr 20m if the weather's good. But senior's rugger is out of the question. I've managed to get quite a lot of shooting and fishing and hope for a stalk later on.

Tony Fasson in training

I hope the new house will be a success, how far from town? It's a pity you're going to Switzerland in January, altho' it's the best time, but a party up here including "moi" have a good idea of going for a fortnight about Xmas time. Snow or no snow we'll have a fairish time!!!

Bun, I believe you are almost as sentimental as I am. In a world like this I find there is no room for it, "Isn't it heavenly" was quite well named I always thought!

I saw "Full House" and "Short Story" a try out in Edinburgh the other day, the latter well worth seeing I thought. Good luck with your steps, I will have to polish up my reels!

Love to your family and a "wee" bit for yourself!

Tony

Letter from Peter Medd, a friend of Tony Fasson's, after the flying accident

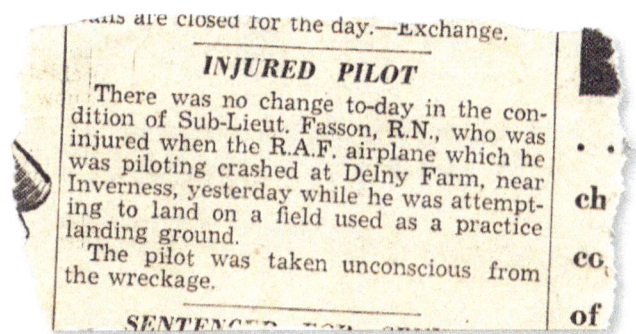

INJURED PILOT

There was no change to-day in the condition of Sub-Lieut. Fasson, R.N., who was injured when the R.A.F. airplane which he was piloting crashed at Delny Farm, near Inverness, yesterday while he was attempting to land on a field used as a practice landing ground.

The pilot was taken unconscious from the wreckage.

Tony was badly injured when his plane crashed at Leuchars

No 1 Flying Training School,
Royal Air Force,
Leuchars, Fife

Telephone, Leuchars   16th November 1935

My Dear Bunny,

I expect you will be getting as much information about Tony as I am. I heard today that he is now conscious and out of danger, but that his skull is definitely fractured. So it will be a long job.

I drove down from Novar last Tuesday, a week before the remainder, to play rugger. I had a shocking drive: the roads were a sheet of ice, it was snowing and blowing like the North Pole. At Blair Athol, I skidded and put the car through a fence. But she managed to crawl home, and is now in dock.

I went to London on Thursday, and had a riotous two days, except that my conscience troubled me as to whether I ought to return to Leuchars for Saturday's game. In the end, I went back and have been cursing myself ever since. I might have stayed until Tuesday!

I got your letter on returning.
Very many thanks for it.
Yours ever, Peter

My Dear Bunny,

Many thanks for your letter. Yes: poor old Tony!
I'm afraid I can only give you a vague idea of how it all happened, as
nobody actually saw it, except a few mad yokels.

We have a small field here, in which we practice forced landings. Tony was gliding down in S-turns to get into the field. He got too slow in one turn, stalled and spun in from about a hundred feet. And here I must congratulate him. His machine was smashed to atoms, all except the back seat, in which he was sitting. It was really miraculous and also miraculous that the machine didn't catch fire as they couldn't get him out for some time.

I'm glad to say he's better again today and is nearly conscious but not quite. They are not certain whether his skull is cracked, but certainly it is not dented, which is the dangerous thing. Apart from that, his nose is broken but the rest of him is all right.

His poor family are having a rotten time of it up here. All this waiting and uncertainty but I have been more optimistic all along. The hospital doctors are naturally reticent, but our doctor says that if he gets over the first 48 hours he is all right and that it is probably better if he stays unconscious from 4-6 days. So I am glad to say that I think Tony is almost certainly out of danger now.

That's about all I can tell you at the moment, Bunny. If there's any big change, I'll let you know.

You ask am I still keen on flying. Most certainly. One can't allow accidents to shake one, but it's taught us a lesson. We shall all be twice as careful now. Well, I hope Seaford is sunny and that the sea is not too cold!

I'm afraid this is a bit snappy, but I wanted to answer your letter at once, and am just off to tea with Tony's people in Inverness.

Yours ever,

Peter

Artwork from Tony Fasson's Midshipman's Journal 1932

My Dearest Bun,

You must excuse this awful scrawl. But I just had to write to you and "wee Janie" to thank you both enormously for your presents. Funnily enough my Navy tie has got a bit shabby, so you could not have chosen a better present. Thanks a big lot Bun. Also for your most welcome letter with all the news of the South. This place is not all bad and everyone is very kind to the "old sinner". I'm in the female wing which I don't think I really should be, do you!

I have ordered a new record for you from some shop. But as it is just out I think, you may not get it for years. If you've got it, or have heard it please send it back with a "curt" note!

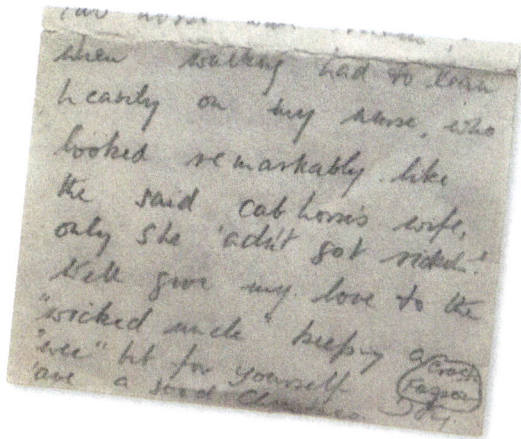

We are all to be at a local hotel for Xmas, which will be nice, but my table manners have gone to blazes and I don't think I'll be able to drink out of anything but a saucer! Which may rather shock the proprietress!

When I first got out of bed I felt like an oldish cab horse with rickets, and when walking had to lean heavily on my nurse, who looked remarkably like the said cab horse's wife, only she 'adn't got rickets'!

Well give my love to the "wicked uncle" keeping a "wee" bit for yourself - 'ave a good Christmas

Tony (Crash Fasson)

1936

Shortly before the end of 1935 Bunny's parents moved to The Mare Cottage, Bovingdon and built Reedlands in Thorpeness as a holiday home.

The Mare Cottage, Bovingdon

Reedlands, Thorpeness

20th January 1936 King George V died in Sandringham and Edward VIII became King. He was never crowned, as he abdicated in December 1936 to be succeeded by his brother, George VI, our late Queen's father. In the summer of 1936 Berlin hosted the Olympics, an opportunity for Hitler to show off Nazi 'efficiency'. 49 countries attended. Radar, pioneered by Robert Watson-Watt, moves to Bawdsey Manor on the Deben, Suffolk.

January 1937

Bunny accompanied her cousin, Mary West, on a recuperative 49-day cruise on the SS Duchess of Richmond to the West Indies, visiting among others, Kingston, Havana, Miami, Nassau, Martinique and Barbados. I think it was Aunt Lil Fasson who gave her the introduction to the King family, when they dropped in to Barbados for a fleeting visit of 2 days. This was where the long, passionate and then enduring friendship with Robert (Bob) King first began.

On her return home

SS Castalia (Anchor Lines)
22nd May 1937
Nearing Bombay

My Dear Bun,

Lumme I'm sweatin' something 'orrid! Well we are nearly there, for which God be praised.

There are a very small party onboard – Coronation and Thomson responsible. In a way a good thing, for I have been well "suited" and there is no crowding, tho' the less fortunate males are fairly bored!

The "affaire" is blonde, dances most beautifully, and a figure that looks very well on the boat deck! Unfortunately she is 26, married and with one kid. She joins her husband at Bombay, and I continue my journey to Purgatory!

The voyage has been "assez amusant" [quite fun]. For the first 36 hours I didn't say much – found myself at the captain's table, amongst the average type of Anglo Indian, and thought a good deal. Then as we began to unfreeze, I found to my astonishment that altho' we were only 29, we were quite interesting – an army matron, who knows everyone, is highly amusing and is now known as "the Duchess". Needless to say, I'm Don Espinoza, the butler [enforcer for the Granados crime family]. Then Joan Austin, my wife: Miss Luard, plays the cello and contrives to be sick, tho' the weather has been flat calm all the way, good at deck tennis. A newly married couple, who altho' acting "suspiciously" contrived to keep their secret for a week. And various Colonels and wives. We celebrated "Coronation" [King George VI and Queen Elizabeth on 12 May 1937] at the Company's expense, very nicely thank you. "The Navy" had to make a funny speech and did!

Hope you are all well.
Yours Affectionately.
Tony

6th May 1937 The German airship Hindenburg explodes in the United States of America at Lakehurst, New Jersey, 36 people are killed. Herbert Morrison's recorded eyewitness account is now a classic and still played today. Neville Chamberlain became Prime Minister in May 1937. 12th May 1937 George VI and the Queen Elizabeth were crowned in Westminster, the date planned for Edward's coronation. It was the BBC's first outside broadcast, having only been in operation for the previous 6 months. Glen Miller debuts in New York, Frank Lloyd Wright builds Fallingwater and a prototype antihistamine to treat allergies is produced.

Bob King and his mother visit first Europe then England

21st July 1937
Hotel York
Berners Street   London W1
Telephone: Museum 6862

Dear Bunny

Thanks so much for your letter, and should I like to come or should I? – Sorry there goes my American!

You say nothing of time, and do let me know where would be most convenient for meeting really anywhere, not specially near here.   What about dinner? Anyway just arrange that you haven't got dinner waiting you at home, we can arrange where, when we meet.

Had a super time in Italy and except for the strikes a rather hectic 5 days in Paris. All news when we meet, really it will be grand seeing the Davis Cup – thank you so much.

Yours Ever, Bob

p.s. Don't forget dinner on Tuesday, we may be able to "drive up and down" waiting for a "table"!!

Letter, marked' Important', posted to The Mare Cottage, Bovingdon, Hemel Hempstead, Herts and then forwarded to The Dolphin Inn, Thorpeness, Suffolk and then forwarded again to Rathmore House, Hoddesdon, Herts.

31st July 1937
Hotel York, Berners Street, London W1
Telephone: Museum 6862

Dear Bunny,

Just a line to say how much I enjoyed Tuesday, and also to say that I have seen Hugh who is even more vague than you!!!   Anyway, he is going to go into the matter and let me know.   Of course the most important thing is what the Bank think about it.

Drop me a line sometime and let me know what the weather is like, also it will give me your address so that I can send you a rude post card!

- Bye – Love Bob

Hugh Rowe was Bob's old school friend from Sherbourne who married Bunny's best friend from Bedgebury, Rhoda Garnett. The four of them were planning to drive to the south of France in a Bentley later in the year.

Hotel York, Berners Street, London W1
Telephone: Museum 6862
Thursday

Bunny Darling,

Enclosed are a few letters that have been sent on from Paris. Sorry I opened the large one but as you will see it was addressed to me.

What are you doing on Sat: can you come up? Anytime just arrange what you would like either lunch and show or dine – why not both? Will expect to hear that it's OK!

Just off to the city again.

With love, Yours Ever, Bob

Hotel York, Berners Street, London W1
Telephone: Museum 6862
Tuesday

Bunny Darling,

Just a line to thank you for the photos, and also that I have arranged about the place for your dressing table set – we will now have to consult the Little Book and see when we can go.

I hope you got home quite safely the other night. I spent rather too long in bed next morning so did not get down to Byfleet till about 1'oclock.

Can't think of any exciting news, - looking forward to seeing you about 6.45 tomorrow.

With love, Yours Bob

HMS Shoreham, Persian Gulf
Basra 1st August 1937

My Dear Bun,

You are a sweet young baggage – fancy remembering the day I first saw light! You know it's strange, because I can't remember myself – but I'll take your word for it.

Life has just started to get really blistering, tho' we can't complain. For usually June and July are impossible too. We spent a "socketing" 10 days down at Karachi – the pace was quite incredible. I worked out my "sleep curve" and was horrified to see it registered about four hours/day. There was a wicked lot of "jug trouble" which in addition to dancing every night at one or other of the clubs, did the "bod" a drop of no good!

Very trying! I'm getting quite a married complex. This time it was a sweet little thing whose husband was away all week flying an Imperial Airways Plane. So naturally she was lonely – purely platonic of course. But one falls it is not the right habit to achieve.

You seem to have that Globetrotting urge, which they say may end one up anywhere. It sounds a trifle obvious to me but I envy you and would like to take wee Janie's place.

The Pet appears to be having a quite delicious time and I can't help feeling that now we Fasson's are "in" at Court, it is only a matter of time before I hoist my flag.

Well we're off to Bombay (the house of my blonde) officially for "scraping the bottom" – but I hope to get in something rather more exciting personally!

This job is very interesting at present – we have in two months captured a naughty sheik without much trouble. Towed an oiler who had gone aground safely to sea and various other unusual jobs, but doubtless I shall get bored with it all in time.

Well I must away to count my "bullets" so goo'bye and enjoy yerself. Love to the wee Janie *[Bunny's Mother]* and wicked one. *[Bunny's Father]*

Tony's signature (FABF)

12th August 1937
Hotel York Berners Street   London W1
Telephone: Museum 6862

Bunny Darling,

Thanks so much for the invitation; and I am going to accept! That's a shock for you.   Actually I will have to leave early, but anyhow I shall arrive as early as is possibly polite to make up for lost time.   Enclosed are my photos which have come up to scratch this time – obviously the bad light at first was what was wrong!!?

No news except that already I have spent two busy days in nasty offices and no-one has given me the lunch at the Mayfair yet. (Sorry I keep putting odd letters on the end of words, but anyhow I find it so hard to write this ANGLAISY language).

Are you coming up to town soon? Anyway, you will have to come up to let us find somewhere for Blené. Will get in touch with you soon – Rien na Pu! With love, Yours, Bob

Post card from The Queen's Hotel,
Penzance Telegrams:
Seaward, Penzance Tel Nos. 471-472

This is the best I could find after holding up a line of determined buyers! So far am going well to schedule but am rather tired of it already. Any further developments as to the continent? I suppose not – knowing Hugh. Will send you a line later on the trip – Oh   *[continued on The Queen's Hotel notepaper]* excuse the weird continuation but suddenly realised that you wouldn't know an address to write and thank me for this masterpiece – for thanks

Post card from The Queen's Hotel, Penzance Telegrams: Seaward, Penzance Tel Nos. 471-472

I must have!!

"c/o R Arthur Esq., c/o Barclays Bank, 84 Osborne Road, Southsea."

We shall be there on the 18th for two days. I'm sorry about the rather weird address, but it's the best I can do when going to odd places every day!!

Must be off and find the car - it is lost in the fog which has been laying about all day.

Be Good, Love, Bob

The continental trip was finally organised and in September Bunny's brother-in-law, James Curry, lent her, Bob, Hugh and Rhoda a Bentley (named Juliet) to drive down to the South of France.

Bob at Windsor Hotel Juan-les-Pins

"Juliet" the Bentley, Rhoda, Hugh and Bob between Juan-les-Pins and Cannes

Postcard dated 8th October 1937

What an impossible person you are to get hold of! I have been ringing you and could only get through this morning to find that you are away. Will ring you again but in the meantime keep Wed 13th night free for a show. Will give you all details when I get in touch with you – love – Rien – na – Pu!

21st October 1937 was Bunny's 21st Birthday. She had a party at which the St Thomas's Hospital band played and Mr Richard (Dickie) Battle played the trumpet (a medical student who became an eminent plastic surgeon and trained with her brother Ronald) – Cole Porter's 'I have got you under my skin' was one of his many tunes.

30th October, 1937 posted from Dover
Koninklyke,
Nederlandsche Stoomboot Maatschappy, Amsterdam

My Darling,

Have just got on board after having been round and round the harbour. The sea is terrific and so I expect most people will soon be ill. No news Darling except that it was sweet of you to see me off. I would give anything to be staying.
All the best my sweet,
Your loving Bob

Tuesday Nov: 2nd 1937
Koninklyke,
Nederlandsche Stoomboot Maatschappy,
Amsterdam

My Dear Bunny,

It was awfully sweet of you to send us those lovely carnations, thank you so much. It was too late before we sailed to write to you to thank you.

We have had the most marvellous weather – down at Dover on Friday night the rain poured and such a gale. I thought we were in for an awful time. Fortunately, we were delayed and we never actually sailed until 7pm having got on board about 2 quite ready for lunch – By then the wind and sea had gone down and we have all felt very fit and we have lovely cabins.

I have been very energetic and entered for lots of the sports and this morning I have had a good practice at deck tennis. They have Bob on the Sports Committee, so instead of being able to sleep late he has to get up early, as there are huge entries, so I expect they will be worrying everyone at 10am to start.

It has been very interesting so far as we saw land (of course only in the distance) up to yesterday afternoon and passed crowds of ships. We are due at Madeira at 12ish tomorrow and suppose to be there until 5 so we should have plenty of time to go up the mountain. Two friends of mine offered to put me between them and hold me tight, if I would toboggan down but I still declined with thanks!!!

We thought it so nice of you coming to see us off at the station. Hurry up and take another trip to the West Indies.

Much love, Very sincerely yrs,
Gwenyeth M. King.

Koninklyke, Nederlandsche Stoomboot Maatschappy, Amsterdam
Tuesday 2nd November 1937

Bunny Darling,

Thanks so much for your wire which I got just before sailing; it was sweet of you to send one. God! What an awful day we had. It was most awfully rough and the boat had two shots at getting through the break-water at Dover before she actually made it. Then we were hung out until 7 o'clock before sailing because a lot of cargo that had to be taken on. As a matter of fact by the time we did sail the sea was much calmer and has remained so all along.

Yesterday we were sailing along the Spanish coast, but no-one had a shot at us!* The crowd on board are a little heavy although lots of them seem to be getting more lively today they have been ill, how I don't know, I think they would have died if they had been on that channel crossing.

The first few days I slept until lunch, but unfortunately I will have to get up early from now on as I have some work to do on the Sports Committee. All the Wilkinson family have been too too hearty for words but I think they will soon have to quieten down. I told Grace that I thought she had been damn rude over the telephone but it appears that I made her understand that that Wed: we went to the Berkley Arms was a night we might have gone to the London Casino, so when she heard from Cunliffe that I had been out with him while she had refused another show for that night she was mad. Of course I laughed like hell when I heard that because it really is very funny Ha! Ha!! Anyway I danced with her last night so I don't think I will be murdered in my sleep now.

I have been playing a lot of dice without making much. I haven't lost mind you, but just wasted my time. Mummie won the ships sweep today so I will have to see what I can do about it. It was her birthday on Sunday, another one of these common October birthdays.

We hear now that we will not be arriving at Madeira before about 3 o'clock so I may still get a chance of getting to the Casino. If the weather is as it has been it should be very nice for going up the mountain.

Mummie is writing to you also; darling so very sweet of you to send her flowers; she loves them; so as it costs 4d a letter I thought I would put mine in her envelope and save 4d for the Casino!! This pen is working fine now with just a little more use it will have got used to the speed at which I have to write while in the office! The one bright spot in the future is the renewed acquaintance of "Romeo" and the fitting of lights horns etc etc which I change my mind about every day.

I think you should get this early Monday morning as I believe the mail will be leaving as we arrive at Madeira, anyway I will write soon again to get the first B'dos mail after arriving. Actually I don't believe there is one leaving for almost a week after arriving there. I have made enquiries about an ocean wire, but there won't be a boat, apparently only the same line will do, after Madeira until just as we arrive in at B'dos. Anyway will see what can be done, especially if I break the bank tomorrow.

Darling, I'm afraid this must be a very boring epistle as really there isn't much news, but anyway I have written whatever I could think of. Do hope that Cunliffe will get you a nice fog lamp, and that the dressing table set has arrived by now. Must close sweet, and I do so wish you could be here, do your damndest to get your people out to the W.I. next year.

With Heaps of love, Take care of yourself, Your loving Bob

P.S. sorry putting these pages one inside of the other will make it difficult to find where I have continued, but do your best – love B.

The Spanish Civil War was fought 1936-39

Darling Bunny,

Just a short note as we hear that there is a mail leaving just about the time we arrive in B'dos. Well at last we end this trip we are arriving about 6o'clock tomorrow evening, an awful time to arrive, we would sooner stay on board and land next morning, but are not allowed to do so.

I have worked quite hard with the sports and managed to get into the final of the men's singles. I have I'm afraid done just a very little flirting but she is more or less engaged to a fellow in T'dad, *[Trinidad]* and so sweet don't worry as I never quite forgot that I should not flirt, I'm afraid I had a guilty conscience (is that how you spell it?) I do hope you will have to report something of the same soon as until we are even I will always be guilty.

Darling, we landed at Madeira but only for about two hours, but what with bullock-carts, fast V8's and wine, we saw an awful lot of the place. I do hope some of my photos come out nicely.

Must close now, as this has to be at the purser's office in just a couple of minutes. Will write soon darling, am longing for your letter and PHOTO!!!!! With lots of love,

Your loving Bob

POB.26, Barbados, B.W.I.
Thursday 18th November 1937

My Darling Bunny,

Am starting this today as the idea of writing to you makes me feel better. You see I am just a mass of nerves today having run over a small boy yesterday afternoon. He is still in hospital, but I think and hope will be OK, anyway it's a hell of a shock and I'm almost wishing I could go off for a long weekend and be right away from it all. So much for my miseries.

We never got ashore until late and there was Romeo, but unfortunately not working well enough to drive away. I left him in town and next day found that there was nothing very wrong just some joints wanted renewing and the plugs were oiled up. So, I got him by Saturday and until yesterday have been very pleased with it. I have even put on some lovely trumpet horns and had the dip switch fixed. And yesterday when the police tried my brakes, which had to be reviewed, they were 100% OK.

I have I'm afraid been roped into the show that is being put on Dec: 4th so have got numerous rehearsals such a pity you won't be here to hear me singing!!!

There is a mail that arrives on Friday so hope to hear from you by that, although it left rather soon after I did. What about the photo, as a matter of fact I hope you will have already had it taken, did mine arrive OK? Darling I am enclosing the photos I took that morning at your place, they are good except for the two of us. I also am sending one of myself taken at The Crane, I thought you might like the setting as there are lots of coconut trees in the background.

Sorry I have to write on this typewriting paper, but it's the only one that I have here at the office. Will close this for the time being, as there should be more news before the mail goes on Monday – so for the present goodbye sweet. Well I must end this off for the mail.

Since last, I have been to a couple of tennis parties and of course numerous rehearsals, and so far have not heard anymore about the accident, so I really hope that it will all blow over quietly. The boy of course is still in hospital but I think is getting on well.

Tomorrow is a big private dance at the Bowrings – Jim knows the son; - the daughter's 21st and I hear that she is announcing her engagement!!! So we are all eager to see if it's true. On Saturday is the Poppy Dance, the first dance at the Marine Hotel that starts off the seasons dances. I have tried to get hold of a publicity pamphlet to send you, but unfortunately they have not got their new ones out yet.

Darling I must end off this now as I have got to go out and do some work. Do write soon darling. With tons of love, Your ever loving Bob

P.O.B. 26 B'dos November 30th 1937

Bunny Darling,

Thanks so much for your long letter which I got a couple of days ago. I think I had better start by answering the various questions, and then see what news there is.

As to mails there are two good mails – The Dutch and Hamberg American Line both of these sail about the same date, every two weeks. The air mail is really quite useless until they finish our own airport which may be in the next 10 years or so!!

Oh! you mentioned dice, well last weekend I was staying with some people at the sea side and they have just got a roulette board so you can imagine the fun I had. I offered my services as bank but in the end came out about 5% down. Cant think why, as I was remembering how we had seen that all the Casinos had made huge profits last year. What I now want is Bool (is that how its spelt?).

So sorry you haven't got the brush and comb set yet, damn slack business I call it. From what you wrote your photo should be grand it sounds rather as though you were having a strip-tease done with only a fan on!!! We are just 4 hours behind you now, and in the summer 5 hours behind. That business about the banana boats is OK! Only they are very small, and do not come here! Ha! Ha!

About cabling me – just wire ARTHUR. BARBADOS. That's our private cable address so eliminates all other addresses. That's the best of being famous!!!

No Darling there is no need to be jealous as there is absolutely no one that I give two dams about in this place. The dance at the Marine last Saturday was rather a big affair but it rained like hell and I got very wet – outside I mean!

Have been rehearsing like hell lately as the show is on Sat: Darling I must close now as there are a file of letters on my desk to sign for this mail.

Will write soon again.
With lots of love,
Yours ever, Bob

My Darling Bunny,

You won't be able to read this, but still you may be glad to get the letter and know that I'm still thinking about you!!

As you will guess I'm in bed, it's just about 3.30 and I have rather too much lunch after a soak in the sea at the Yacht Club. The weather has been bad lately, rather hot and much too much rain. In fact, yesterday was quite the exception being very bright and sunny, it was lucky as it was the Bazaar. I don't think they did as well as last year but they say the show was good, and once more yours truly scored a hit!! What conceit, OK I know it! After the show everyone seemed to want to go home, so the other staring man and I went up to the Marine Hotel where we discussed the worlds politics over a few drinks until sometime around 1.45am. I'm really very glad it's all over as we have been at it ever since I arrived and have not even had time to go to but one flick. No, there was no making love this year, I was merely the fool, and had to sing a few songs with hits at local people and things – do you remember my showing you the various things hung on the wall at the Y. Club? Well one verse brought them in for they have been trying to prevent the owner of the articles from displaying them on the tree and wall.

Since last I wrote I have had the pleasure to be in a burning car, Yes Romeo. Not Romeo's fault though, a boy in the garage forgot and left an oily rag on the exhaust manifold, just next to the carburettor, so the rest quite clearly can be expected. I must admit it was a hell of a shock when I saw flames come leaping out from the side of the engine. Anyway with the use of a hankie and burning my hand I got it out, then I realised that I had it insured for £150!!

The boy I ran over is out and about again just ready to be run over for the second time. There was no police case and so just through kind heartedness I gave the father a little money when he had signed a paper to say that he would never claim from me again.

We have been discussing whether we are going to launch our yacht, you know the one I told you I shared with a couple of fellows, but I doubt if we shall it would cost quite a lot to do the things we want to, so I think I will race in a snipe which a friend of mine owns and I know he wants a crew.

Well Darling I can't think of any more news so I will see what questions there are to be answered in your letter. By the way thanks ever so much for it, but I need hardly say that, need I?

No sweet, I can't say that either of those photos do you justice, but still I agree 7 is the better; perhaps this other place will be more successful. So glad the dressing table set has arrived at last – it's the least they could do to charge less after keeping it all that time.

So far the land is only bringing in a small rent for we find that we cannot sell any of it for two years, some stupid law that was passed to prevent people like myself ruining the country side with houses! "I told you so" OK darling I deserve it I know, but you will be glad to hear that she does not live in B'dos, anyway board ship is rather a difficult place, I think you will agree? Sorry to disappoint you, Darling, but there's nothing to report yet, I must be losing my technique!!

I must really close now as its 4.30 and I must go to sleep as George and Hilda are dining here tonight.

This, my sweet, is the Xmas mail, I'm sending off a few stupid things that you will be able to stick on the mantel piece if even only till the New Year. The thing with hankies it is known as "kiss kiss" grass (not sure if it's K or C) and is meant to make them smell nice, please note I say "meant to". Didn't you say you liked guavas, well here is a guava cheese – shouldn't be surprised if you tasted it when you were out this way. Next time I hear of a friend going to England I will get them to smuggle in a bottle of Rum for you.

Must go to sleep, darling. A very very happy Xmas and all the best of everything for 1938. Do wish you could be in our party for the New Year at the Marine, we start off at Denise (Lucille's married sister) with cocktails, then dine at the Marine, dance there and at the Y. Club and after have bacon and eggs at a friend of mine who is a planter 14 miles out of town. I shouldn't be surprised if we stayed on for breakfast too!

I off to sleep! With heaps of love Darling, Yours ever, Bob

My Darling Bunny,

Thanks so much for your letter and photo received today. It seemed ages since I had got a letter, not your fault Darling, as there had been no boats. I can't understand you not getting a letter from me up to the time you wrote, I mean a letter from B'dos, I can't think why as I have never missed a mail. Darling, I like the photo awfully, a little serious, but I'm not sure if you are trying to make your mouth look like Myrna Loy's or if you're just serious!!

Well we are nearly at Xmas now, and I'll be glad when we do get to it as we are always terribly busy just before. To add to the fun an agent of ours from St Louis Miss: had to turn up on Sat: so I have had to be going around with him and with the mail closing at 4 o'clock this afternoon I hadn't started any at 2.30. Anyway I have made arrangements to have these sent off to the boat so am writing this at home after dinner – tinker on my right, and Prince on my left.

There has not been much excitement lately, I have been to three films since I've been back, so Darling you see I have become the complete hermit. There was quite a good dance at the club (Yacht) Sat: before last, I dined with a cousin of mine and then had a very prim and proper night dancing with numerous married women, although I must admit very few had their husbands with them!!!

Yesterday I had a small picnic at The Crane for a young cousin of mine who is passing through on her way home (Toronto).

On Wed: I'm going to a dinner and then on to the newly opened night club, the first to be heard of in B'dos. I don't think it will live longer than this tourist season. I'm wondering how the party I'm going with will like it as I've told them, and they believe me, that a girl has been got down from the States to do a strip tease. Since I told them other people have told me they were told it was true, so now I dare not say it was I who started the rumour!! What it is to be a liar? On reading that though I seem to have used a hell of a lot of "tolds" but I'm trying to listen to a funny man from the English programme and write at the same time.

I'm taking Jim at his word and sending him the bill for fixing the brakes on Romeo, and there were a few other things they did as he would not work. I'm going to have him cleaned early in the new year as I feel that is sorely needed, the petrol consumption has a regular average of 11.2 MPG that's without the free wheel, anyway they say when she (I beg your pardon) HE has his valves ground in and what not that he will be quite different, I personally am very satisfied with the way he works, especially when I have the hood down.

Well Darling I seem to have come to the end of the news. I have just heard that the roads in and around London have been ice bound, what a contrast, we have been having glorious hot days with rather cool evenings; I actually wished I had a blanket the other night.

Darling, again thanks ever so much for the photo, I love it, and you too. With lots of love, and all the best for 1938. Yours ever, Bob

PTO: How did you know it was Jan 13th? I shall be most annoyed if you send me a present, really I'm not being funny, I forbid it. Fancy thinking it was the 14th – don't you know that the only lucky thing that ever happened for the world on the 13th was my timely arrival!

Mummie sends her love and the best wishes for the New Year. Oh hell the others beg to send theirs also.

Love B

Upton
28th December 1937

My Darling Bunny

This will be a rather short letter as I have not had much doing since last I wrote. I have now finished with Xmas festivities what they were; actually, I spent most of the time sleeping – a weakness of mine!!

On Friday night I was dining with some friends and they went on to the newly opened night club. Oh! By the way last time I wrote I had not been, had I, well its very good indeed, and as a matter of fact we had a strip but not exactly a tease on Friday night when a tourist, who was very well lit, insisted on dancing with most of her dress off. So you see my forecast that there would be a show like that was merely a little late in coming on!!

I don't know if it's worth reporting but I will so that, you will see that nothing is left out, I did a little necking at the club, but as you will realise everyone "makes a lot of sport" to quote a Barbadian expression on occasions such as Christmas, and not the merest idea of seriousness is attached to it by either party, and anyway, Darling, definitely not by me, you know that don't you?

Well to return to my Christmas holidays – I arrived home from the night club at about 4am on Xmas morning and was up again at 8 to go to church with the Mater. Anyway that proved too much for me as I went to sleep in the drawing room when I was waiting for the King's Speech, when I awoke at about 12 to find that the family had turned off the wireless and gone to the 11 o'clock church, so I thought it better to sleep in bed so then I went and awoke at about 6.45 just in time to dress and go to Hilda and George (Challenor) for Xmas dinner. Next day it was rainy, so I slept late and then stuck in about 50 of my photos. I still have some 40 odd to stick in. That night we dined with my aunt – on Monday there were yacht races, I wasn't racing but I went down to see them, and damn glad I was that I wasn't racing as there was a hell of a haze and the sun was very hot. I went to various friend's houses and begged meals and drink arriving home about 7.45pm

I have been playing tennis this afternoon, tomorrow I have to go to a cocktail party and then if I think I'll go to a cinema at night, it just depends if there is anything good on. Have just been asked to another private dance on the 19th. The other is the 5th can't help feeling that it's because they are short of men, because I have been rather rude to both families since I have been back – I have got too too blasé!!

I haven't had a letter from you for ages sweet, but there is a mail in on Saturday so will get a letter on Monday, we get New Year's Day as a holiday out here, very nice it being a Saturday that means that Sunday will be there to sleep on!

Tinker has just insisted on getting up and seeing what I was doing – the scratch on the page is his claw mark with his love. Darling I must close now - long for your letter.

With heaps of love,

Your loving Bob

My Dearest Bun,

Thanks a million for your long letter filled with front page news! Well – crack out of it kid. And let's talk sense – sorry I'm slowly going mental. So bear with me a little longer.

Now you'll probably think I'm talking nonsense, maybe you're right. But here you are –

1. I don't think you've ever been seriously in love before

2. If you were well and truly in the pond – you wouldn't care where you were going to live, the Pole or Bloomsbury, as long as the boyfriend was about.

3. You would be (at present) quite certain that neither of you would mind waiting till doomsday if necessary. All this you'll say, is the mutterings of a rather soft cynic – then you're certainly wrong.

But I'm romantic enough to believe that there is a "right" person somewhere, and that when he or she happens along – nothing will matter as long as you can get together in the end. Candidly, I've only had it badly once, and as I think, like you, it was the first time. Miss Barcelona it was! I mean I actually went about trying to help people and be extra nice to them – quite probably it affected you much the same. But Margot died, while I was at Greenwich, which was sad, but heaven knows what I'd have done if we'd ever got together again.

I'm telling you all this, because I'm rather fond of "the rabbit". For because, altho' it sounds horribly cold and gruesome I did heal my aches – yet I've never felt the same about any other girl since. And don't intend to until the real thing comes along. And that's straight from the hip Bun. Anyway, you must have had a super time, and I honestly do believe everything happens for the best. Look at my crash – I thought life hell, when I gave up the FAA *[Fleet Air Arm]* and now I wouldn't be in it for anything!

Talking of flying, I got my flip at Basra all right. In one of 84 squadron's Vincents, who are stationed there. I went up in the dual with a fellow I know. He took off, then – the whole world suddenly belonged to me. My nerves haven't been touched, and after an hour, in which we 'shot up' the *[HMS]* Shoreham and landed at the civil airport to see the Aga Khan, I did one landing at the aerodrome. It wasn't a three-pointer; but considering I'd never touched anything as big as a Vincent, I was absolutely thrilled.

Bombay – is so perfect, because life is fast and fun, and there are so many pleasant people to share it with – I've suddenly gone all platonic – and like it. It's fairly essential as they are nearly all married! I do see my blonde bombshell, but she lost something about the Red Sea, and it's never been so hot since! I know Bill Agnew quite well – he threw me out of the Navy side! He's nice tho'.

Lots of fun and love,

Tony

H.M.S. COLOMBO.   H.M.S. ACHATES.

Drawings by Francis Anthony Blair Fasson (FABF) From his Midshipman's Journal

Office

3rd January 1938

Darling Bunny,

A very Happy New Year, and when do you decide to bring your Mama out here? Darling thanks so much for your two letters that the family got out of the Post Office yesterday after church. I'm so glad that Hugh and Rhoda will be able to get married soon, but I think they are quite mad if they are going to have to live like a couple of church mice!

Well, the New Year party was quite good and much more a sober affair than usual; I actually never had any wild flirtations, although I did seem to kiss more people than I can count. After the dance I went down to a plantation for bacon and eggs where I eventually stayed until about 5 o'clock the following afternoon.

Since then I have been at home except yesterday when I was down at the Yacht Club and had a lovely bathe. Some people are already making arrangements for an Easter party, nothing like being well in time.

My sweet this is a lousy letter but I'm rather busy and I have to go out to a meeting in a couple of minutes so I can't think of any really good news. Will write all news next time.

With lots of love darling, yours ever, Bob

Upton

Sunday 16th January 1938

My Darling Bunny,

Thanks so much for your letters and that lovely blotter. Darling it's sweet of you to have sent it and believe it or not I will use it.

It is ages since the last mail but with the exception of a weird cocktail party or two I have not been doing very much. Last night I had to do a small show at The Marine. They had a sort of cabaret in aid of the local charities all this business of acting for charities is becoming a damn nuisance. Yesterday I got Hugh and Rhoda's Xmas card, a very good effort on the B'dos Post Office I think or perhaps it is because of being rather famous?!

Since I last wrote I have had Romeo thoroughly cleaned and overhauled and now he is going like a charm, when he is just ticking over you can't hear a sound and of course the power and speed is terrific. I want to go down to Bathsheba and see what he will do in those hills, I don't think you ever went that way, but they are pretty terrific.

Darling, I haven't got any odd photos of the house, but I will buy a film and give you all the various angles of this abode. As for myself I don't expect that there will be any until there is some weekend party, the first of

---

March: Hitler marches into Austria; Nazis destroy Jewish communities, about 30,000 sent to concentration camps. May: Admiral Sir Hugh Sinclair, Head of the Secret Intelligence Service, privately bought Bletchley Park (from the Sebag-Montefiore's family) for use in the event of war. Orson Welles creates nationwide panic in the States with his broadcast of HG Wells 'War of the Worlds'. Biro pen invented. In late August 'Captain Ridley's Shooting Party' arrive at Bletchley Park – a secret team of MI6 and code breakers – one of the best kept intelligence secrets of the war.

which will be Easter. As a matter of fact we have already begun making enquiries about a house for it, and I am just off now to the Yacht Club to discuss where we are going as the house we went to last year has been booked for that month.

The tourists are now beginning to arrive, we had two tourist boats in last week, and there were one or two dizzy blonds at the Marine last night, cant think what has happened to me, as I am being cut out all round, when the dance was over and a suggestion of going to the Moyan Club (night club) was made I found that they had all left already, getting too old and think it was very seldom that anyone got one up on me. Anyway, one never knows perhaps some film star may be coming down soon and then I will do my stuff!!

I am going down the leeward coast, opposite end to The Crane, for a bathe and supper party this afternoon, should be quite good fun, as the people who are giving it always have bright wild shows, such a pity that I can't have a few Rum cocktails just as a primer.

No doubt you will have heard over the wireless that we are getting a new Governor, we hear that he is very keen on dancing and parties, and as he is single we hope that he will be having rather good parties. The man who is suspected of causing some of the disturbances locally has just returned to the island and has again been elected for the "House". We hear that he is saying that it is through him that our other governor, who by the way has had a grand promotion from £3,000 to £7,000 a year, has been moved down to T'dad. I have got hold of one of the books with all the evidence on the riots and am sending it over, your Papa might like to read it if it is too boring for you. The R Challenor in it is George's brother, commonly known as Laddie.

Darling, I have been writing too much dribble (do you spell it like that) so must close, just off to the club in roasting sunshine.

Longing to hear from you soon, with lots of love my sweet, Yours ever, Bob

Romeo

Upton 24th January 8.45 p.m.

My Darling Bunny,

I have just come in after giving the dogs a run after dinner. The London news is on the wireless and here I go to try and remember anything interesting that has happened.

On Saturday we had one of Barbados' society weddings, not a very terrific show, although quantities of champagne were drunk. After the wedding we had a dinner at the Bridgetown Club, and so on to the Marine when we danced amidst much American Navy. There has been an American ship in for the last four or five days, so all the girls have been all spit and polish!!

I am now having the fun of collecting the money from the people who were at the New Year's dinner. I hear tonight that one of them have measles. We also have a few cases of diphtheria so we do get our spot of infectious diseases! Just lately I have been playing rather a lot of tennis, this afternoon I played so badly that I think I will have to take up some sort of indoor sport, the quieter variety I think would be best.

I'm enclosing a piece of a cutting from the paper which gives a short account of our cabaret show at the Marine a couple of Saturdays ago. I'm now feeling like doing some show, but as "George and Margaret" are not released yet I don't know what to go in for.

Darling your blotter is grand and I do believe it makes me do more work for it is completely inked up, and I'll have to tear off the first leaf.

So far we have not been very lucky with the land that the "Old Man" bought for us, but still I think that eventually it will be worthwhile. Did I tell you that I have bought some more "stock" – Canadian copper mines this time, so once more I am trying to make my fortune on the Stock Market.

Darling I haven't taken those photos yet, but I will soon, I hope to get a photo in time to enclose with this letter taken on New Year's morning, yours truly still in his Turkish what not, it's not very flattering. Either by this mail or the one later in the week I hope to get off some more guava cheese, as I happen to know the guava cheese in London, specially the one from the City, isn't a patch on ours. Grannie is getting some stuff known as shaddock rind and as the name says it's the rind of a shaddock or rather overgrown grapefruit which they do something to.

The Mount Gay Rum is not by any means the best B'dos rum, but I think you will agree that its streets above any Jamaica stuff.

Oh! I forgot to say that after the wedding on Sat: I had to go to the funeral on Sunday, the father-in-law of the fellow I was to be best man to, quite a contrast!!

I have now gone one step farther as I have got to the end of my bed, and had to come up to see if there were any questions in your letter and that reminds me, I haven't thanked you for it, of course darling you know I love them don't you?

When I take those photos for you, I must get one of Romeo, you wouldn't know him, not that he has changed in looks but his tummy is so improved. I have just spent about £10 in cleaning him and generally tuning him up and now he's terrific. Prince has gone to sleep already so I think I'll follow suit. Goodnight my sweet, with lots of love, Yours ever, Bob

Upton 1st February 1938

My Darling Bunny,

Ever so many thanks for your letter and photo. As a matter of fact, I don't like it as much as the other one although Mummie and the family think it is better. It arrived with the corners rather broken, but still, that doesn't spoil the actual work of art.

Now let me try and find some news, I don't know but just lately with the exception of lots of tennis I don't seem to have been doing much. Last weekend I had two women staying in the house so I have had to be the perfect host; God, what a strain. It was a cousin from Canada and a friend of hers. On Saturday we went to a very good dance at the Yacht Club then on Sunday afternoon I took them for a drive round the north of the island, Romeo did her stuff well in Tuff Hill districts. On Monday afternoon I took them sailing and had a lovely afternoon with a good wind blowing that brings us to the end of their stay, so once more the homestead has returned to its normal quietude. I saw Broadway 1938 the other night, have you seen it, I thought it very good indeed that Powell woman dances even better than before I think.

I begin my tennis lessons on Thursday it's a fellow called Blair who is at Selfridges usually. He has been out here the last two years and has been pretty good. I am going to have 12 lessons, so look out for terrific results when I have finished!

I'll look through your letters and see if there are any questions to answer. Say if you don't get a letter from me by next mail you will know that it's because I would have written it in the office!! Since when did one work in an office anyway?

I am awfully sorry for your father if he is going to depend on your housekeeping when your mother is away especially now that you can make a milk pudding or whatever it was you said you could make!

Thanks darling for the kiss, I haven't had it yet, I will wait till I can find some startling tourist. Very nice of you, sweet. I have no intention of giving you such a good excuse!! Although I would love to give you several personally. Darling, I have not taken those photos yet, but I must try and remember to get a film soon. Must go to bed Darling as I have to be up late tomorrow night as taking a party to the theatre to see some dancing can't remember the people's names – I think something like Zola and Paula, supposed to have danced in the West End! With heaps of love sweet, yours ever, Bob

p.s. Thank your Mama for her message and give her my love. B–

Upton February 13th 1938

My Darling Bunny,

Who said the 13th was my lucky day, I have just got home from the club where I lost about $5 in the most remarkably short time. So now I have come home to sleep. As a matter of fact I have to go out to tennis this afternoon, so sleep won't help much. Not that I think anything could spoil my tennis these days, I am in the hands of the pro, and find that by the time I've thought what I should do correctly the ball has gone!

Went to a private dance this week, a hell of a show, don't mean bad, but colossal. Oh! Have to report one case of necking, but darling I had to find someone to give me that kiss you sent.

On Thursday night went out on a sailing trip, we had lovely winds but only got one fish, it was in the yacht owned by the Commodore of the RBYC which was sailed out here from England. When I was sailing her home I thought well how the devil people can be so foolhardy I don't know, she rolls like a tub. I don't think I will ever come home that way darling.

Must go down and get a bit of lunch, and will get you a piece of bougainvillea, cant think what it will look like by the time it gets to England.

Next week we shall be overrun with Navy. There are seven Americans going to be here all at once and they have a show at Government House for them. Then we start with driblets on HMS York, being the first on Friday. All the girls are getting worked up already and the Navy list at the club is showing signs of wear!

So sorry to hear that your Pop is ill, hope he is quite fit again now. Darling thanks for your letter, you poor thing you do seem so depressed, never mind sweet, things always have a way of brightening up.

Everyone out here is getting the blues too for the price of sugar is going down and down, and after the conference we expected great things. Anyway I'm sure we'll get a good price in the end or at least hope so for we are having short crops this year to droughts.

By the next time I write I hope to have won some money on the local races. I have got interests in numerous tickets, not that that means anything it seems that the people who win are the ones who have only bought one ticket. If I win I will be able to pay off all my debts.

My sweet I can't think of any more news, Prince is walking round and round my bed with a ball in his mouth making the most awful slobbering noises. It's the great joy of his life to be given a ball to chew especially when Tinker isn't around to try and get it.

Longing for your letter by the boat on Tuesday take care of yourself. With lots of love. Yours Ever, Bob.

Office 21st February

My Darling Bunny,

Thanks so much for your letter which eventually arrived before mine left the island. I posted on Monday as the Columbia was supposed to sail on Tuesday morning early, it however didn't go till Thursday.

I didn't know that this mail was going tomorrow or I would have written yesterday, knowing how you disapprove of my writing in the office, but as there are local races tomorrow, and we always shut down at about 11.30 for them, and as I will have lots of office letters to write before that, I am writing today.

There hasn't been much doing this week, tennis every afternoon, and for the bright young things HMS York has been here since Wednesday. On Saturday I went to a dinner at the Bridgetown Club given for some Canadians, there were 32 of us, and with very few exceptions the most boring 32 one could have found. After dinner we went on to the RBYC where we had a dance for the York. Quite a big affair with the Admiral and HE (His Excellency the Governor) with lots of gold braid and medals. I decided to leave about the 13th dance 2.15am, but as usual got talking to a great friend about the newly married people, and those who were about to be married – she by the way is married and has 2 children, so no need for alarm – and learned that there was one girl here who was apparently madly in love with me, and as I didn't appear to like her she has got engaged to a very morbid lad. They are all trying to get her to break off the engagement as it can never be a success, all very exciting cant think what I am meant to do, for although I quite like her, I can't think that anything I tell her will cause her to think I know best – rather fun being brought in as an adviser – you see Darling what sway I hold even advise people who or when to marry!!

This isn't very interesting but still am letting you know, it's the only bit of gossip this week.

Am now off to my 6th tennis lesson after which we have a cocktail party. Tomorrow night is the dance on the York, I have written and thanked them and said I should be pleased to come, but haven't the least idea of going. It used to be good when I could go off and drink the King's whiskey, but now why worry, all the girls have the Navy to look after so I stay on shore, it's safer.

Darling must be off or I'll be late for the lesson. Lots and lots of love sweet,

Yours ever, Bob

26th February 1938
Addressed to The Mare Cottage, Bovingdon
and forwarded to 7 Chepstow Mansions, London W2.

Darling there isn't much news since my last letter on Tuesday but I have at last taken the photos of Upton, and hope to get them soon so will enclose them in this.

Except for tennis every afternoon I have nothing to report. This afternoon is a show at GH [Government House] one Governor has returned from T'dad on his way home.

Oh! I never answered your questions about Andrew's factory and Laddie Challenor. Laddie alias Robert, I mean the other way round – his name is Robert, is the one that you probably met he has just been appointed on the Council and so is now the 'Honourable' in name only I'm afraid.

The Duchess of Richmond is in this morning, so I am sending this note by her. There is also an English mail in so hope I will hear from you.

With lots and lots of love yours ever,

Bob

28th February 1938

My Darling Bunny,

This may catch the Dutch boat, or if not the tourist boat "Arandora Star"*. Thanks my sweet for your letter, your cousin must have had even worse a time than we had going to France.

Saturday wasn't so bad at GH after all as I was asked to play tennis so didn't just have to wonder around aimlessly. Yesterday I spent the day with two of my best friends a young married couple who live on an estate. I took down all my photos and showed them, it made me very homesick seeing all those photos of the South of France!

Darling, Bajan is the Barbadian for Barbadian if you see what I mean!!! I have got the photos of Upton, not too good as most of them seem to have been taken looking into the sun, anyway I have written on the back of each explaining. With lots and lots of love my sweet,

Yours Ever, Bob

Office March 14th

Darling Bunny,

Thanks so much for your letter, and I'm so sorry to hear that your Pops isn't quite OK yet. He really wants a change Darling, and I can't help feeling that a month at least in B'dos would just do the trick?

Don't tell me you know all there is to know about cooking already? Personally I should say you have only got to the Caramel pudding stage!! Anyway I'm sure that you'll be glad if you haven't got to go up to town.

Good old Hugh so glad he did the only possible thing, no doubt Rhoda must be trying to persuade him to give it up, tell him from me that we are having a rather good landing ground so why not try to see what about coming out this way.

Darling this is a lousy letter, too early in the morning I suppose. There isn't much local news. I was badly beaten in the "singles" and have much the same fate in store for me tomorrow in the doubles – as I think I told you I have been very unlucky in the draws this year.

Had two dinner parties this week, one of which was with the Gov: General of Newfoundland and today

---

* On 2nd July 1940 the SS Arandora Star was struck by a torpedo off the Irish coast and sank. 800 lives were lost.

and Wed: I have got a rehearsal for another charity show. On Friday we have the annual meeting of the Dramatic Society and soon should be thinking of another production – unfortunately "George and Margaret" is not released for amateurs yet.

Darling I must end off now and do a spot of work.

With lots of love yours ever, Bob

Army and Navy Club,
Pall Mall SW1
Telephone Whitehall 9721-8
16th March 1938

Bunny, m' angel

It would appear that we've missed each other by a head – for I've tried to get hold of you but failed.

Aunt Cara told me your future moves, but I've forgotten 'em. I'm coming south for a board at the Admiralty about April 14 and hope to get a month's leave after that.

A. Could The Mare *[West family home at Bovingdon]* harbour me over that weekend?

B. Will you help me to forget Heart throb No 1. Ex Viceroy – and make a party on the 15th. I producing one Godfrey Darling, sailor, and you producing yourself and another lovely.

(God, I fell badly, but with your aid hope to recover poise!) Excuse short note – which show shall we go to? Yours an' all.

Tony

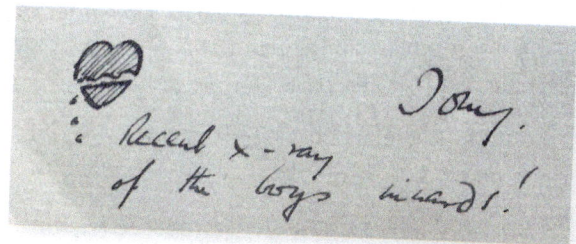

Recent X-ray of the boy's innards

23rd March

My Darling Bunny,

Thanks ever so much for your letter and also for the music which I will give to Gittens and no doubt in a few weeks we will have it played at least three times each dance, it's a weakness that he has when he hits on a really good tune.

We have had our annual meeting of the Dramatic Society and it seems as though they will be putting on a show soon. I'm waiting for George and Margaret to be released, and I am sure it would be a great show, although the president is against it, he is Mr Wilkinson, and doesn't seem to fancy his daughter, for he would naturally want at least one in the lead, to do the modern daughter's part: we will see though as we are having another producer and he swears he won't have any Wilkinsons in it.

Lord, what terrible luck I have been having lately. I have done nothing but loose, I think it must be wrong of me to play polka during lent!? They have put in a new 1/- in the slot machine at The Crane Hotel and that seems to be the only thing which I can recover money on.

Well all preparations are going swimmingly for the Easter weekend. I have got the servants and am now trying to get hold of cots for people to sleep in. There are only 6 beds and a sofa, and as there are 16 people going you can see that we will have to get the cots?

We have sold one family a large piece of the land that we bought, but as I told you we have to wait 2 years before selling all - if however we care to we may sell one piece every year prior to the two years. There is one big chance however, the Government are trying to buy some land for playing fields, and with a little propaganda we hope to be able to get off the whole thing. We wont of course make as much, but still we will get about, or should, £300 an acre which would be about £1,400, my share when paying off all debts would be about £350 clear profit, just enough to pay off for Romeo and have a little money to buy some very good shares that are going now at 4%.

Darling, on going through this it is a lousy letter, sorry have hit on a diary line this time.

Do hope by now that your Pop is very much better, you will no doubt be in the north now.

Must be off Darling, with lots of love, Yours ever, Bob

POB 26 undated

My Darling

Thanks ever so much for your lovely long letter. So sad to think of poor Juliet going off to South Africa, Romeo is very sad!!

Have been very busy lately as we have another charity show, and they have me singing in a trio in 2nds and I can't sing 2nds so I'm all in a flat spin. The Dramatic Society as decided to put on 'Turkey Time' yours truly being in Tom Wall's part: - funny peculiar?

Last night Gittens played through your music, he likes both of them very much so we should hear them soon, on his behalf thanks very much.

Darling sorry that this is such a short letter, but I couldn't write last night owing to a rehearsal and so have got this sent off late to the boat. As a matter of fact, the boat is a day early, so you see I have a perfect alibi!! The firm has just gone in for another real estate purchase, buying a large plot of land which we intend to build some 20 houses on purely for the tourist element, wish I could have gone in for it but it cost £2040 already without the houses, these will cost about £600-800 each so naturally it's a little above my limit.

Darling will make up for this short letter next time! My love to your family, and do hope that the change has made your Pop ever so much stronger.

With lots of love my sweet,

Yours ever, Bob

Upton
11th April, Monday night
Forwarded on to C/o Mrs Lewis, 25 Stockwood Crescent, Knowle, Bristol

My Darling Bunny,

Thanks for your lovely long letter, and I do hope you are quite better by now. What do you mean by being ill?

Since my last letter I have again been on a cabaret show, this time doing harmony, fancy me singing 2nds, personally I thought I was flat all the time, but they say that it was right so that shows my ability for 2nds!!!

I have not had so much tennis this week and have only one good cocktail party which ended about 12.45. I'm afraid I did a little flirting that day, and one awful dinner on Saturday night.

Darling, I have had rather a bad week; did I ever mention a girl by the name of Monica Pantin. Well years ago we were very friendly and then I wrote and said that I wasn't really in love and she promptly got engaged. She suddenly arrived here on her way to see her family in Grenada and so I took her out to lunch. I think she had too much to drink, not that she was tight but just enough to make her talk freely. She said that she was not in love with the boy she was engaged to and wondered if I couldn't fall in love with her again. I told her that I wasn't in love with her and that even if I was, I couldn't marry her for years. That didn't seem to matter as she said she didn't mind when once I would eventually. Darling, don't let this bore you as you must realise the way I feel. It's a hell of a shock and as she says I am getting to the stage when I have had too many people in love with me to be good and gradually, I'm beginning to doubt that I really love anyone enough to marry them.

It's all very difficult for I suppose she may be right it has certainly had the effect of depressing me beyond all measures. You see Darling I am not in love with her, but this damn separation you in England and I in this spot that makes me begin to fear that again something might bust this up. If only we could get married, for Darling does time make such a difference or not? That's what I dread. My sweet when we are separated, we find each other's changes all at once and they don't grow on us together. I am dreading when she passes through on her way to England as I feel such a cad, and yet it's her life that she is throwing away, but why in hells name should it always be I who get this sort of thing let on to them, this is the second, the other I told you about some time ago.

Darling I very nearly tore all this up on reading it through, but I want you to know exactly what's happening and how this sort of thing affects me.

Now for some other brighter news – let me think. They are having pretty bad strikes in Trinidad again and they fear more rioting. They expected a big strike here today with the wharf "rats" as they are very rightly known; but up to now (9.35pm) everything is quiet. A friend of mine had a robbery last night and had only a gold ring and a revolver and 50 rounds of ammunitions stolen, rather amazing as they left numerous good things that they should have wanted behind. It's quite a different job going at a burglar with a revolver than one who is probably as frightened as you are!!!

Yesterday a few of us went down to the house that we have rented for the Easter weekend. They have done it up and now has running water in all the rooms, and electric light, we move in on Thursday afternoon and leave on Monday night. I'm quite looking forward to it; I intend to have a really lazy time.

My Darling sweet, I do hope this wont bore you too much but I feel much better having got it off my chest. Longing for your next letter, with lots of love, Yours ever, Bob

P.S. Romeo sends his love and says he would like to have you drive him.

Office (Undated)

My Darling Bunny,

This will not even be termed a letter, as I have arrived back at the office after a very hectic Easter Weekend to find that the mails close in a few minutes. As a matter of fact I will send this on board to make sure that it goes.

My sweet thanks so much for your letter, which I got as I came into the office. Will write and give you all news by next mail as the messenger is fidgeting about. It's quite OK about Monica as I have heard from her and she says she is sorry and that it must have been the drink that made her do it, anyway all news when I write. All love my sweet, Bob

Upton 25th April 1938

My Darling Bunny,

Thanks ever so much for your last letter, as a matter of fact I am going through a couple of your last letters and see if there are any questions I have not answered.

Did I ever thank you for the page from "Men's only" I laughed quite a lot and so did lots of people in the office. So sorry that you couldn't persuade your Pop to come out here. My God, no of course it isn't "Toots", no they are Bostonians, you know they are the most English Americans, and so are the nicest?? Darling, do be careful loosing 1 ¼ lbs you know it's very dangerous to lose a lot of weight suddenly – sorry my sweet –

No so far have not been able to sell any land, but no doubt in the next ten years or so I will get a little money out of it. Oh! By the way I have had my salary raised to £200 per annum and have turned down a directorship. Sounds mad I know, but it will be more beneficial for the firm if I'm not a director, as a member of the staff I can get much more information and news out of the rest of the staff and as I am trying to clear up a little doubt here and there, some of which has already been fixed I thought it best to remain as I am - not that it really makes any difference to me with the other directors. I have now paid for Romeo – funny peculiar?

Yes – I had a grand weekend no sleep at all I'm afraid people seemed to be arriving to see us all through the night and if they did those staying quite forgot that the idea of night was for sleep. No Darling, very little flirting I'm afraid, the old technique must be failing.
I hope to get some photos to send you soon.

I won $6 (25/-) over the weekend, but unfortunately lost about 35/- last Saturday, must do something about that.

Monica passed through a couple of days ago on the Harrison boat, and I went off to see her. I told her that I could not possibly feel about her as I might have done years ago, and that I was sorry if she must go and marry someone whom she really didn't love, but that I couldn't do anything about it.

Have got a dance in the country tomorrow a distant cousin of mine comes of age. Then on the 10th of next month the Trinidad tennis team arrives for 10 days to flag the annual inter colonial tennis matches every year then flag at each other's home (if you see what I mean) hear rumours of some very snappy Trinidadians coming up but don't worry Darling I'll tell you if I flirt. Talking of that, you must have gone off on your motor tour, hope you have a grand time, and remember to tell me of all the little diversions. Isn't that the cousin you used to be keen on once? I'm not jealous Darling since it's not serious.

Mummy and my young cousin, who is going to school in England this year, have gone to see "Wee Willy Winkie". I saw it in England but Pam wanted to see it so Mummie has taken her. She has been staying here to practice her piano she is taking some exam or other in a few days, you see she has taken after her cousin and is very musical!!!! Ha. Ha.

Funny how small the world is – met a girl at a tennis party the other day who was at Sherborne Girls School while I was at Sherborne, she knew Rosemary Rowe quite well.

What about Hugh and Rhoda when are they getting married? Must close now Darling, good night and all my love, Yours ever,

Bob

Hugh Rowe and Rhoda Garnett married on 7th May 1938

Upton
In bed 9th May

My Darling Bunny,

Thanks so much for your two letters which arrived together. I was beginning to wonder if you had changed your mind and gone off somewhere else as I didn't hear from you for some time. As a matter of fact it is almost two weeks since I last wrote, and as your book of words will show there have been no boats.

The tennis team arrives on Wednesday: but I don't think I will have to report any flirting; the girl I came out with whom I told you I had flirted with is coming up here but to get married, must be my technique that has got her married!!

As a matter of fact it looks rather as if Trinidad will win as our side is not up to standard and they are bringing up a pretty good side. Usually we always win at home and loose down there, so if we lose here too we shall be always one down. George and Laddie Challenor are playing, not together this year which is unusual, they have played men's doubles for the last 10 years and were beaten for the first time 2 years ago when T'dad were up here. Have been to a couple of very good dances lately, just things go up at the last minute and the men pay for drinks and the band, someone lends a house and the girls bring supper. The last was on Saturday and everyone was asked at various times and told whatever they were wearing when they got the invitation they had to come in. It promised to be a very good show as a girl and a boy were given their invitation when under the shower: Anyway they all seemed to compromise and arrived in pyjamas. I went in shirt and trousers with sleeves rolled up as I happened to be in one of the bonds when I was given mine, very nice and cool, I also had a shower and borrowed one of the host's shirts half way through the night!

Everyone seems to have either flu or whooping cough, my young cousin being one of the last to join the whoops, hope I don't go and get it too.

If I remember I will stick in a couple of photos which show an amazing chalk mound, I didn't know that we had anything so wild looking in the island.

Well my Darling, I'm almost asleep – Lord knows what this letter would read like. Do hope your Pop is much better, I still think he should be ordered out here. All the best my sweet,
With lots of Love,
Yours ever, Bob.

My Darling Bunny,

Thanks so much for your letter which I received this week. You must have had rather a good time, I envy your cousin!

Darling, it was grand getting your views on the subject of Monica, by now you will have got my letter in which you will realise that we both have the same ideas on the subject.

We are having a most exciting time – the T'dad tennis team are giving us the works, and yesterday afternoon we did a grand recovery by winning all + matches, we now stand B'dos 7 – T'dad 8, so the crowd should be terrific this afternoon. I think it's the best of 25 matches of men's doubles & singles, women's doubles & singles and 2 mixed doubles. I have just returned from The Crane where we have been having a bathe and drink with the team. They are a very quiet crowd this year, most of them seem to be on the wagon and taking the tennis too too seriously!!

*Bunny had a trip to Cornwall and
The Scilly Isles with Tony and his mother.*

Our new play has just arrived, but the day before it did we discover that an English touring company will be here in June doing all the latest things like George and Margaret* – I'm most disappointed, as I had hoped to put that on at the end of the year.

The Yacht Club tournament starts as soon as T'dad leaves and although I haven't got too good partners I hope to get through one or two rounds.

Darling, I must get this off as the mail soon closes. Write soon, with heaps of love, yours ever, Bob

Upton -22nd May Sunday Afternoon

My Darling Bunny,

Thanks so much for your letter which arrived yesterday also the photo. I had no idea that Hugh and Rhoda were married, give me their address, I must write them sometime soon. How long did you lean over the engine, of course you look as though you have dropped a hairpin somewhere before you could get them to snap you?

Well I'm sorry to say that we lost to Tranquillity, that's the name of the tennis club in Trinidad that sends the team up, I've sent a cutting from the paper in which George's brother who was captain made a few good remarks. The team left on Friday night or rather Saturday morning about 3am. I'm afraid I can't take all these late nights I have been sleeping all day today, and as you may have guessed am writing this in bed. I

---

* George and Margaret was a comedy written by George Savory and had a successful run in the West End and Broadway

have ordered a few photos which may be ready tomorrow, but I don't know, anyway I'll send them as soon as possible.

The boat that this letter is coming home on is the one doing its same run home as we came on, you see it just happens to be a little earlier, that's all. What makes me all envious is that some people who came back with us are going again, not world's workers obviously.

We are going up to The Crane for Monday night and Tuesday returning on wed: morning. Tuesday is some bank holiday, I'm having 14 people up to breakfast that morning, of course a bathe and egg flip first!!

Darling I'm still half asleep and seem to be writing the same thing over and over again. Somehow there doesn't seem to have been anything but tennis lately and I haven't even got any real necking to report, it was a bad team, except for tennis!!

Darling I must close for now as I have to get up, there is a cocktail party in the country and I have to go and see some people who live quite near first. Will keep this open in case there's anything to add. Bye for the present my sweet –

Have not been able to get the photo yet, so will send them next time.

With lots of love,
Yours ever, Bob

Office – Monday 30th May, 1938

My Darling Bunny,

Thanks for your letter which arrived on Saturday. You say you are away for a tennis tournament, but you don't mention how it's going?

I have not been too successful in the Yacht Club tournament; I lost in the mixed doubles on Friday 6-8 7-5 4-6 a grand fight in which I have ricked a muscle in my leg. Have been to a few other plays very good indeed, tonight is the one that is meant to be so vulgar, of course the house is sold out, "The Greeks have a word for IT". Mummie is going just to see if it is really bad she says. As a matter of fact the one on Saturday was quite good "The Old Folks at Home" rather subtle I don't think she understood half of it.

Had a flat tyre on Romeo the other night. Just when I was late and in most unsuitable clothes to fight with one. This month is the time when one hates a car, for we have the taxing and insurance to pay out about $110 for Romeo all in one month!!

I have taken to reading. I can hardly believe it, the truth is darling I'm losing my technique, I was accused of it on Saturday night when they said they couldn't understand how it was I wasn't taking out one of the actresses, very charming too.

Thanks for Hugh's address – our letters will have crossed in which I asked about it.

I'm rather sunburned and uncomfortable today, was sitting about on the club beach too long yesterday reminiscing about the "City" with a lad who is in the Police out here, and who used to be in the city, and knows most of my old haunts.

Darling I must close, as there really isn't much news.
Write soon my sweet, with lots of love.
Yours ever, Bob

7th June 1938

My Darling,

Thanks so much for your letter, I expect there is another one in the post now, but it is raining like hell and the mails have been closed suddenly, yesterday being a holiday did not give us any warning, so I'm writing this and having it sent off.

We have had nothing but rain for the last week, and the Yacht Club tournament is not too far on. I'm enclosing a photo taken at the tennis picnic at a rather lovely spot called Chancery Lane; this morning I've heard that a boy was drowned there over the weekend, it's a lovely spot, but a little dangerous.

We get another holiday this week; Thursday is a holiday, such a pity they couldn't have run them all together.

On Friday the theatrical company start here, I think they begin with George and Margaret, I am not seeing anything that I saw in England but am definitely going to "The Greeks have a word for IT"* don't know what "it" is but they say it is a very vulgar show, naturally the house is almost booked up!

Yesterday I took four people down the hilly side of the island and Romeo did fine of course – 2nd was all that was needed. Darling I must send this off – with lots of love my sweet, Yours ever, Bob

Upton June 12th, 1938

My Darling Bunny,

Thanks so much for your letters and the photo of the bridesmaids. I don't think I met this girl, but anyway I never remember a name. What are the younger generation coming to making a dog show an excuse for a drinking party!!

Well I must admit that I thought the last thing Hugh would do would be to visit the "Old School" on a honeymoon. By the way can you suggest something that they might like for the flat that is something all tropical like which I might get or have made? Write and give me some suggestions. You might also give me their address as I must write them, anyway in the mean time give them my love and tell them I wish them all the best.

Rain, rain. That all it's been doing for the last few weeks, very depressing, but of course very important for the old sugar crops. I seem to be working much harder than I've ever worked before, but that's probably my imagination. There is nothing on nowadays, no dances, or rather regular dances, and the theatrical company are putting on so many more things that I have seen before. I went to see "Love from a Stranger" last night, they are very good and I liked it a lot.

That land that I told you about has not been so good – there was some mess up about building and water supply so we thought it best to get rid of it, the Government have taken it over for either playing fields or local housing - we hope it will all be fixed up by the end of the month and I think I should make about £75 profit, still better than a kick in the pants as the musicians might say.

Yes, I'm afraid things on the whole are far from being settled in the West Indies, I don't think that we are as badly off as T'dad and Jamaica, but one never knows, it is obviously foreign propaganda working them up and one can't say where it will end. All this bilge that is talked by a bunch of nitwits in the House of Lords

---

*1930 comedy written by Zoe Akins about trio of money grasping ladies with sugar daddies

etc, about bad conditions and the lack of education is tripe. That is given out on the wireless and does a great deal of harm. The majority of the people who say all this haven't the vaguest idea what the real conditions are, or the types of people we have to deal with. Sorry Darling that's all rather like a speech.

Darling as to the business of stop writing that's for you to decide, I would far rather we didn't, I'm still terribly in love with you, and as a matter of fact it is one of the real bright thoughts that I have. I do so wish you could come out, it's so depressing thinking how terribly long it will be till we meet again, and of course the longer it is the more changes we will find in each other. In real fits of depression I like to fancy myself the confirmed bachelor, but I don't think we will change with such wide variations, anyway I hope not: and so darling unless you think it is best, please keep on writing, I love your letters so.

Might I point out my sweet that I do not number both sides of my paper, and although you will say you have written me 8 pages time before last that this would be 10!! Now compete with that if you can.

Longing to hear from you, and don't forget about Hugh and Rhoda. With all my love, Bob.

July 4th

My Darling Bunny,

Thanks so much for your letter and photos, which I think are quite good. You do look well don't you my sweet!!!!? You have no idea what hellish heat we are having, don't know what's in store, if it's a storm or what, but it's so steamy it seems to be hard to breath.

All last week we had rains, so there isn't much news. On Saturday I went to a very good cocktail party after which we went on to the Aquatic Club where they had a rather poor dance, anyhow I did a little flirting to pass the time away. Yesterday I played badminton, the first time out here, it's not very good as the sun was in your eyes at one end and the wind was most peculiar at the other.

It's a pity if Boyle is blasé already, as he will get worse when he has been here for a year – the ADC is a very sought after man? The new road traffic regulations have just come out and they seem to have got almost all round Bridgetown has now been put to 15 MPH a most impossible speed.

Did I ever tell you, you were spoiled? That new camera [new Voigtlander] is a lovely sounding thing, but you will never get to know all those gadgets, anyway I shall be most disappointed if you don't send me that photo in the bath, I need hardly say not to bother with the soap, as the results will be probably very decent!

My god, I'm melting, I think we should get some excitement if this lasts. Oh! By the way there are great rumours that they are going to have riots again this month. The 27th is the anniversary of the last show, so you never know how we may be shooting soon.

Darling, I must be off and see if I can find something cool to drink. Sorry you are only "rather fond" of me? Anyway write soon.
With lots of love my sweet,
Yours ever, Bob

My Darling Bunny,

Thanks so much for your letter which I got this week. Can't think of anything nice and yet local for Hugh and Rhoda, that doesn't sound very complimentary to the island does it? What about reading lights, have they got hundreds of them? They make rather a nice light with the shell of the "konk" as a shade, its rather nice and of course very local, but generally people don't want lights anyway not when first married – funny ha! ha! let me know don't tell them I want to send it, or they will say yes.

Darling if you have a spare photo, I should love one, and your others have not been put into the draw, one reposes on my dressing table, the other I have cut out and that is in my desk. I'm afraid that I haven't any of myself somehow except for weekend parties, one never has ones photo taken, and there is no one who can do it properly anyhow.

I have been playing a little cricket again, not too good yet, but may be able to make a grand "come back"! Somehow I seem to have got a damn cold, I might lose my voice, and wouldn't that be awful?!

We are just waiting to see what's going to happen, as there are rumours of strikes and/or riots either about the 17th or they may wait till the new governor arrives, just a friendly welcome for him, I hope Boyle can shoot straight!!

I'm giving Romeo a new hood, the present one leaks like a sieve, and as the rainy season isn't really here yet, what can one hope for.

Have been more lucky lately at poker, won about 30/- at a shilling a play the other night, its quite good going.

My sweet there isn't much news these days, everything is very quiet. I still love you, by now I thought you knew that? See –

With all my love, Yours ever, Bob

My Darling Bunny,

Thanks so much for your lovely long letter, I'm so sorry that your Pops is ill again. How awfully disappointing for you my sweet, I do hope he will be quite better by now.

Fancy you as a cricketer, funny peculiar I call it. A very good effort the 24 bottles of champagne, can't say I've ever done better, and I thought this was a hard drinking place and England the quiet rather sober parties!!

You seem to have been hitting the high spots lately, Wimbledon, tennis dinner, parties, it's all too grand and nothing happening out here now, not even any dances, it's too hot.

Darling don't come out this year, or rather not yet as the Uncle and Aunt are going to England in three weeks and the two small brats are coming to stay here, so there will be no room in the house, and as for you staying in hotels, well that's madness – see! What I would like to arrange is that you come out and stay early next year, in our gay season! Think this over, after all you should see what B'dos is like, passing through doesn't give you a good idea. Darling my powers of transatlantic telepathy are still good, probably I was thinking of you, believe it or not I still often do, there's a Ripley one for you – sweet .. I have just been spending the weekend at the sea, in fact you very nearly had the pleasure of sending flowers. I went out fishing at a rather dangerous spot where you have to go over bad reefs, all went well by day light but coming back I had the first experience of these locals uncanny sight in the dark. This fellow brought us through a zigzag channel in the pitch dark, if any one of the waves breaking on either side of us had hit us it would have been too bad. They will never get me going there in the dark again!!

Romeo has disgraced himself, he has cracked his manifold, and is now in dock having it welded and a new hood and wood struts fitted. He is also being polished, so with the new hood he will look like new.

In spite of all the rumours and nasty speeches there have been no strikes or trouble yet and so I think they will probably wait till the new Governor arrives.

Darling there is no more news so I will go to bed, have just been listening to dance music from the Pie Hotel, very good it sounds too.

Good night my sweet, I still love you.

With all my love, Yours ever, Bob

Upton
26th (no month - from the writing paper probably July)

Thanks awfully for your last letter, so glad to hear that Pops is well enough to go to Thorp, though I'm awfully sorry for you having to go up there at this time of the year.

I've just arrived back this morning from Bathsheba where I've been staying Sat: half day till today. That will be my holiday for this year, or perhaps I may be able to wangle another day next month when another friend goes to the seaside. I was with Sis and Jack this time, and was unlucky that yesterday was a filthy day, it rained hard all day, so I never went out of the house. I seemed to play bridge most of the day, and as try bridge is somewhat weird it was quite a strain.

Grannie tells me that she has written to you about coming out – something about March and April – that will be grand, but I had hoped in some way that perhaps we might have wangled it to be just before the old people sailed for England and that you would have stayed on with Mummie and I. That is of course taking it for granted that they are going to England which I don't know for certain yet. Anyway there wouldn't be much doing then, and of course it's hot. I think Grannie wants you here while she's here, but we will see how things work out, and then make definite plans. Don't think that this will be one hell of a party Darling, for there will be lots of rather quiet days, of course you will have my car, I think I can manage to get "Plunks" (Police Officer, Irish, quite mad) to give you a licence to drive in this very difficult Island!!! So you would be able to go down to the club for a bathe during the day. Tennis most afternoon, and of course the odd party that would so make for the very friendly existence that exists out here.

There is still a chance that I may be going up to St Lucia next month on business, it should be good fun, but St Lucia is rather a "dead alive hole".

Romeo is still going quite well, just approaching its 37 thousand miles, and I hope good for another 30 thousand. The paint is beginning to wear so I might paint him before you come out, what colour would you think? Silver grey with black wings, and aluminium wheels should be quite good?

Have been working much too hard lately, there are still people sick with this weird type of 'flu', if it is flu, so

I have all sorts of odd jobs to do. I hear that Cunliffe may be off to Jamaica this winter on business, but no more news of Busty, have you ever seen anything of them since I left?

Have just started rehearsals of the theatrical show given at the annual bazaar in aid of a local charity, don't think it will be any good, too many Wilkinsons (do you remember) in it. But I've very little say in it as Grannie is the president or something so I more or less have to do something.

Darling can't think of any more news, hope this hasn't bored you – must be off to bed. With all my love, my sweet, Yours ever, Bob

Royal Barbados Yacht Club
Barbados B.W.I.
August 1st 1938

My Darling Bunny,

Thanks so much for your last letter, I will see if there are any questions to answer when I get home, but as you see I'm writing this at the club.

Life has been very boring of late, and to add to the monotony I've been on a vegetarian diet for the last week. I'm feeling grand, but the doctor thought it would be a good idea. There is absolutely nothing happening here now and today most people are at the races, I've been for a swim and now decided to write here before going home.

The "Ajax" has been here for the last few days, as today being the anniversary of the "Emancipation of Slaves" they thought they may have some rough stuff. So far everything is quite OK. I can hear the roar of the crowd as they have just had a race.

I've been working rather hard for me of late, we are short staffed, and with one of the directors, my uncle, who goes to England on the 8th, I can see even more work in the future.

The new Governor arrives this week so I expect there will be great festivities soon after his arrival. Romeo has been in the wars! He burst his manifold and so I gave him a new hood while they had to do a bit of welding. Darling, I have a little necking to report, but it was very mild and really one must have something to break this boredom!!

I'm thinking of going in for a motor boat, only thinking Darling, as I'm told that the expenses on a motor boat are pretty high, but I have sold my share in the yacht, and thought that with a motor boat I might have some aquaplaning or even water skiing, so you never know my sweet that if you come out next year I may not be a super skier?? Oh! By the way saw a very nice thing in an American paper the other day –

> *There was a young girl of St Paul*
> *Who wore a newspaper dress to a ball*
> *The darn thing caught on fire,*
> *And burnt her entire ....*
> *Front page sporting column and all!*

I must try and find something for Hugh and Rhoda, as I could send it over by my Aunt and Uncle. They are taking the eldest girl over to school, St Margaret's Bushy, I think, makes me feel quite old as I remember holding the brat in nappies!!

Darling sweet I must end off now, will see if there are any questions when I get home. With all my love my sweet, Yours ever, Bob

Thanks for the photo they are jolly good, especially considering you took them!!! So glad that your Pops is much better, he has been laid up rather a long time. Darling, never tell a Barbadian that you are looking forward to drinking Jamaica Rum, we just don't recognise it when you compare it with ours!

Must cut my nails couldn't do it yesterday as it was Sunday, so must miss my sleep now.

All love my sweet, Bob.

Upton August 8th

My Darling Bunny,

I've just scribbled off a line to Hugh and Rhoda as I'm sending a "conk" shell lamp by the cousin who leaves for England tomorrow. Darling thank you so much for your last letter, I'm so sorry to hear that Pops is still ill, from what you say he sounds worse, anyway with nurses it means that your mother won't have so much to do and you can get away for weekends.

The weather is terrific, all yesterday it poured 3 inches if you know what that is, and today the heat has been awful.

The "Ajax"* left us on Saturday night; it stayed on to welcome the new Governor, a very fine looking man too. I saw Boyle in the distance, but haven't met him yet, I rather fancy that he is busy learning what an ADC should do.

On Saturday night they had a "not outs" dance at the Yacht Club so I went along, as a matter of fact there were quite a few not outs a lot older than myself there, it was quite good fun, only too hot, my dinner jacket hasn't dried yet.

There is nothing very exciting in the offing, one private dance for some young people out from the varsities on Friday, and another for some school girls also out from England on Wednesday week. Then the last ADC is getting married soon, can't remember the day now, otherwise rather hard work is all I can hope for with John going on leave, I would like to stowaway tomorrow morning when I go to see him off.

The brats have come up here tonight, so I've been good and played 'sticks' with the eldest who is very upset at her sister going to England.

Haven't played tennis for ages, although I've got in a couple of afternoons cricket, it seems to have been doing nothing but rain. By the way, I heard tonight that there is a hurricane moving north around Puerto Rico, that probably accounts for this.

Oh last week we had two days races, I never won a thing, not that I go, for I wrote to you on the first race day, but I had bought lots of tickets that they have on a sort of lottery, and never got even a cash prize, anyway I can't complain as I collected about 20/- at dice during the two afternoons.

We are having two new police officers extra appointed here from Palestine; we have one fellow already, if they are like him they should be great fun. This lad has bust up and turned over his car four times in a year. Of course, it's all hushed up otherwise we may go and say if the police do it why not I? But even so out of a car, he is even madder. Must close my sweet and go to bed, all my love to you darling, with lots of love. Yours ever, Bob

---

* 13th December HMS Ajax was involved in the Battle of the River Plate, the first naval battle of the war fought in the South Atlantic, when HMS Ajax, Achilles and Exeter engaged the German heavy cruiser Admiral Graf Spee.

Upton 14th August 1938

My Darling Bunny,

Thanks so much for your last letter and especially for the photo which is very good. I couldn't get used to the new way of doing the hair, but have got used to it now, although I think the way you had it done before, flat on top of the head, was nicer!! So glad to hear that Pops is much better, and thank your mother for her love, give her mine too please.

Oh! While I remember it, if you should ever be sending another photo, one piece of card isn't enough with the rough treatment they get out here, luckily the photo itself was not much bent, the outside thing however was badly cracked.

Very surprised about people not liking the choice of the commission, the official opinion out here is that they should be very strong.

We have had quite an exciting though rather sad few days. The Hotel at Bathsheba, don't think you saw that side of the island, was burned flat, some wild rumours that it was done to get the insurance. The next day two rather prominent people were drowned on that coast. It has always been dangerous if you can't swim, and more so if you don't know the places to go in. One of the people, head of the W.I. oil company had only been married to his second wife for 5 months. He was divorced and married this girl of about 21 he being about 56 or more!!

Gad I'm working too hard!! Doesn't seem possible does it, but we are short staffed and a hell of a lot of work to do. Lloyds are making a nuisance of themselves with insurance so we have lots of alterations to do.

I met Boyle at a private dance last week, and introduced myself saying that I had heard of him from you, he seemed rather surprised. Don't know what he is like as I never got a chance to have a drink with him. He seemed quite OK, but will have to liven up a lot for these people.

Darling, have got a little necking to report with an old flame of mine. Nothing serious darling, so don't worry. A great friend of mine said the other day that I must be in love as they had never known me so quiet. Not from the noisy point of view, but because I never seemed to be going off with odd girls to the flicks or Club Morgan (the night club) so you see darling you can trust me, although I will do a little necking every now and then, it's just my nature but I still love you.

Darling I must go to bed as there is no more news. With lots of love my sweet. Yours ever, Bob

Sent to The Mare Cottage but forwarded to
Dryburgh Abbey Hotel, St Boswells, Roxburghshire
Upton 29th August 1938

My Darling Bunny,

Thanks ever so much for your letter, hope that there will be another boat in this week. Hope you feel very honoured as I refused to stay on to dinner tonight after rehearsing for a show on the 17th of next month, as I had to write to you. Just think of that see!!

So sorry that your Pop isn't better yet, but anyway if one leg is better it shows that he is really on the way to recovery. No darling, it's not the Challenors who are going over, but my mother's sister and her ex-army husband.

Fancy having another Joan West, seems quite unbelievable? You'll have to bring the cactus out with you, but it has grown quite a lot already. Why didn't you tell me that you liked mangoes? Its rather late for ones that could be shipped but I could have sent some over for you, you must let me know about these wild fruits as I can go out into the 'interior' and get you some!!

Grannie has been ill for the last two or three days, some trouble with an ear, the rest will do her good, as with the children up here she is always fussing around. Anyway one goes off to school again on the 20th. Don't you think that you will get in the way, for you won't, no one will fuss over you, I hope you won't find it too boring, anyway, bring your driving licence and if you're good, I may let you drive Romeo, mind you he doesn't like women!

We have just had a hell of a fire, last Friday night, it burned out an entire block and only luck saved two petrol tanks from exploding, if they had gone up I think most of Bridgetown would have gone. I had to go over as we had £9,000 on the stock of one of the places, a nice year for the insurance as this is the 3rd big fire, there is some talk of having been set, but I don't think so. We are now doing private detective work as there appears to have been some drums of petrol in the store in the middle of the building, if we can prove that we are exempt from paying.

There has been nothing but rain lately and so except for a little bathing there hasn't been much outdoor sport. Went to a dance last week where Boyle was nicely tight and caused much amusement by dancing the can-can and big apple with a rather wild girl who, not too sober herself, thoroughly led him on. On Saturday there was a huge wedding, the last ADC, a rotten kind of a show, most people feel that it was a present grabbing affair, as it resembled a garden party or cocktail party much more than a wedding. It seemed that anyone who had ever been here was asked, even Tom Sopworth who had passed through here on his yacht some months ago.

Darling this is rather a boring epistle, but there isn't much to write about. I'm working too hard for my liking, in fact have never worked so hard before.

With all my love my sweet, Yours ever, Bob

p.s. as I can't see the nightie, why not include a photo of yourself in it while taking those you promised me of you in the bath. Better let me have the film developed here. Bob.

Upton 5th September 1938,
also forwarded on to Dryburgh Abbey Hotel, St Boswells

My Darling Bunny,

Thanks so much for your letter which I got a few days ago. No good enquiring about the water skis as the boat that I was thinking of buying has not been sold. I made enquiries and found that the hull was not as good as might be expected. Anyway, I've invested in some local shares so haven't much money for luxuries!

I think that advertisement you answered about photos is really funny – I laughed a lot over that.

I've been in bed for the last few days with fever. I'm much better today, cant think what caused it except it may be a type of flu, it was all very sudden and then almost as quickly it went back down to about 100° again. There is nothing much to report, rain, rain and still more rain. I missed what I should think must have been a pretty good cocktail party on Saturday and had to put off a bathe and cocktail show that I was giving at The Crane on Sunday, so have been ill at the wrong time. We are meant to be having meetings for the dramatic society and we are rehearsing for a rather more elaborate cabaret which is due on the 17th. At this rate I shall have to do a lot of overtime.

Must close my sweet, as I can't think of anything interesting. Hope your Pops is up at last he has had a hell of long go of it. Grannie is going to write to you about coming out, don't know when though. I hear it rumoured that they may be going to England again next year. I don't know if its true as I always thought the old man was not going back till 1940, anyway don't think I would come over, especially if you are coming out. It would be rather fun if you were out for the time they were away, Mummie and I generally stay here so you could stay too, anyway I will discuss this with them, of course there isn't much going on then and it is hot, while in January and February its cool and there are dances.

Must end now darling, as the Old Man has to take them to town.
With all my love my sweet.

Yours ever, Bob

Upton – September 12th 1938

My Darling Bunny,

I'm afraid that this will be a lousy letter, there is very little news for since last I wrote I've not done much. I started work again on Thursday when I did a few hours work, I started in full again on Friday. I haven't been doing anything except two rehearsals one on Friday afternoon the other Thursday afternoon which didn't end till almost eight o'clock.

I like your paper darling even the brick red letters, I'm afraid I can't raise to such style. You see I don't write enough letters yours being about the only ones.

On Saturday we have a dance at the Marine Hotel and there is a new type of cabaret, two lots of piano playing on two grand pianos, then some tapping and songs, I'm doing the thing "Oh, how I hate women" Ha! Ha!

Fancy you doing office work for your Pops, so glad he is so much better. Who is driving to Scotland – you? Oh! By the way have you still got that awful little Beep! Horn on the Vauxhall?

We have been having terrific rains and a few bridges have been broken down, the heat is really good now, and it's not much fun in town just now.

What fun we are having with this European situation, I'm now listening to Hitler's speech, what a man, he seems to think that he has the whole German nation behind him I wonder? Well I somehow feel that there won't be war, anyway not yet.

Laddie Challenor leaves for England by this mail, he suddenly decided that he would go, we didn't expect that he would be going till October. The Governor's eldest son who was going to Sherbourne, and into my house funnily enough, for the first time this term, has been kept back here owing to European conditions quite a lot of people with children in England have called them back!

Well my sweet I must close, this is a terrible letter but except for reading "The Rains Came" I have done nothing. Longing for your next letter.
With all my love my darling.
Yours ever, Bob.

My Darling Bunny

Thanks for your lovely long letter, I'm afraid that I missed the last French boat, but her mails were to be closed at 2pm, instead the boat sailed at 10am on the same day. Sorry darling, but you see I have a good excuse, and my sweet it's the first that I've missed!!

Everything is in a flat spin, the news seems to get worse and worse, but of course we get the concentrated stuff which I think is rather inclined to make things sound worse than they really are. I can't help feeling that even now there won't be war, although I can't quite see how we will stop it.

Yes it's rather amazing that this time last year we were having a super time in the South of France. I wish we were there again now, without the European troubles. Thanks for the heather – I have the white one in my desk, a couple of the staff were very interested in it so I gave them a couple of bits of the other.

Yes darling, I have your AA route, if you would like it I can send it over for you. You know talking of that I can't find anything that you might like for your birthday, and there is some talk of writing by the German boats or sending parcels, for if there is war of course everything would go.

I've bought myself a new racquet, and played with it this afternoon for the first time, I can't blame the good old fish net anymore!?

Our cabaret went off very well and people seemed to enjoy the show. We have had lots of rain again, and even some good thunder storms – one house got struck by lightning twice, this side of the island was not troubled much though, and just as well as Grannie is terrified of it. I may be going off to St Lucia on business early next month, but nothing definite has been fixed up yet. Various friends have gone off to the sea-side for next month, so I expect I should get a weekend or two away.

The flu, or whatever it is, is still raging, I'm sure it is some germ carried by mosquitos (don't know how it's spelt) after the line of malaria. Don't worry my sweet when you come there won't be any going this is the time of year for those things when the rainy season is on. I'm enclosing a cutting from the paper, the first part should be taken with a gram of salt for nothing could make the Marine look like fairyland except lots of "fizz" which as a matter of fact I did have, so you see you aren't the only person who can go to bottle parties!!

My darling I must go to bed, I can't think of any news for life is really rather dull at this time of year – so my love with all my love. Yours ever, Bob

p.s. Afraid David Boyle isn't doing too well. People don't seem to like him, he rather gives the idea that he is brainless, and except when he is a little under the weather, which I might say isn't infrequent, he is dumb without a cause! I hear rumours that he isn't doing too well at GH either. We are now getting two additional policemen (officers) from Palestine; they should wake the place up a bit.
Love B.

Musical Entertainment At The Marine Hotel

A Fine Programme

ON SATURDAY NIGHT LAST the Entertainment Committee of the Marine Hotel staged a cabaret supper and dance the principal feature of which was a sparkling variety entertainment in honour of the increasingly popular Maestro, Mr. Lionel O. Gittens, who has become the bright figure in the musical life of the island's leading hotel.

As usual, the Management explored every avenue to ensure that their patrons derived the utmost from the musical fare. The ball-room was transformed into a gorgeous background of elysian grandeur, the artistically arranged lighting making of the grounds a veritable fairyland in which the Dance Hall stood out a brilliant palace of splendour.

Before the entertainment proper began six dance pieces were played and the bumper house attuned their spirits to the transporting atmosphere in preparation for the delightful treat to follow. After the fifth number, the dancers revelled in the "Lambeth Walk" the dance that has taken London by storm, and was then introduced to the island for the first time.

THE PROGRAMME

The Programme proper began with a lilting song by Mrs. George Challenor "I want to spread a little Sunshine," in which she was assisted by a Chorus. Familiarity has not bred contempt for this talented singer, who was well received. The next number brought down the house with cheering. It was Chopin's Polnaise in A Major arranged for two pianos in which Mrs. Lawrance Bancroft and Mr. Gittens further endeared themselves to their audience. A Tap Dance to the music of " A Toy Trumpet" was next perfectly executed by six pupils of Miss Murray and Miss M. Wilkinson. Then came the highlight of the evening "Excerpts from 'n a Persian Garden' " (Liza Lehmann) with Mrs. Thorne and Mr. Evans as solists and a chorus. It was most realistically rendered, and was a personal triumph for Mrs. Thorne, who came in at the last moment to take the duet with Mr. Evans vice Mrs. Sisnett whom illness kept away. Mr. John Skinner made his first appearance in a Tap Dance, which was followed by a Selection of Dance Numbers, arranged for two pianos and also rendered by Mrs. Bancroft and Mr. Gittens. Their playing of "You and I Know," "Did Your Mother come from Ireland," and "Love Walked In" brought them resounding demands for an encore, which took the form of a most novel arrangement of "Humouresque" and "Swanee River." Each of the pieces was rendered by one of the players; they were then played simultaneously; then they were played as a waltz and finally as a fox trot. It was all too good for a single helping and the audience cheered for more. The pieces were played over again. The Musical Monologue, which followed, Mr. Bob King was exceptionally good as the world's greatest mysoginist in the song "Oh, how I hate women;" only he was too sincere to be true. Miss Norah Bowen, the rhythmic phantom, gave her audience an ethereal display in a Classical Tap Dance. More at home, the bigger the occasion, Miss Bowen tapped away in perfect harmony to Rubenstein's Melody in F, and then amazed her audience by tapping to a waltz 'Tippitin' which she gave as an encore. The finale "Medley of Old Tunes" was a gay, appealing, hilarious medley of excerpts from popular songs, rendered by the Chorus, joyfully rounding off a delightfully arranged Programme of high entertainment value.

Bob was a enthusiastic amature dramatic participant

My Darling Bunny,

Thanks so much for your last letter, I rather doubted if I would have a mail this week for with this business of war, the German boats were not calling here. Anyway, there seems to be calm again, so the boats will call as usual. We were damn near war, and even now there seems to be a split of the Government as to if it were right not to fight. Yes, darling, the colonies generally send troops over. As a matter of fact, there was quite a lot of chat about it, and there was a movement afoot by those in the Government to see who would go. The chief idea being that if only people like me went then the future of the island would be hellish. The idea seemed to be that we would go only if large numbers of locals went, otherwise we should stay as there would be lots for us to do before the war had gone too far!! Anyway, my sweet I think that is over now, anyway let's hope so.

Yes, my sweet I agree with your brother, I should have been up there with you to look after your behaviour. I too have a little necking to report, we have just returned from The Crane after spending the week end there. The hotel was full and a girl that I really hardly ever see was there and well darling, there was a moon. Anyway I too have returned without any heart aches and I think by now my sweet that you know that I do love you.

Darling, this business of a photo, you don't know how bad my mother is at taking photos, anyway I'll see if anything can be done – tell you what I'll wait till I get that one of you in the bath and/or nightie and then I'll promise a really good photo!!

There hasn't been much happening in the last week, I've played a little tennis, but we haven't ended the rains yet. I'm meant to be playing tomorrow, it will be a hell of a rush as I will be playing up in the country and I have to get home, change and get to the Bridgetown Club by 7.30 for a 'stag' dinner for the lad whose getting married on Thursday. I've lost about $16°° at The Crane on the slot machine and tomorrow night I suppose there will be dice, or poker, hope I win.

The news is just on and they say that you're having gales, we are being quietly cooked.

Darling I must go to bed all my love to you my sweet, I think the next mail will arrive in time for your birthday. Yours ever, Bob

Royal Barbados Yacht Club
10th October 1938

My Darling Bunny,

Very many Happy Returns of the 21st. I expect this will arrive on your birthday, I hope so.

I haven't been able to find anything nice for you, but the tortoiseshell book marker struck me as being rather unusual. The clothes hangers are made with a local grass "kuskuss" I believe the French make a perfume of it, anyway they use it out here to make ones hankies or clothes smell nice, that is if you like the smell.

Grannie sends you some Guava Cheese with her love and good wishes. She is at the moment in a flat spin as Elizabeth the eldest of the two cousins at home has been brought home from school and what with a temperature and cough the fear that she will develop some chest trouble or the other.

I have been away to the seaside again this weekend. Bathsheba this time staying with Sis and Jack (Mr and Mrs Thorne) and Den and Bert (Mr and Mrs Sisnett). Den is Lucille's sister. The former two are the grandest couple I tell all my woes to Sister in fact I am always in and out of their house. You will meet them when you come out. The two families are sharing a house so I went down on Saturday and came up this morning. I hope to go down again for a long weekend.

The wedding on Thursday came off very well; I was beautifully lit and really enjoyed myself. Next Sunday I have been asked down to spend the day with the newlyweds. They are also at Bathsheba so all the others are always going round the house and giving them hell!

Haven't played tennis for ages, it always seems to rain, anyway have just been asked to play at the Savannah Club on Wednesday so you can bet it will pour. Last Tuesday went to a dinner for the bridegroom, rather a drunk and I lost at poker. I'm meant to pay my doctor an occasional visit, think I better give myself a week to recover from the hilarity.

There are no dances just now, too hot, but the film "Hurricane" is on for tonight and tomorrow so I think I must go tonight. I got an invitation to Old Year's Night dinner, nothing like looking ahead. Suppose I will have to accept, but will curse if the usual crowd haven't been asked.

My Darling must go and change from these damn hot town clothes. Will think of you on the 21st. With all my love, my sweet.
Yours ever, Bob

Letter from James Fasson, (aged 29), who eventually joined the Lanarkshire Yeomanry
Borthwick Mains, Roberton, Nr Hawick, Roxburghshire
[Date unknown but Partridge Shooting time and prior to the West Indies trip]

My Darling Bun

It was very sweet of you to ring up last night. I am sorry the line was so bad because I could not hear you and nice Mrs W. How are you my dear – fatter than ever?!! But the same old Bunny.

I have at last got my wrist out of plaster and I do not think it is really any better. I went to the bone specialist, and he injected some dope into my wrist and said "Oh that will be all right" so it was for one day. I think half the time they just say anything these ruddy doctors! Anyway, I am back in the saddle thank goodness. We had an excellent hunt last Saturday. The ground is absolutely bottomless. Kim has just come up on my knee so sends masses of love – he is up again so sends more, my dear. Since I last wrote I have done very little except stay at ?Teri of bank with the Sperlings last weekend. A good peaceful change. A naval friend of Tony's was staying there also.

The Mackenzie's have asked Sheena and myself to go to the Highland Ball on the 16th. And we go to a private one, two days after in the Old Burgh. Hope I find a sweetie to hop round the floor with! Why the hell do you stay so far away darling – a great pity.

When are you going off to the West Indies? I expect you will have a darn good time but darling for heaven's sake don't make your home out there – it is far too far away from the Cheviot Hills.

I hope Uncle Gilly is better and the old girl full of life.

We had a dreadful shooting accident here the other day. John Ingles shot Col Kennedy out partridge shooting. He got the full charge and has been very ill besides loosing the sight of both eyes – tragic isn't it. He is a very great friend of Dads.

Darling, since I last wrote I have got a new housekeeper – she is most awfully good and very clean. So far she is looking after me very well indeed what a difference it makes to me I find – getting your food properly.

Well darling there is no more news at present. Goodnight, darling old girl. My best Love.

Jim

Office 2nd November 1938 letter forwarded on to
The Dolphin Inn, Thorpeness, Suffolk
[Bunny has written 49 on the envelope – most envelopes were numbered]

My Darling Bunny,

Thanks awfully for your last letter, this I'm afraid will just be enough to let you know we are still here! You see Darling, Monday night I had to take Mummie to the flicks as it was her birthday. Last night there was a rehearsal and so I had to leave it until today, or rather this morning as the boat sails at 10am.

Went down to Bathsheba again on Sunday, all this side of the island was washed away, but down there it was lovely and the sea very calm, with just ordinary swells for surf riding.

Grenada has been badly hit, floods, and lightening damages all the bridges out of the town have been washed away.

I had two photos taken of me, but the light was bad so don't expect that they will come out, anyway still waiting for the one of the nightie and bath!

Romeo is in dock, the kingpins on the front wheels are worn and the wheels rattle! Nothing very much, and as the Old Man is laid up with a bad throat I am using his Armstrong, don't like it too much.

My sweet, must end off as I really have a little work to do. With all my love, Darling Yours ever, Bob.

Office 7th November 1938

Thanks ever so much for your two letters. Mummie asks to thank you for your letter and sends her love. You don't know what you are asking when you ask her to take a photo, she is hopeless, anyway I enclose two bad ones taken lately, the one with "Prince" trying to be camera shy was taken by her. Anyway Darling I will try and have a couple of good ones taken soon. So sorry to hear that your Pops has been ill again, do hope that he is better again, rotten luck about your fall, didn't know that you ever rode, or rather fell!! Must be most painful, such an awkward place!

I've got an awful week before me, a rehearsal every day till Friday then I go down to Bathsheba for a weekend. There is a charity concert on Thursday night and the other rehearsals are for the Bazaar on December 3rd. That is the day that my Aunt and Uncle arrive back from England, so the family will be in a flat spin, as they have a stall which they have to go to at about 12 o'clock.

Darling this is awfully untidy, but there is a business discussion going on which I'm half listening to so hence the mess. Will finish this at home tonight.

Oh! You know I've never heard from Hugh and Rhoda, suppose they got the lamp OK. I think you said that you had heard about it? Bye for now sweet will write tonight.

Have got home late after a miserable afternoon, and none too good a rehearsal. I was meant to be playing tennis, but got a spot of work to do, and never got away from the office till about 5.15 and at this time of the year it is dark by 5.45 so I only got three games of tennis.

Darling you must do your damndest to come out, as although there may be a vague chance of my going over next year, it wouldn't be a good move, for A) it means a break in the office, which is really most detrimental, for being away for 4 months means that there is an awful lot to thrash out by the time one gets back. B) it takes at least a year to get the budget balanced after a trip to England, and then by next year I wouldn't have saved much money, and anyway if you can come out it wouldn't do to go throwing away money coming home again so soon.   You see if I'm ever to have any money to get married I must try and get some saved now, for I'm damn poor just now.   Darling I'm sure you will agree with me about this, for I've got to know all there is about the business, which, covers all sorts of jobs and lines, as when the old man goes I'll have to know, and not learn them.

Funny that you should ask about Audrey Branch (that was) Mrs Dix now, for she was out here only last month, I don't really know her, but I know her sister a little.

Talking about Xmas presents can't think of anything to get you. Don't bother about sending mine, bring it! When you write do tell me something you would like if not I shall send you something stupid.   You can send me a silk hankie for evening, you know the type you wear for show, and girls to wipe lipstick off your collar with!!

Oh! There was an eclipse of the moon tonight, you wouldn't have had it, only visible in the West Indies. You see we can see things that you people aren't blessed with.

The "Columbia" arrived back a day or two ago, this time last year I hadn't arrived yet we get here on the 11th. It doesn't seem like a year in some ways, yet that trip to the South of France seems an eternity. Now I'm rambling, must go to bed.
With all my love my sweet.
Yours ever, Bob

Upton 23rd November 1938

My Darling Bunny,

Thanks for your last letter, are you a 'film star' yet?   If not why not, don't say the old technique is going!!

Well, we have almost been washed away, I've never seen so much water, and it's not over yet, although it doesn't rain more than an hour or so now.   They say it's due to two planets being in consternation (the polite word for 'on heat') wish they would stop it or we will have to build a raft.   Nearly lost Romeo in this, fell into a river!! Not as bad as it sounds, but the water had washed out the road and Romeo fell in – removing front jack, flattening in exhaust pipe and denting the petrol tank, anyway he came out under his own power, and did the run home with the exhaust sounding like a tenor sax!

Have been playing a little Bridge, not that I have any idea what's happening but for some time now one hasn't been able to go outside.

The Uncle and Aunt should be leaving England today, Pam must be somewhat depressed although she likes her school awfully.

Last Saturday was the Cricket Club dance, we were very lucky to have about 1150 people for it rained from about 11.45am until well after 3am the next morning.

On Sunday had to go up to St John's (the parish near The Crane) for a cocktail party. I left early, but when most people had gone the remaining 14 people found, that owing to cars failing to go, that they only had 2 cars for the lot so the hostess had to turn out her two cars, they eventually beat up the island not getting home till Monday morning.

Giving hell with rehearsals for the Bazaar show, don't doubt that people will start throwing things right from the start – it's bloody.

Darling must end, will have this sent off to the Dutch boat, for the other will take longer.
With all my love, Bob.

Upton 28th November 1938

My Darling Bunny,

Thanks awfully for your last letter – it was a lovely long one. About coming out – Grannie seems set on Feb: so I suppose it had better be then, you mentioned Feb and March, don't make any definite plans for the return, as we may work it in for some of April, Easter is early in April and we could probably arrange for that long weekend that is always got up around that time of the year, so that you could sample a real wild Bajan party.

Yes, that girl at the Spanish restaurant was Lucile MOURRAILLE (a hell of a thing to spell), I'll get her address for you, she would love to give you any information, and would be one of the best people as she always dresses well. As to the Costa Rica don't know when she sails, but I think she is an awfully nice boat and the Captain is very nice. I believe a cousin of ours – Sybil Arthur – the Old Man's brother's daughter, will be coming out by that mail. She isn't bad, quite amusing and I quite agree that it would be nice to know someone before you start. No, there are no small boats except the Harrison Line, but they are awful - bad food, dirty and awful sea boats, don't tell any Harrison owner that of course or I shall be had up for liable!! [sic]

By the time you come the highlands will have all disappeared, we have had terrific rains more than has ever been recorded before and the hilly district have all begun to slip-slide, or fall over. Very nice to see but all roads have gone, and several estates have lost their canes and works. It is amazing to see how where they had ground crops growing they now have canes, or roads the man at the bottom gaining by collecting all sorts of fields!! One fellow who owned coconut trees made a good story out of it. He said that he backed various trees as they went passing out each other down the slope. The trouble is that there is so much clay, and if the sun dries it too quickly they fear that they may have a damn landslip!

Owing to the weather conditions the bazaar has been changed to the Marine Hotel, so the show will be held later (the 8th) at the Empire the huge (?) town cinema, and theatre. Don't agree with that idea as what may go down at a bazaar I am sure will not be liked at a theatre.

Today was the first day of the races, they have had to be put off twice already because the track was under water. I never go, but I passed round the Savannah today and the horses seemed to be fairly flowing their way through.

Well darling, must go and have dinner, have been sleeping all afternoon, now I have to go to a rehearsal. Will ring Denise and get Lu's address, the mail doesn't close until afternoon. Quite a change for me to get a letter in the mail in time. I generally have to write 'late fee'. With all my love sweet, Yours ever, Bob.

Lu's address: - Lucile Mourraille, 9 Barkston Gardens, London SW5

Office 6th December 1938

My Darling Bunny,

Thanks so much for your letters, sorry that I have to write this at the office, but have been so busy with rehearsals, and getting Xmas cards off that I've not been able to write.

Darling, Sybil Arthur is definitely, or as definitely as anything that she ever does, coming by the Costa Rica, so you would have someone on board that you know, anyway you will soon get to know the people - onboard ship is like that!!

I've just sent off some guava cheese, it's not as nice as usual because of all the rains it isn't as dry as it should be anyway I hope it won't go bad before you get it!

Sent a card to Lucille and told her that you would be getting in touch with her for clothes. You will want some slacks and shorts for going bathing, but cotton dresses are worn mostly. As to evening things just the same as England, without too much coating etc for coolness. You would be able to get a good racquet here but probably cheaper in England, get them to string it with Armours Varsity gut, not spiral; I find that it lasts better. Don't let them string it too tight, I think armoured for this is quite good, I'm not sure about this pressure.

I've got two paintings done for your Xmas, they are of a bay on the north part of the island, and should go quite well with the one you got at Age. The Bazaar went off quite well, at the Marine, the show is to be at the Empire Theatre on Thursday. The bookings are good, but don't think the show will be liked, too may novices. Darling must close, sorry this is so short – all my love my sweet. A Very Very happy Xmas and New Year. Yours ever, Bob

RN Hospital
Haslar
17th December 1938

My Dear Bun,

Thank you for your 'noos' – glad to hear the wicked Uncle progresses favourably. From one crock to another give him my salaams.

They have got tired of mucking about with me without any satisfactory result. So at last I've persuaded 'em to give me 3 months sick leave to be put right by a clinician. So I'm off on Monday to go into a home in Edinburgh. And hope that a specialist will do the trick. They haven't said so, but I gather its "Gulf Starvation"; to be treated by Horlicks and complete rest. I'm ready for anything as long as they put me on the track again!

You 'immoral hussy'! I wouldn't dream of another trip to the Scilly Isles – much! I hope you are right about the West Indies; I shall await the inevitable postcard informing me that my wife proposes bigamy. But Bunny try not to make a mess of things! You said once, he was something like me – I felt of course quite pixilated – but on thinking it over, I know "I'd make a hell of a husband". So "ca' canny my sweet white nymph!"

Tony Fasson at The Mare Cottage

The family seem quite well, althou' Papa seems to have been pretty shabby. So I'm telling them nothing about my move until I arrive in Edinburgh. 'Fraid I shan't see you before you go but rest assured your hubby will pray for you when and if he remembers.

Love to you all. Tony

My Darling Bunny,

Thanks awfully for your last letter, I can hardly believe that you will soon be here, this will go by the Costa Rica and Grannie has written to Captain Tea Klooster to tell him to look out for you. He is a grand person and will introduce you to people. We went home on her last year. I like her the best of the Dutch fleet. Tea Klooster was in the British Navy during the war and is one of the few foreigners who still has RN OBE after his name.

Now darling, the family would like you to be inoculated against typhoid – that sounds very terrifying but there is really no more typhoid out here than in England, but we happen to be one of the many families who are inoculated every 18 months. See Dr Gregory and he will fix you up - it's no trouble - I never even have a swollen arm, the only snag is that you shouldn't take any alcohol for 24 hours after having the stick.

Give Rhoda and Hugh my love and thank her for her long letter, tell her she is quite forgiven! So glad to hear that Pops is so much better, you must be glad to see the last of the nurse. Who are Jim's friends in T'dad, I may know them? Oh! By the way bring your driving licence, as then I should be able to wangle your driving here without a driving test. What have you decided about a racquet? For you should get lots of tennis as we haven't had any for weeks owing to the rain. Do you play bridge? I don't, but I try and play at it, not seriously of course, hardly ever for money, so you may guess how little I play!

Now, while I remember it you won't have to wire what time you are arriving as I will know all about you from the Agents, and I will be off just after you anchor, if its early don't eat too much as the meals out here are – tea and toast 7.30 – breakfast at about 9.30-10.30 a very light lunch at 2.30 that's with tea then dinner at any hour between 7.30 & 8.30. Do you think you will manage that!

I'm going to another wedding on Wednesday a very bad time as we are terribly busy this week, I worked like nobody's business today, you know darling I really think that I'm one of the worlds hard workers!!

Last Friday, there was a stag dinner for the lad who is getting married, we met at the Bridgetown Club (men only) at about 8 o'clock and after a very hectic dinner we began playing poker, I got away at about 3.50 and I came out square, having won at poker and lost at dice.

On Old Year's Night I am in a party of 30 at the Marine Hotel, have been asked out to dinner on Xmas night and then on to Marine so I'm fixed up for the festive season. Xmas dinner is at George's that won't be too exciting, I do dislike family dinners, you will see how terribly boring they are.

I hope by the time you arrive the house will have been done up. It should have been done before Xmas but with all the rains it was quite impossible to paint anything, anyhow the old barn of a place should be looking a little more respectable by the time you arrive.

Bring some old clothes to wear in the house during the day as no one wears respectable things in the house unless there are people coming in.

My sweet can't think of any more instructions so will close – am too excited for words – hope to hear by your next letter that you are booked and have been lucky in getting a good cabin. With all my love sweet.

Yours ever, Bob.

My Darling Bunny,

Thanks ever so much for the lovely hankies, they really are grand. What sort of Xmas did you have? We had quite a quiet Xmas dinner with George and Hilda. The night before was the dance at the Marine, I went to a dinner at which David Boyle and I generally broke up everything, then on to the Marine after which I went home as I had been at work until 6.20 that evening so couldn't take it. I believe most of the other people went on to the Morgan (night club) where they were until Xmas morning.

The wedding was a very good show, got nicely tight but went home fairly early. Went down to the Yacht Club this morning but before I got into the sea Plunks, police officer, arrived to arrange about a dinner for tonight so I went off to the Windsor Hotel with him, there we sank a few beers and on to inspect country police stations, I've only just got back, will have a little lunch and then go to sleep. We dine and then go up to The Crane for a dance. Tomorrow is a holiday too so shall make up for the extra late nights. Have been drinking too much lately, shall have to go on a strict wagon for January 1st!

The weather has been grand, I've slept under a blanket for the first time (at home) since I've been out, it's been down to about 65° at night, with bright sunny days with a cool wind.

Must see if there are any questions to answer in your letter. You won't have to worry about being too functional with Tea Klooster, he is really nice, and anyway he may put you at the 1st Officer's table, if he is the same fellow that we travelled with you will like him. Look out for one Sybil Arthur and tell her you're coming here, she is fattish and not too bad, nor too old. Why are you getting in touch with Cooks. They won't be any help to you, deal with the Van Ommeren people, the agents, direct, and give them hell till you get a good cabin!!

I will take this down tomorrow and have it sent off to the ship, there is another boat on Friday, but thought I would get this one so as to get in early. Rather think there will only be one more mail before you leave - what a grand thought.

Must go and get a spot of lunch, darling I'm getting all excited already.

With all my love my sweet, Your Bob

All the best for 1939.

1939

Upton 3rd January 1939 (No. 56!)

My Darling Bunny,

Thanks so much for the calendar, I think one of them looks something like Tucker, also for the letter. Can't think of any questions that I should answer, anyway when I go up, I will read it through again and see. Not quite sure Darling but rather think that this will be the last letter before you sail – grand!

What a New Year, we had a very good party at The Marine, and I sank lots of Champagne. David Boyle, Plunks and others came on from the Yacht Club and then we booked a room where we had Champagne on tap all night. I then went home with Sister (Thorne) where I got into Jack's pyjamas and went to sleep in her bed. On the way down a fellow who was rather tight ran into me, I got into the ditch and so he came off second best, I am really hardly touched.

On reading back think I had better put in that Sister was not in bed with me, but in the next – Jack's her husband!!! We all went on to breakfast with some people at a nearby estate; I then got down to cocktails at George Challenor's mother and so home. Laddie Challenor arrives from England tomorrow at about 2pm. The Intercolonial Cricket tournament (B Guiana, Trinidad and B'dos) starts on Saturday, this year it is here. An Elder, the senior Director of Gillespie Bros, arrives here about the 14th at one time Cunliffe thought that he might have been coming, which would have been much nicer.

What about your clothes, did you get hold of Lucile Mourraille? Well darling, can't think of any more news, will be off to meet you as early as possible on the 31st, mind you are awake!! Longing to see you sweet, with loads of love – Yours ever, Bob

Borthwick Mains, Roberton, Nr. Hawick, Roxburghshire

12th January 1939

My Darling Bun,

Thank you for your long epistle just what I needed as I have got over my weekend in Dumfries! I enjoyed myself not a little – all above board though. I suppose that is why I enjoyed it so much. I have been hit badly although up to last weekend I tried to pretend I was kidding myself – I am still doing it and trying to make myself believe it. The annoying part is that I used to admire her when I was at Castle Hill when she was fourteen!! She is twenty now far too young, so all will be well with luck. I feel like a rabbit in frosty weather searching for food and can't get or rather I can't settle down for long. My goodness I thought I had

---

1st September Germany invades Poland. 3rd September Britain declares war on Germany. Codebreakers at Bletchley Park start urgent intelligence work. HMS Courageous, rebuilt in 1920 as an aircraft carrier, was torpedoed by a German submarine and sank with loss of 500 lives. Albert Einstein wrote to President Roosevelt about using uranium to initiate a nuclear chain reaction – the atomic bomb. 'Gone with the Wind' premiered.

passed that stage years ago – it is hellish. Thank goodness I am dining with the Thompsons tomorrow a dinner dance so will endeavour to enjoy myself. Sorry Bun Darling for writing all this nonsense, but I feel that you do not mind me airing my feelings to you darling. For goodness sake all this what I've told you is just between ourselves and no one else darling. But because I've told you this probably at an inopportune moment, but it has just happened really last weekend. We are just the same as ever and always will be Bun darling.

I think the Rollers are going on one of these cruise boats – but if they are on board just introduce yourself as they are the greatest fun.

I am glad you are going out with a very level head. But as I always say to myself there are plenty more very lovely fish in the sea. But at present my theory is rather upset. Now Bun, not a word old girl. I do hope you have a wonderful time out there.

Of course, do write as your letters and none other keep me alive in the hills at this time of year. I'm afraid this letter is sentimental like – it must be Victor Sylvester Band as he is playing at this moment.

Goodnight darling, with much love. Jim

25 Belgrave Crescent *[A nursing home]*

Edinburgh

14th January 1939

My Dear Bun,

This will surprise you perhaps! But dear Ma has told me of your whereabouts, and I thought I'd catch you before you sailed on 'the Big Adventure'!

I hope you'll have a good trip out without having to use too much Mothersill's *[seasick remedy]*. For the first day or so, I'll bet you think – Coo'er when have I ever seen such a lousy collection as you fellow passengers! And yet by the end you'll have found they ain't so bad – I believe this is always the case – but then I forgot, you are an old voyager.

Malcolm Buist has just fallen to the tunes of one of your sex. He's done well too, for she's an heiress, and very nice too. We used to fish together as Snotties in the Rodney, at his father's place in Rosshire. So, I expect I'll have to assist the old devil.

I am beginning to get irritable again, having been fairly good for a week or so, but this "cure", so-called, is hellish tedious.

D'you remember "Madeline Carroll" who came back in the Viceroy? Well, driven to desperation for a little sympathy, I wrote to her; having sworn that I wouldn't. Now of course I am once more "up to the hocks" – but what the Hell! She's just off to Switzerland, but will be back in time for me passing thro' town in March – So what? "Quit chose épouvantable" *[What a terrible thing]*

Well Bun, try and use your head as well as your heart. I know it's impossible, but still try! And my blessings go with you. Give David a crack from me.
Affectionately,
Tony

Letter from Helen West, as Bunny departs for two months in Barbados, having not seen Bob for over a year.

The Mare Cottage,
Bovingdon, Hemel Hempstead, Herts Tel. Bovingdon 3212

January 19th, 1939

My Darling Bunny,

Just for fear you are hence – sick – not had lunch yet surely! Here is a nice letter from us both with all our love for your happiness and Bob's of course. I don't know when you will receive this darling, but I shall post it anyway.   You have been to us, what few if any daughters could have been, in this last very trying year. Dad's illness has been a great worry but has brought us 3 more than ever together understanding each other, helping each other in so many ways.   I do not think I could have carried on so well, had you not been with me to talk to and ever give advice – very sensible advice too, on so many occasions - not to speak of taking the nurses out, and so off my hands so that I could be alone sometimes! All the many little things you have done for us Tiddie dear – we do know – now is your time to have a repayment and may it first be one glorious sunny holiday from day to day.

The days are longer light now, Dad is stronger and well on the mend. We shall just be cosy together and get around a little and have one or 2 of your nice young things to see us. So, all is well love, all I will say now is first thank you for all you have done to help your very loving,

Dad and Mum

January 28th 1939

Bunny wrote a letter to her parents from on board Koninklyke,
Nederlandsche Stoomboot Maatschappy, Amsterdam (Royal Netherlands Steamship Co.)
on her way to Barbados.

My Darlingest Mummy and Pop,

Just got your wireless tonight, it was sweet of you.   Actually I had been wondering if I'd get one before we arrived. We will be just a day late on a/c of the bad weather we had at the beginning. It really was very rough indeed. One person very nearly got killed – she slipped and fell injuring her throat badly. She had to have ice all round it and couldn't speak or eat and nearly had to be operated on.   She's up now although still heavily bandaged. Poor thing it must have been beastly. Another person threw a bad heart attack almost immediately after sailing and has collapsed several times since. But everyone else is in fine form now and the last few days have been busy with deck sports. I was only sick the day after we sailed. Got up for breakfast and then parted with it soon after – Spent the day on deck under rugs. Felt awful in the evening buy stayed out as long as possible. The Captain came along to us on deck – we were the only two survivors – and had a chat. Col. Allen then kindly bought us a brandy which settled me well but made the other girl sick! Her name is Marion Butcher and is travelling with Col. A and a very nice person called General Farrar. The 3 who were on the Duchess of Richmond.   It has been nice having them as they immediately asked me to sit at their table and I spend most of the time with them.   Had dancing for the first time on Wednesday. They screen in the Promenade Deck and have it out there. No one much to dance with, but I had one with the

Captain. He's a sweet old fellow, with a big sense of humour. The Purser asked me to be on the Sports Committee, so I've been very busy of late – my main job was to collect subscriptions for prize money. So far, I've got £12-6/6 not bad? We have to arrange all the tournaments – bridge – Treasure Hunt Children's Party etc. The Purser is very nice, and dances well too! Tonight, we had a film with Mae West in it. Of course, I got ragged having the same name. I'm almost used to it now. Mummy darling, I only found your note today when I pulled out my blue sandals. It was sweet of you to stuff it in there. I wish I had got it before, but I have been living in sandshoes and never unpacked the others.

Do hope your arthritis is better and that Greg *[Dr Colin Gregory GP and old family friend]* has given you something for it and see that you behave yourself Gilbert and do what wifie tells you and don't eat so much Pork. (Had a very nice steak for lunch thank you!) We have a drink most nights with Col. Allen before dinner and he insists on us helping him with his wine at dinner, so we are being very spoilt. Then I manage a few Beers throughout the day!

January 30th

It's really getting hot now and I've discarded some blankets. I think I must have been the only person to sleep under 3 while passing the Tropic of Cancer! The Officers and Stewards have all changed into white today – we have had a wind the whole time which has kept it cool.

Today there will be some finals of the sports – tonight a film and tomorrow night a farewell gala dinner. 21 people land at B'dos 37 at T'dad. We had some priceless motor car races on deck the other day. You sit in a wooden car affair and have to pull yourself along a rope turn round and come back. The wheels are set crooked so it's very difficult and people get in the most extraordinary positions and they're very top heavy. I got to the finals and was then beaten!

I really have been terribly lucky with my cabin. It's a lovely one and I can't thank you both enough my darlings – Had Mrs Murray come I should have been livid as there's no one in 47. They had several cancels before sailing. I have my porthole open all the time (except of course when it was rough then I slept with the fan on and the door ajar on the hook, so that anyone who wanted to be a Peeping Tom damn well had to be!) Enclose a photo to give you some idea of how rough it was – it is looking right forward.

My inside is v. troublesome on this boat! It must be lack of exercise – However Alophen and a pill of Marion's has helped and we're OK again now! I was told the other day I was looking a different person from when we sailed – bright eyed and more colourful! Can hardly wait till Wednesday morning – we get in at 6am so I don't know when Bob will arrive onboard – I'm bound to throw a fit I should think. There's a man here who knows old man Arthur *[Bob's grandfather, Alleyne Arthur was the old family run firm of rum distillers and import export]* He says he's a wonderful old chap and a big noise in B'dos. The firm has been there over 100 years apparently. Enjoying this very much but am getting fidgety to arrive now. I love life on board – it suits me well – will finish this off tomorrow – must go and eat now.

January 31st

No more to tell you now will write after I arrive – Have to take this to the Purser's office so goodbye just now darlings.
V Best love – Bunny

On arrival in Barbados, on Tuesday 31st January, early in the morning, no time was wasted in getting settled in – Bunny became a member of the Barbados Yacht Club, Flying Fish Club, and Aquatic Club not to mention acquiring the driving licence which was issued without delay.

No letters from Bob, obviously, for the next few months except one during her trip to Trinidad, but usefully Bunny's letters to her parents were all kept.

Barbados
Yacht club

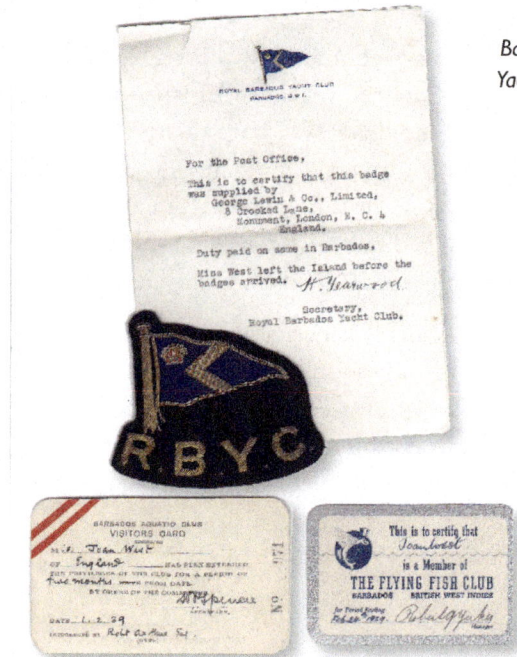

Acquatic Club

The Flying Fish Club

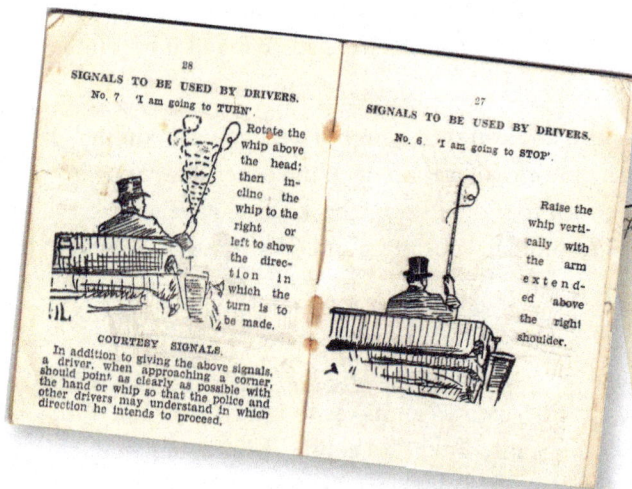

Driving licence

Upton, St Michael, Barbados
February 8th

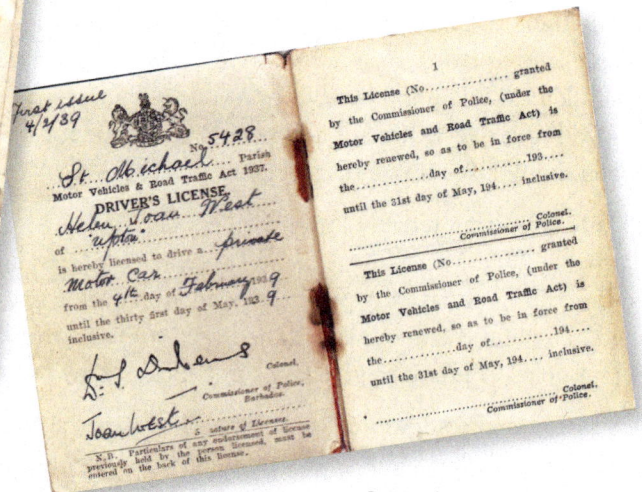

My darling Mumsie and Pop,

Was very pleased to get your letters, I'm afraid you would have to wait longer for my first one, although I got the Costa Rica to post it air mail from T'dad. We arrived in a day late as you probably know. Bob came on board just after we anchored and when the Port Authorities had finished with us. I watched him coming up the gangway, looking somewhat pallid in appearance! And I had a funny feeling right from the start that I'd never marry him. Well, it's quite true, I shan't - ever. We both realized before we'd even left the boat that there was just something missing and that things would be different between us. So, you see you'll be getting your small (?) daughter home heart-whole and with Freedom still her middle name! It's a good solution to a problem which has been worrying us all for a long time. I knew in my heart of hearts that I didn't want to live here but I felt I simply had to see Bob again before calling the whole thing off. And he says that right up to the time I arrived he felt exactly the same about me, and he also says never before in his life has he ever taken so much trouble over anybody. I know that we did really love each other very much and it was pretty near 'the real thing' only once more time has told. Bob doesn't agree with me there, he thinks its conditions and general atmosphere of the place you're in that counts more, and that here amongst his work and general routine he wouldn't feel the same way about anybody as he would away from home, which to my mind is rubbish. Of course, I think he's still too young to think of married life. That may sound funny coming from me aged 22, and it may be the result of spending a lot of time with someone older like Jimmie who obviously has older ideas.

Mind you I think I shall always love Bob a little bit or at any rate be very very fond of him whoever else I devote my affections to in years to come. I can't love someone to that extent and then just forget them. At first, I thought it would be better to come right home, but we are having a very happy time together and he wants me to stay on. Now I'm here it seems silly not to make the best of a marvellous place and in any case the boats are very full and I doubt if I'll get a single cabin now. Bob was finding out about it yesterday. I'd rather like to go down to T'dad and Bob suggests I stay here till the end of March go down to the Wrigleys and catch the Columbia, which is the best of the lot, from there about the end of the 1st week in April. There's a Tennis Tournament here that they want me to enter for in the middle of March and we've already been asked to something on the 25th. Anyway, we'll see what the shipping agents say. If there is a hope of a decent cabin before that I'll come perhaps!

Life is very gay here just now. The very 1st day I was taken to call at Government House – calling only consists of writing your name in a book and leaving cards. But I met H.E. and his wife at a party on Sunday. It was tea, bathing and cocktails given at The Crane Hotel which is up on the other coast. A perfect place and the colouring was unbelievable. The 1st night I was here B and I went off to a cinema together. The 2nd a cocktail dance where I met David Boyle. He's very nice and quite mad like several others here. There are a couple of wild policemen from Palestine, one of theme is a Plunket (Lord Plunket's son or grandson or something) and in charge of all Traffic and Fire Brigade arrangements. They are having a lot of trouble just now with cane fires – the crops have just started and the locals set fire to various people's cane as they want more money. They say that this Royal Commission has caused a heap of trouble and stirred up feeling, and it will be ages before they do anything to help if they ever do. The only thing that will do any good is for England to pay the people more for sugar so that the owners can give the labourers more. But they can't afford to at present as they get next to nothing for sugar.

Some of the people here are awfully nice. Mrs King's sister and her husband are very sweet. They have a child at school at Bushey so I must go and see her. I don't like all the people though. Some of them seem almost a different race of people of living out here – they are bound to be different especially if they don't get home often.

I'm writing this in bed – so excuse the writing please – Bob has just been in and is off to the office. He comes in every morning about 8.15 and takes my mosquito net off and discusses the days doings etc. We have breakfast about 9.15 and B get back about 10.30 for his. Then he messes about, has a potter in the garden and so back to work till about 4. We have a light lunch about 2.30 – sort of fruit – cheese – tea, bread and sling which is a lovely treacle stuff. No afternoon tea which I don't miss at all – and dinner 7.30-8 if we're in! We have a lot of queer vegetables which I rather like – yams, eddoes, rice and a pea thing, sweet potatoes, plantains etc etc. Breakfast is a big meal and I can't always cope with it – I should think I'll put on weight here as all the food is rather filling and of course Rum is fattening and I drink buckets of that. In the mornings I often drive down to the Club (Yacht) in the singer or in Bob's and meet the others for a bathe. By the others I mean the General, the Colonel and the girl. Saw Mrs Daincourt yesterday, I'd forgotten about her. They are all in the same Hotel. Cocktail party tonight and something tomorrow. Then HMS York will be in soon and there is a big dance for them at the Yacht Club. I think Bob and I are dining and dancing at the Marine Hotel this Saturday, but I get so muddled with all the arrangements!

They've put me up as a member of the Yacht Club and I hope to be elected by Friday. Then I have the privileges of the Aquatic Club as well. We wangled a driving license through "Plunks" (Plunket) without doing a test and with paying 2/6 instead of 5/-! They are awfully sweet about lending me cars. The old man has his Armstrong, the family one is the Singer, and then there is Bob's. They have a chauffeur who's been here 21 years, a garden boy, a garden girl, a cow man, a cook (18 yrs) a parlour maid and a house maid - all black of course.

We see the sugar canes being carted down by mules and cow carts. You see this is a big estate, but the old man sold most of the land some time ago. I am getting brown, but don't want to do it too quickly as I was a little sore the 1st day. Of course, some of the people aren't tanned at all – the ones that don't bathe a lot are quite pale. They like to keep that way as they're living here, otherwise they'd get very dark.

I haven't got used to the cold shower yet! No hot baths at all, you wash under the shower. I just run round and round it shrieking! There has been a strong breeze all the time so far which helps to keep it airy, but its terrifically hot right in the sun in the mornings. We usually have a snooze sometime during the day, either before lunch or after if there is nothing on. Bob needs a lot of sleep and doesn't get enough. He's looking pretty well but still has to visit the Dr as his kidney trouble is not cleared up yet – He seldom drinks which is a very sore point with him poor lad, for it does make a difference socially. It shouldn't, but it does.

Well darlings, I must stop this and get up. Don't like the sound of all the bombing at all. Hope it'll stop. Love to everyone please and I'll send some P.C.s when I get time. Bestest love to you both. Bunny

p.s. Hardly ever need a blanket at night at all! Bob sends love and thanks you for the ash tray very much.

Upton
St Michael, Barbados BWI
14th February

Darling Mum and Pop,

Got your letter yesterday Mumsie for which very many thanks. I was so sorry to hear about poor old Jim – still it must be the best thing now that he's done so much harm.

Well your rabbit is extraordinarily happy – I haven't enjoyed life so much for many a day and wake up in the mornings feeling just grand and full of joie de vivre if you know what that means. I adore this weather and all the things there are to do. I go and mess about at the Yacht Club most mornings, either going down with Bob and using his car, or else in the singer – Bob's in fine form now and we have a lot of fun together. He's a darling and I'll always love him a little bit I expect – he's spoilt here but he can't help that. He's looked on as very eligible and mothers and daughters chase him alike, but I fancy my coming out has acted as a sort of brake to that. My coming was heralded for a long time and we're always asked out together and put next to each other at dinners – even at GH! Can't remember when I wrote last but now since the dinner and dance at GH for some of the Navy. It was a very good show – quite small and informal. When we arrived we found David still in plain clothes. There had been a panic as a machine was reported down in the sea and the York was under sailing orders, but luckily the plane had landed at St Lucia and the officers were able to come off the York – very late for dinner.

When we arrived at GH we had a chat with David in his office downstairs and then we all foregathered in the hall. The men all get given a card with the name of the girl they are to take into dinner and a plan of the table. Bob was to take me and our places were marked with x's and an arrow to "Cad's Corner". Of course David writes them all out and fixes the places so we 3 were all next to each other at one end, and on my other side was a boy called Cooper off the Vindictive who knows Tony well. There were about 32 of us. Dancing afterwards in a lovely ball room upstairs with little balconies off the French windows. H.E. and his wife are awfully nice and not a bit stiff. I had a dance with him. They are both keen on dancing which is nice for the young people. Oh! I forgot to tell you that after we all arrived we file upstairs and David announces us and we are received by the Gov and Mrs then we have drinks before going down to dinner.

The next night B and I were out at a dinner at the Marine Hotel. It's a lovely place, with a huge ballroom open at the sides leading off onto a terrace and then a big garden. They have a huge local bank there – there are always locals but at smaller shows people only have about 3. I left the party for a bit towards the end as our officer off the York introduced me to the Flag Lt. who is John Lawrence – Col. Lawrence's eldest son. He is very nice indeed also his wife – they were most amusing about Polly and don't think much of her at all! They say she's a silly ass and damned bossy! I'm going to a cocktail party on the York tomorrow without Bob – they don't want local men much – only girls! The next night is the Dance at the Yacht Club for the Navy. The Governor turns out for that and the Admiral. On Saturday we have a dinner here of about 12 and then on to a dance. Yesterday was an At Home at the Yacht for the cadets off the Vindictive. Some played tennis some bathed some danced and most of them just ate and drank, greedy little devils. I played tennis only not with the cadets, as luck would have it, but with various officers from the York. Bob had had a tooth out so wasn't playing but was there sitting about. Drinks with various people and so home. Tonight, after tennis I am going to the concert party at the Empire Theatre given by the Ship's Company of the York. Bob and another man are taking me – his wife is out at some bridge do and he wants to come.

Mrs Daincourt is ill again I'm afraid. I must go and find out about her today. She has been moved to a nursing home I believe as she had a haemorrhage – the other day when I saw her she had had a temp of 100° one night but took aspirin and rested a lot and was down to 97° next day. Someone else in the same hotel is ill and is having a nurse come out from England. It's difficult to get white nurses here – there are a few in the hospital but that's full just now. Poor girl it's rotten for her. I don't know how bad she is but I know she'd intended going home at the end of the month.

Bob's Uncle and Aunt have asked me to stay on with them for another 2 weeks after I leave here, but nothing definite is fixed yet. I had thought of going to the Wrigleys in April – You'd better let me know what your views are. If all is OK with you both I may as well stay out for as long as they'll put up with me! Lil [*sister*] is a devil she never sent me the Wrigley's address and I can't write till she does. She promised to catch the mail after I left but of course never did. Give her a smart tick-off from me please. She'd adore it out here you know. I'm getting quite brown but can't do it too quickly and you blister so very easily.

A lot of the people I came out with are going back on the Costa Rica on the 28th I shall go and see them off I think.

I have bought one or two little things already – I may send bits of things home in envelopes to escape customs so you can make a collection of them in my room and we'll sort them out when I get back home. The local crochet work is lovely also the mahogany trays. There are thousands of mahogany trees here and most of the furniture is in that. Very nice too.

Don't know if you've seen anything in the papers about cane fires here but they are still having a lot of trouble. The idiots don't realize that it means less work for them and the owners merely claim from the insurance – and get very good money at crop-time. Something will have to be done to stop them though or they'll get more out of hand. People say they were settling down very well after last year's riots, until this Commission came out and stirred up feeling again. The locals thought the people were coming to give them more money and of course when they went home just telling them not to strike and that's all, they got upset again. The Commission apparently found that conditions here were far better than in the other islands but the damn fools hadn't the sense to tell that to the people.

Well my darlings the sun is out and I must be off for a bathe and I don't doubt it will be followed by a rum punch or egg nog! This letter probably doesn't make sense but Bob has been sitting here talking rubbish and reading stuff out of the paper non-stop! He's gone off now to do a spot of work – time being 12 o'clock!

Am meeting him at the Club for tennis at 4.15. Had 3 singles with him the other day but couldn't beat the brute.

All best love to you both and mind you keep fit and happy. Will try and write to Lil, if not time let her have this will you?

Ever your very loving Rabbit.

PS forgot to tell you the Old Man has made me a proper member of the Yacht Club and if I ever come back I just have to pay so many dollars a year. Am also member of the Aquatic and the Savannah. Shall have a fight with him over the subscription. Never delivered your letter to Mrs King. No need.

HMS YORK
AMERICA AND WEST INDIES STATION
(no date and hand delivered)

Dear Bunny,

"Man proposeth" but a riot is under way somewhere so we are off in a hurry to examine same: the usual round of West Indian fun and games.

I'm afraid it will have to be England, so

À bientôt   Attie

[*Who later became Admiral Sir Arthur Francis (Attie) Turner RN KCB DSC Chief of Fleet Support*]

Upton, St. Michael,
Barbados BWI
18th February 1939

My darling Mum and Pop,

I am beginning this today although the mail doesn't go till next week. But if I leave it I shall only have to do it in a hurry. Never have I known time fly so fast! I can't believe I've been here 3 weeks already. The days seem gone before they've begun. I suppose it's because I get up fairly late and then usually wait till Bob comes back for breakfast before I go off down to the Club for my bathe.

The mail came yesterday and I got all your letters – for which very man thanks. Poor old Ron [*Bunny's brother*], it is rotten for them all – I hope by now he's over the worst of it, but I'm afraid it will pull him down a lot. Had he had any idea that it was getting bad again, or did it just suddenly arrive? I suppose that will do in their Norway holiday too. It's all a damn nuisance and very worrying.

HMS York left in a hurry yesterday morning as there is a riot somewhere in Demerara – it was a pity as I was going on board for lunch – I've made a big hit with a certain Lieut. and have promised to help him buy a bowler hat when we both get back to London in April! He's quite a nice chap and lives at Chorley Wood so might be useful for tennis in the summer, if he gets any leave then. I met John Lawrence again the other day, he was on his way to a game of golf. His wife was here and now I suppose she'll have to pack off to Demerara.

The York had their concert party at the Empire Theatre on Tuesday. It was quite funny in parts and the whole thing was written and produced by a lad on board. Bob and I went with a friend of his called Bert Sisnett, He's a b-in-law of Lucille's, the girl I met in town before I came out. I may have told you this though. After the concert we went into the Morgan Club for a drink and a dance or two. It's the only night club here and doesn't really get going till 12ish. They have a superb band and it's a lovely place, but no cabaret like a London show – it wouldn't go down well here, and it wouldn't really pay them.

The next day I bathed as usual at the Yacht, then had lunch at the Ocean View Hotel with Marion Butcher, Col Allen and Gen Farmar. It's a lovely hotel – not enormous but right on the beach. You step out of the hotel on to sand and they have a pool in front of the hotel for bathing. It's actually in the sea but the water is so clear you can see where there is a bank of reef all the way round. It's not very deep but enough to have a good wallow in, and beyond that it would be dangerous. You cannot possibly imagine the colour of the sea here at times it really is perfect. I have put a colour film in my camera and hope for some good results. They cost 4/- each and you can't get them developed here – so I'll either send it up to the States to be done or keep it till I get home. Now where was I? Oh yes - Wednesday. Well after lunch I went back home and changed for tennis at the Club with 2 off the York. I had been asked to their Cocktail Party so Bob arranged to take 2 cadets from the Vindictive and show them a sugar factory. The Cocktail party was v. good indeed. Various boats went off from the Aquatic Club to the ship from 5.50 onwards. They had it all decorated with flags and little lights and their Marine Band played for dancing. There were very few local men asked as they have 50 officers on board. The Governor was there, of course, and the Captain received us – I never saw the Admiral at all. I could have got the most perfect picture if only I'd had a camera. Just as it was getting dark with the sunset almost over, a schooner came out of the harbour and sailed by quite close to us. She really looked wonderful silhouetted against the pink and grey sky. The sort of thing you see in a picture but seldom in reality. 'The King' was played at 7.30 and the last to leave got a boat back to shore. As we started both ships began a searchlight display which looked rather good.

Thursday was Mrs King's Tennis and Cocktail Party at The Savannah Club. We had about 3 courts for tennis. Played till the light went and then people arrived for drinks. Unfortunately there were various dinners on and several people had to go early. Bob and I were changing and dining with John and Kitty Hudson (his Uncle and Aunt) and I went back with them. Unfortunately, Bob's gum began to bleed where he'd had his tooth out – it was rotten for him as it was the Yacht Club dance. We arrived there late – he had a dance or two but it wouldn't stop and he looked a picture of misery. I wanted him to come home as I wasn't enjoying it particularly but he wouldn't do it, simply because I had about 2 more dances booked up – I didn't care 2 pins about missing them, but he wouldn't even go when I said I'd get a taxi home. However, in the end he went to the car and fell asleep. The next morning it was still bleeding and he had to go down and have it plugged. That made it throb and he had a mouldy 2 days. He should never have played tennis so soon after having it out, but men are funny creatures with their little ailments and seem to me just like small children! There was nothing on Friday afternoon so after lunch we both went sound asleep on my enormous double bed until about 7.15! That sounds a long time but lunch wasn't over till 3ish and then we sat around in my room doing nails or rather I was, and looking at books. Always when there's nothing on the family go to their rooms and flop on their beds. All of them sleep with their bedroom doors wide open so as to get a draught through. I don't actually, as I'm very seldom too hot – in fact lately I've had my blanket on. But out here the houses are built with rooms leading out of each other often without doors at all. In some rooms downstairs they have sort of shutter things. Saturday bathe at the Club followed by egg flips – very good! Rum, egg, milk, angostura and nutmeg. Lovely after being in the sea. Bob picked me up there as he gets home early on Saturdays. He went to sleep for the afternoon and I did too in the end although I meant to go and watch some tennis tournament at another club but the girl I was going with had fallen down some stone steps and hurt her knees. I did some ironing – an evening dress - and when Bob 'came to' again I was given the job of giving his head a damn good brushing and general clean up! He should have had it washed but on a/c of his tooth he hadn't so little Bunny had a good scour round with alcohol. Then if you please I had to cut his toe nails! I told him I'd refused to cut yours Pop as they were so huge. When it came to cleaning ears and finger nails I struck quite firmly and retired to attend to my own toilet!! It was the night of our dinner here. There were 12 of us young people and the other 3 had a separate table. It was a very cheery dinner – David came and two very nice young married couples – great friends of Bobs and various others. We had two butlers in, to attend to drinks and help with the waiting. They look so nice with their black faces and white uniforms. We had one man extra as the girl with the bad knees couldn't dance. Bob was going to come home early but in the end he didn't as his gum suddenly got much better. I think it was because he'd finally been persuaded to take an aspirin and that did the trick. It was a dance at the Marine Hotel. I danced everyone except one, which I was thankfully to have free, for someone had been throwing a sardine sandwich at me and I really needed a bit of a bath! We got home round about 3 o'clock. There is always a glass of iced water waiting for me in the fridge and we collect this on the way upstairs. Arrived in my room to find quite the largest spider I've ever seen on my wall! It must have been about the size of a tennis ball, legs included. Bob clambered up on a stool, armed with one of my tennis shoes. He took good aim – then wonk on the wall. But the spider was too cunning for him and he missed it! He had another crack at it with the same result! We then got the Flit can and chased the poor brute from one end of the wardrobe to the other and finally it shot under the door into the Arthur's room! Gosh how I laughed – we both loathe and detest spiders and nothing on earth would have made either of us pick it up. Got up fairly late yesterday (Sunday) had breakfast and went off down to a bathing party at quite the most lovely house I've seen yet. It was built about 2 years ago by a very wealthy Englishman who was once staff officer out here. He married an American and has a wonderful place in the USA and now this. It is all built in stone in Spanish style. A lot of wrought iron on these off white walls looks very nice. In the long lounge room they have a huge open fireplace filled with logs – an unusual sight here. Its only once ever been lit and I should think they must have been also! There is a swimming pool just outside the house in a walled in bit with hibiscus bushes all round – I took a coloured picture from the flat roof so hope it will come out. Their rum punches were very acceptable thank you! And they have a lovely cocktail bar off one room. I also took a photo of one of Bob's orchids. He has two pots of the most lovely mauve ones. There are several growing on trees in the garden with sprays of little white flowers. The others he has in a little house, open except for 2 walls of wicker – then they have the little yellow bee orchid which is a tiny bloom but very pretty.

Things aren't too good out here, and they blame the Commission for everything. There have been many acres of cane burnt as you've probably seen in the papers and lately various people have been striking – the entire staff of The Marine Hotel struck last week and had their wages increased 100%. Whereupon two other hotels struck and were promptly dismissed – the visitors having to wait on each other. But I hear since that they've been taken back with 75% increase. Some of the factories are not working as no one will bring in the canes, and the ones that are can't get the sugar carted to the wharf and Bob says shipping is at a standstill. People are just hanging around in town – quite good humoured about it but just asking for more pay which I don't see that they can all get. It's a difficult problem and I don't see what is to be done for them. One thing is they can't strike for long or they'll starve. Some people think that there's money coming in from outside – some communist affair, but I dunno I'm sure. People say there won't be any serious trouble as they had their lesson last time. Anyway the police force is very loyal and these locals can't seem to organize a proper riot. It's all very interesting – for God's sake don't get it into your head there's any serious danger and that your daughter had better come home early 'cos she ain't coming! Not till my time's up and I have to. Bob is back having his breakfast – he's just had a grain of rice stuck in his tooth hole, so we've had to do an operation with my eyebrow pluckers!

Just off down to the Club so will stop this. Pop, I do hope you're behaving yourself properly. Di says you're as mad as ever so I suppose that means you're pretty well. Mrs King has been using a lamp on her leg as she had sciatica – but it's better now. Hope your hip is behaving itself Mumsie and you're able to get over to old Ron alright. A friend of Mrs Daincourts has flown from Havana to look after her. She's a girl who was on the Costa Rica and was doing the round trip. I must take some flowers in for her soon. I think she is better and may go back at the end of the month in the Costa Rica. Don't bother to mark any more letters Airmail darling 'cos there isn't one! The only way you can do it is via USA and airmail to T'dad and on here but it isn't much quicker. I only sent your 1st letter like that as we'd missed the mail.

Have got accustomed to the food and it suits me well or else the Rum does, anyhow the old inside functions like clockwork! You might tell Greg the other trouble is very nearly gone altogether. It had by the time we arrived at B'dos and I've only used about 5 of the pills altogether since I left England. Must have been the sea-trip.

Have you sold the pups yet? Hope so. Di is being v.g. about writing – haven't had a word from Lil yet. She is the limit and I want that address badly.

Very much love to you darlings, from Bunny

Upton
St Michael Barbados BWI
26th February, 1939

My darling Mummy and Pop,

Have had masses of letters during the last few days. One mail came in unexpectedly via Martinique or somewhere, then yesterday's was the usual German boat, and the Old Man suddenly produced a letter out of his bag that had been sitting there for about a week! It was the one from you Pop enclosing the photos of the Sanitary Inspector! Thanks for sending it; it is very good I think. Glad to hear Ron is going along alright. I had another letter from him yesterday and he sounded pretty cheerful. You seem to be having a bit of an upheaval one way and another over his practice! I wonder how it will all turn out. Shall look forward to hearing the result! Len seems to be being a little difficult and not exactly helpful when the poor lad is laid up. It's funny because I always thought he was so fond of him. I think he is really, it's just his peculiar way of tackling things.

You do all sound in the wars you poor dears. I hope by now Juney [niece] is better again. It would be a change for her anyway to be at The Mare for a bit, as she never got her week before. What a mut that girl Mary is to go and get ill again. She can't manage to stay fit for long, can she? Had my usual report from Di on you two. You sound OK to me. Tell Greg not to be too hard on the dieting while I'm away, though I must say it doesn't sound as though you're being exactly starved. I'm eating far too much here and have put on flesh I think. They tell me I'm looking far better than when I arrived – so you can imagine I'm pretty well bursting with health.

Glad to hear your pups are doing well Mum. You ought to be able to get rid of them you know. Perhaps you've had some answers by now to the ad especially after Sir Galahad winning a prize again. Ron says you immediately raised the price!

Don't think there's very much news for you this week, except that I'm still enjoying life enormously – I have a passage definitely booked in the Columbia – leaving T'dad 10th April here 11th, so I shall probably come by her though I can always change to another boat of the same line! However, the next decent one would be the Costa Rica's next trip beginning of May which is too late. Anyhow, I'm not sure I want to go and stay with these other people now. I wouldn't be so independent and I wouldn't see so much of Bob anyway. I am writing to Dick and Bunty Wrigley to see if they can have me from about April 3rd – 10th. If not I dare say they'd put up with me here – at a pinch! The Columbia arrives back home about the 21st I think, that's a bit later than I originally intended but the one before is too early – as there is a party on here on the 25th

March that we were asked to ages ago!

Everything has settled down again here, and everyone is back to work. They did fear a general strike some time ago but nothing happened and they have had various increases of wages and seem satisfied now. There were two race days last week. We drove around in the car and saw a race but didn't go in. Of course they are all coloured jockeys. I had various sweep tickets but didn't win a cent. (Sorry but I'm beginning to think in Dollars and cents now!) Went to two films last week. One was "Bluebeards 8th Wife" which Bob and Mrs King and I saw and the other was "Robin Hood" in technicolour. Both very good – a whole party of us went to the latter and then on to some place for drinks after. Had 3 days tennis last week – 2 good 1 bad. On Thursday we went down to an estate the other side of Bridgetown called Sandy Lane. It's where Jack and Sister Thorne live. Think I told you about them – anyway they are a young couple with 2 kids about June and Jill's age and are great friends of Bob's. They have a lovely house and Jack is the Manager of the Sugar factory there. He used to be in the Navy years ago and then came out here. Had lunch with them and then a bit of a snooze and then tennis at another house up in the country. Friday I was a very good girl and sold flags from 10-1 in town for the voluntary Nurses (coloured). It was damn hot I can tell you strolling up and down Broad Street. I went into Bob's office and worried them all there, and finally sat down to look at some very nice photos the secretary man had taken. He is very keen on it and does all my films for me. Later on I sneaked off with another girl and had an ice cream soda and later still someone took me into The Flying Fish Club and gave me a drink. I'm a member there now and have a tiny badge in the form of a gold flying fish. The men have silver ones. It's quite a small place but you can get drinks and snacks there and it's a nice room looking out over the wharf. They get a coloured chap in to play the piano – even at 12 mid-day! The 'Normandie' was in that day so everywhere was full of tourists, nearly all Americans. Sonia Henje [*Norwegian figure skater and film star - three-time Olympic Champion 1928, 1932, 1936*] was on board and caused great excitement here. The Normandie is the largest ocean-going liner ever to have been here so of course there were crowds out to see her. We wanted to go on board but were too late in getting tickets. 400 were issued and no more. So instead, 5 of us went for a sail in a Star Boat and sailed round and round her. Can't remember ever having sailed properly before – I loved it. I was so intent on not getting my head hit by the boom thing when I was changing over sides, that the other girl and I went crash into each other! – Not very hard luckily. Then I kept sitting on cleats which apparently is an unforgivable sin in sailing! I also managed to be on bits of rope just as the critical moment, but still we survived somehow without capsizing (spelling OK?). It was a darn small boat for 5 people though and 3 of them great hulking men. Still I thoroughly enjoyed it. Arrived back at the Yacht Club about 6.30 in time for drinks. Of course they all ragged the life out of me over my 1st sailing effort – I must have looked a bedraggled sight – in shorts and with my hair all windswept and damp. Bob and I have spent the last few days fighting over anything and everything. He started teasing me over something the other night so I tried to tackle him and bring him down but couldn't and then of course he says something which makes me weak with laughing and I collapse on the floor in a heap – where upon he sets the dogs on me! He is a sulky devil at times (bit like Tony!) and I tell him he's desperately spoilt here at home! He knows it too – he says I am too, must be 'cos I have my own lavatory seat at The Mare!

You know I can quite see how all these many marriages fail, because supposing Bob had been living in England and there'd been a bit more cash floating round, it's just possible we'd have done something about it last year – and really it would never have worked. Still, we might not have done, because as I told you before, I never was absolutely certain I wanted to marry him – he says he was but I doubt it. He's not old enough yet I'm sure of that. Perhaps I'm not either – I dunno.

Last night we were out to dinner at some people called Hutson. He is the family Dr. The party was really for the daughter who is a nice girl and a great friend of mine. We bathe in the sea and have rum nogs together in the mornings! The party was about 12 and after dinner we went on to a dance at the Yacht Club. David was there too and since the place was a trifle quiet to begin with he thought he'd liven it up by finding a bicycle, a thick hockey sweater, a boater and a rudder which he attached behind, and went cycling round and round the garden and across corners of the ballroom! You see 3 walls of the ballroom are outside ones leading onto the veranda with open spaces at intervals down each. Not a very dignified proceeding for an ADC! But it went down well and anyhow he wasn't there in an official way at all. During the evening I lost my lipstick and then my ring – someone came up to me with the latter which I'd apparently left, unbeknown to me, in the ladies room, but someone recognized it. On the way home Bob produced the lipstick out of his pocket but when I got home I found once more I'd left my ring on the basin! Batty I know. However, I collected it this morning after church. Mrs K, B and I went to early service at the Cathedral. Bed 3.30 up at 7.30 not bad? It was a choral communion service. Choir of about 40 little local boys and a few older ones. The Dean took the service with 2 others to help. Enormous congregation – majority coloured of course. It took about an hour and then there was another service at 9.0'c which Mrs Arthur went to and they then have another at 11.00. Bob just goes once every month to the early. The Old Man didn't go at all as he had trouble with his heart the other night and spent a day in bed. He has been worried lately over all these cane fires and it sort of got on his nerves, but now everything is settled he should be better. He's a dear little fellow and extraordinarily agile for his 73 years. He won't hear of me paying my own subscriptions for the Y Club – and has made me a life member which means anytime I come back I just must pay 12 dollars.

Mrs D'Eyncourt is not at all well poor girl. She is to be taken aboard the Costa Rica on Tuesday on a stretcher from the Nursing Home but must not stay in England I believe or she'll be finished. I hear she is only using one lung and that has 2 patches now. This is only what I am told 2nd hand so you better not repeat it. No one can understand her husband allowing her to come out alone, and if the Island had known how bad she was they probably wouldn't have let her come. I don't think it's fair on the hotel either as anyone is liable to pick up germs from plates and things. I hope to goodness she stands the trip home aright. I sent her in some flowers the other day and hear she was very pleased with them. Poor girl its awful for her and she's so nice too and cheerful. Last night at the dance there was a young lad called Paddy da Costa. His mother is either a great friend or relation of Mrs Roylance who is Phyllis Langton's sister-in- law. B and I are dining and dancing with them next Saturday at the Marine.

Please thank Lil for her letter – can't write this mail as I've spent too long on this. Had a letter from Jimmy Cooper the other day – must send him a PC or something.

Take care of your knees Pop and don't go roaming about the fields too much. See? Oh and tell Greg it's I who should have the Marron Glacé not Mum. Hope he didn't break up the old Vauxhall – or perhaps you've sold her by now have you? When we get a new one I must have some decent horns put on – they all have those lovely deep sounding double ones here!

It's lunch time so I will stop this. The others have all been resting, but I wanted to do this as I knew I wouldn't have time tonight, as we are going down to Jack and Sis and then on to someone else for dinner. Its family dinner night here which we are missing this time! Mrs Arthur's mother comes (aged 90 something) Hilda and George Challoner (her son), John and Kitty Hodson (her daughter) Laddie Challoner the other son and all of us. This happens every other Sunday and in between we go to John and Kitty's alone.

Please keep the stamp thing on this envelope. It's a new ad. they've just produced.

Thanks for your epistles Popski, you've been very good. I'd appreciate it Ma if you'd refrain from writing on that lavatorial paper as it takes me the better part of the day to decipher what you have to say and 1 ½d is sufficient. Air mail is no quicker - in fact often longer as it must go T'dad, New York, England. I only put 2 ½d on when I'm late in posting and must send it late fee.

Best love to everyone please and most especially you two small selves. From your ever adoring daughter, Rabbit.

I'm called Rabbit, Bunty, Bunny or Funny alternately in this Island!

The Mare Cottage
Bovingdon
Hemel Hempstead
27th February 1939

My Beloved, Just got your letter and Mrs King's, please thank her. I had to post yours as the postman handed me yours. So here is another line just before Santer [the chauffeur] posts it at 7o'clock. Oh my little darling, how glad we both are you and Bob knew from the first that it could never be. That was the best thing to know at once, love. I just wondered as I went through the same feeling – once – and I knew it was the right thing. So now just enjoy meeting other people. Rhoda did not want you to marry Bob or even to go out, but you have done the right thing and us for allowing you to go. It will be great experience for you to meet colonial and half casts. Just enjoy yourself now and be friends only with Bob. Give him my love and I do understand you are both loveable people. No more now my darling. We feel so tearful with joy. We have been so very anxious love. Dad is adding a line. Your devoted Mother.

My Darling Rab,

Your very welcome letter came just after we had posted ours.

My dear we are so relieved. We could and would have parted with you even to that d – d spot quite happily if we had been certain it was really right for you, but we have been very doubtful all along.

Anyhow we three did the sound and right thing amongst us and though you may feel in a way sort of disappointed all is very well. Come home when you like old lady and we will be "sent to meet you". In fact, will give you quite a hearty welcome. It will be very good to see you again but you are quite right not to rush back. We shall always be jolly glad you went and made sure. That is just one thing we must be really and truly certain about.

All my love little roman. Your very loving Pop

Upton
St Michael
Barbados BWI
1st March 1939

Darling Mummy and Pop,

Shant [sic] write a very long letter this time as I only wrote a few days ago, and nothing much has happened since. The weather hasn't been quite so good the last few days. Still hot mind you, but not so much of the brilliant sun we have had – some rain as well, which spoilt tennis yesterday – Instead I went round a little museum place with Mrs King and saw an exhibition of some very nice water colours of here – all the ones I liked were sold unfortunately. I've been doing a bit of shopping lately one way and another – one shop has some of that lovely Chinese underwear all handmade – heaven knows what duty I shall have to pay on them. Then I've got one or two little tortoiseshell things – and a mahogany tray. There's masses of mahogany here and some very nice furniture locally made.

Not sure when there is another mail in, but not before this goes out I think. Looking forward to the next to hear how the discussions about the practise have gone.

Played tennis all this evening at the Savannah Club. Played 5 sets with Bob against another couple who are paying together in the tournament – it starts on Monday. I met a girl who was in the Costa Rica in first round – don't know who Bob and I have got in the handicap. Tomorrow I am playing singles with a girl for practise in the afternoon. In the morning Mrs King and I are going to a breakfast party at the Yacht Club. We'll probably bathe, then breakfast at about 1030 then sit about on the beach.

The Costa Rica sailed yesterday. I was going on board to see them off but couldn't get down in time. Pam D'Eyncourt was taken off in a stretcher and had a nice cabin reserved for her. She has a friend with her who flew over from Havana when she got worse here. I do wonder what they'll do with her.

I've written to the Wrigley's and am waiting to hear if they can have me or not. John and Kitty Hodson (Bob's Uncle and Aunt) are trying to get me to stay on with them till the next decent boat after the Columbia – well that would be the Costa Rica's next trip which is May 9th but I don't think I'd care for a month with them – although it seems silly not to stay out here when I have the chance. Still we'll see how things go and how old Ron gets on etc. probably by the end of another month I'll be quite pleased to get home to my Ma and Pa again!

Thursday March 2nd Must finish this soon as I'll miss the boat. Bad news here today, for the Old Man is ill. He had some trouble with his heart a few nights ago and the Dr. saw him and said it was nothing to worry over. But he's got a very bad colour and kept feeling shaky and dizzy – so yesterday he went down to the hospital for some tests and they fear an ulcer like Ron's. He is to have saline injections for 48 hours to stop any bleeding and then down to the hospital again for X-ray. They have no portable X-ray here at all. They say they won't need a nurse in any case, but if they did I think I should probably go to the Hodson's as there is only the one spare room here. Poor things it is worrying for them, for he's no chicken and like Pop he's never been ill in bed before. A nurse is coming 2 a day for the next 2 days as he is to have nothing through the mouth.

Enclosed 3 snaps of moi. Haven't any decent ones of Bob to send you except in colour and mounted and they are too heavy to send. It's the first colour film I've taken and they weren't too bad really.

They all tell me I'm getting like a local – so tanned – hope I don't lose it all before I get home. Pop do you think things are any more settled than they were? Everyone seems to have got the idea of war in their minds again, and no one seems to have any confidence in anything.

I'm writing this downstairs in the drawing room after dinner. Its 9.30 here so I suppose you're both in bed and snoring as it'll be 1.30 with you. It's funny to hear the wireless announcers and Big Ben striking all this way away.

The American navy come on Sunday and there are various parties for them the next day – the tournament begins that day and after the cocktail party I may go back for the night with Sis and Jack as I'm playing tennis with them the next day if I don't have to play more tournament. The following Saturday is a wedding and party after at the Marine and the Saturday after as well. It's rather annoying really as it means there's never a free Sat to get up a party with just our own special friends.

How's To [Tony Fasson] getting on? I haven't heard from either of them, the devils. And what about Aunt Lil and her domestic upheavals? Perhaps Edinburgh will have put new life into her and she'll be fit to tackle the question. Glad to hear Sonja and Ellen are still as nice as ever. I suppose they can speak almost perfect English now?

You know I still can't get over you letting me come out here. You really are rather a perfect couple of parents for anyone to have – but possibly I've told you that before. I feel rather a fraud now, as things have turned out. Still I suppose you'd sooner have it that way than the other. Do hope I don't make a habit of meeting people who live in outposts of the Empire as its apt to become a little expensive. Rhoda complains bitterly of the letter mails to here and says either I must arrange for an air service immediately or else marry the

Sanitary Inspector! By the way have you seen anything of him lately? Possibly he's been in to have a pull at the Cherry Brandy or a little Danish Lager. They have some funny Beer here in cans (i.e. tins) called Budweiser, from USA quite good.

Must finish now as its getting late. If I should ever cable "Money please" you'd send it to Barclays wouldn't you? It's extremely unlikely that I should want any more as I've only cashed 2 travellers' cheques and haven't started on the £20 I can draw from the Bank. But I was just asking in case of unforeseen circumstances cropping up.

Goodnight to you both and bless you. Very best love. Bunny

The Farm Sunday
5th March 1939

My Dearest Bun,

Glory be! I never thought you'd return unengaged – perhaps you won't! But to one who won't keep you abroad always possibly.

Everyone seems delighted, for as you say it being mutual, helps a tremendous lot – Bun, I am so glad for you – and the right person will turn up when and where the Almighty has arranged despite everything.

I bet you're having a hell of a time – for the West Indies is a grand place for a holiday – but not longer than three months I should say.

Sorry to hear David's not so hot. I expect he lives a fairly exotic existence – what with gin and no sleep. Give him my salaams, if you're still at B'dos. Wonder if you came across John Hayes in the Vindictive? I am "attending" his swan song in April, all rigged out in full dress – sight for the Gods and Goddesses who I gather will be attending this function in large numbers.

Of course I know Cooper and Battchy Rebbeck – the latter rather a charmer I think –

How familiar – a trip to the sugar factory and bathe after. I can remember in [HMS] Rodney days doing it all. The "Bobs" who showed one round were always terribly kind.

You'll have a dandy time, in T'dad. QPH nights I can remember fairly vividly or at least the beginning of them, for all those Punches were terribly bad for little snotties. Can remember a very attractive daughter of the head of Police, Du Pass, but he's dead and she married someone – quelle misère!

I am much better and go south for my board on March 20th and look forward to getting back to work seriously at last – for now my plans are cut and dried – It's to be destroyers now and always – hope it comes true!

Lily Blair has found a new lease of life and is in better form than we've seen her for ages. Positively swaying at the hips. It's terribly good to see.

James approaches the age of discretion and the road divides here – to marry or not. If only he'd find someone suitable and really worthwhile. It would produce that effort to succeed which is not too apparent normally.

Enjoy yourself 'ma honey sweetling' probably out of date across the pond but you'll fasten to the idea.

Best love, Tony

If Pop is out, open his as it's a continuation of this. Too fat for envelope!

Darling Mumsie and Pop,

Fortunately the boat that is carrying this is late in, so I have a bit more time to write. The Columbia is also late with your letters so I doubt if I will be able to answer them this mail. This won't be very tidy but as usual I'm writing it in bed at 8.30 am (12.30 with you!) and Robert has just been in and is now off to the office. He has a lot to do poor darling with the Old Man laid up. They still aren't quite certain if it is a duodenal or not, and cannot move him down to the hospital for X-ray until there is absolutely no sign of blood in the tests. He has now been 2 weeks on 1pt milk and glucose a day. He's very bored with it all but is pretty cheerful. I go in and kiss him good morning on my way down and pop in when I come back to lunch and we all usually forgather in his room to listen to the news after dinner. Empire news given from London at 1am when you're all tucked up in bed!

You know I've still not heard from the Wrigleys – I think either they must be away or else the address wasn't sufficient, and Bob swears he didn't leave my letter in his pocket by mistake! I don't really mind very much whether I go or not, as I'm so terribly happy here. Still I shall go if they can have me, as it must mean a lot extra having the Old Man in bed. I could go to the Hodsons (John and Kitty) instead if I wanted to. They are the people who asked me to stay on till May 9th, but I doubt if I'd like it with them all that time. The old people may have to come over to England this year as the Dr. here would rather have a proper examination by English Specialists. Mrs King would have to go with them but I'm afraid Bob would have to stay.

Oh I forgot to thank you for your lovely long letters. I got 2 lots together last week by a French boat. It seems so funny only getting the answer now to something I wrote over a month ago! You certainly sound relieved that I'm not digging a burrow here for keeps. I was relieved myself when I decided, although believe me I still love Bob more than anyone else in the world (immediate family excepted of course) although I do know that it's not enough to contemplate spending the rest of our lives together. He seems very popular out here with everyone. Not only with the people one meets at all the parties but with the tougher club people and business men as well. It's entirely different here from England, for all 'the best people' (as Lily Blair would say) own shops and stores and various business premises. There are a lot of awfully nice people, far more that I thought at first, and everyone has been really very sweet to me. Mrs Arthur is giving me a breakfast party on the 23rd at the Freshwater Beach Club about 3 miles the other side of town. We go down there and bathe and then have Breakfast about 1030 which will probably consist of fruit, flying fish pie, very tasty and really more like chicken than fish, then either bacon and eggs or cold turkey and breakfast cake and marmalade tea or coffee. You can't imagine how much I eat here. Enormous meals and yet I'm often more than ready for the next! Last week we had dinner with John and Kitty and they gave us a little roasting pig especially for me! It was only just over a foot long, and stuffed with green peas. Very tender and quite a delicacy here.

Glad old Ron is getting on well. I wonder if you have got the house business all fixed by now. It will be lovely for them having a court of their own. Yvonne will have to get a whole lot of new curtains I suppose as their others won't go round in a big house.

I have written to Lilo and Ron so you won't need to let them have this. It's a real hard job writing all these letters I can assure you! God knows how many P.C.s I've posted up to date.

Can't remember when I wrote to you last, seems quite a time, so I'd better give some a/c of my doings! Last week the American Navy was here in the form of 2 Aircraft Carriers. They had been at sea for 4 weeks and

US ships are dry so you can imagine how they painted this poor little island pink. I've never met such a wild crowd of creatures in my life. A few were extraordinarily nice but the majority were pretty impossible. However, they all spent a vast amount of money which did the town good. The sailors behaved very badly though and broke up various restaurants, throwing money, tables and chairs into the street. They also walked off with a large amount of plate etc as souvenirs – it's a habit of theirs. They took the telephone from one club place and masses of ordinary Bakelite pepper pots from another. The Police had an awful job with them, as they would pinch bicycles and tear round town. One of them dived off a jetty thing by a hotel – broke his neck, was taken back on board – operated on by a brilliant surgeon (ships) and is quite alright. He slit him open all down his back fitted the bits together again and sewed him up again. At dances the Americans have a habit of 'cutting in' so if you're dancing round and they decide they want to dance with you, they just come up and tap the other chap on the shoulder and they must hop it! Very convenient when you're stuck with a dud but not so good when you've just started off with someone you want to stay put with. I got talking to one officer at a cocktail dance and he asked me to their big reception on board the Ranger. I didn't want to go alone and said I didn't think I could arrange it. Then he said well would it help if I asked the boy-friend there – pointing to Bob, so I said it would.

If Mum is out open hers as it's the start of this

We went on Wednesday. They sent their launches over to the Aquatic Club for us and we were met at the top of the Gangway by some Officers. Then we went into the enormous Hangar Deck where all the Officers were grouped about. Had to walk down a line of Admirals and what-not all with their gold braid hanging around. They had dancing on one part to a superb band which is hired for the cruise and not just got together by the Ship's Company. Some chap came up and asked me to dance and after that took me all round the ship. Saw all the machines out on the flight deck, guns, telescopes on the Bridge, Chart Room and even a Cabin! They have lovely cabins, with wash basins and huge zip things to hang their clothes in. She's a modern ship and beautifully got up. My escort, true to the Navy, appeared to entirely loose his heart to me all on the spur of the moment, and did his best to keep me on board for dinner. I kept telling him I'd deserted the rest of the party and must really try to find them. Bob and I were going down to Jack and Sister's for dinner so I couldn't have stayed anyhow. We took this lad and another back with us for drinks at the Yacht first, and then left them with some other people when we had to go. I got a message, next day, after they'd sailed saying –"Say goodbye to Bunny again and tell her I love her"! the Navy Forever, but take 'em with a pinch of Salt!

On Thursday last we went down to a private beach belonging to one of the big estates. Had a perfect bathe in a pale clear sea with a wood coming right down to the Sandy beach. We bathed and played the fool with a tennis ball and then Bob came rushing into the sea with a basket of glasses on his head and someone else with a huge thermos affair of rum cocktails which we drank in the water. There must have been about 10 of us in. Then we all went up to someone's house on another estate for drinks and eats. The man there is manager of the estate. We passed him one day on his horse riding around the cane fields. He's a young and very good looking married friend of Bob's. Looks so nice on horseback too in his pale clothes and toupee – they have to carry umbrella's on the saddle in case of sudden rain, or if the sun is too hot, as they're out for hours on end. But a gamp looks so funny to me sticking up out of a saddle! Friday was Bob's cocktail party at the Savannah Club. A very good show – all young people about 60-70 and when most people had gone it turned into Poker Dice!

Saturday was the wedding – a girl from here marrying a man from the T'dad oilfields. Good wedding – at least the reception was. They had it at the brides home, which had the most glorious pots of mauve orchids hanging all along the veranda. Each spray had about 15-20 blooms on it. We had dancing which went on for some time. I wore that new pale blue semi evening dress I got and borrowed a big navy hat from a girl and gloves from Mrs. King and bought a little thin bag! Most people wore long dresses. After the reception we had to tear home, change and out to dinner and dance at the Marine. Thoroughly enjoyed it. Bob looked awfully tired by the end, as it was a full day, and he still gets tired fairly easily on a/c of that kidney trouble he had. Sunday was a good day – I got up at 10.35, dressed, spent from 10-15 mins trying to get Bob out of bed – had breakfast, wandered round the garden picking lemons and limes and then went down to the Yacht Club for a bathe. We were so late getting there everyone else had gone except one man called Johnnie McKinsty who is very nice. Lay about and bathed, looked at papers in the club and had drinks (mine a grapefruit juice and Bob's an orange juice – so there!) and rolled up in time for lunch at 3o'c! After that saw the Old Man and then went to sleep from about 4.30-7o'c! Couldn't sleep very much actually as visitors kept coming and making a hell of a din in the next room. The tennis tournament also started last week. As you will see by the enclosed cuttings. I got through the 1st round of the singles. Cracked up in the 2nd set didn't I? My hand got so wet I couldn't hang on to my racket half the time! By the end I found I had a colossal blister on my big toe pad and the darn thing had split down the middle. It sure was painful and it wasn't much fun trying to dance on it that night. The other big toe had a huge blister too but unburst. We plastered them up and I had to play again next day. I met the woman who had got through to the finals. She played for the Island last year v T'dad. I was playing rather well to begin with and should have got the 1st set off her as I led her 5-3 and 40-30 and then let her get it. If only I could have got that set I might have won, for she isn't as young as she was and once I got her on the move she soon tired. Still it was lots of fun. Bob should have won his too. Two days ago Den and I played the Ladies Doubles. There again we could have won but she went to pieces in the last set and I did one or 2 double faults. One day I was serving like a dream and then suddenly it goes and I can't do a thing. Bob says I just get the dithers! The results are all given out on the local wireless but I never heard it – such a pity as I've never heard myself mentioned 'Over the Air'!

The last few days have been warmer and even I can only bear one sheet and not even my little thin blanket on my feet. But I love it and even in the heat feel full of energy. But I am fatter. It's awful as I hoped to lose weight. They keep on telling me how different I look now and how horrified they were to see me when I arrived! So thin! Imagine me ever being called thin. How are your teeth Pop West? I hope they aren't going to give you trouble. Get your blood pressure down by really eating less – biscuits instead of bread and leave that Pork alone and then have a sniff of gas. Much the best way. Mummy what on earth did you mean about meeting coloured and ½ castes. One doesn't even meet them anywhere – not at any social event or even any clubs. Only some of the people in shops are slightly coloured, but the majority are poor whites. Actually, there is one girl and her brother who in England move in very influential circles and yet here up till quite lately were not received anywhere. Now the girl goes to GH to quite a few houses but Mrs Arthur won't entertain her here, although she has been just to change once. Probably English people have no idea, but I've been introduced to her mother who is obviously coloured but I believe a very clever woman. All servants everywhere are quite black some much darker than others. When I come home I shall probably start clapping for waiters in restaurants as here when you want a drink or anything you just clap twice and a waiter appears for the order.

I am having a very nice yacht Club Blazer made like Bob's. It will be useful for trousers in the summer. Well darlings, I really must end off now. This is all very disjointed I expect, but since I started Bob has been in to Breakfast and out again and I've kept stopping to talk to someone or other. Am off now for a bathe and possibly an egg flip at the Yacht, and this afternoon Mrs King and I are going to see some show garden up the Island while Robert practises men's doubles for tomorrow.

Bestest love to you both and I do hope you're OK and behaving yourselves. Expect a PC next mail as this has finished me off completely!
Your very loving Bunny.

Darling Mummy and Pop,

Gosh how I hate the sound of all the news bulletins. It strikes me we're back just where we were before. I wish I knew what you thought about it Pop. I don't imagine we get all the news here – Chamberlain's speech from Birmingham was relayed or at any rate recorded. If there is war and it happens suddenly within the next two weeks this will probably never reach you, as its going on a German boat.

Thank you both for your letters and the photos. They're very good Mum. The pups look enormous now. I hope that man has taken one alright.

I1.30 pm in Bed

Having fallen nearly asleep on the sofa listening to the wireless, I've been dragged up to bed. Now I've 'come to' a bit and thought I would write some more to you for the mail closes tomorrow. I am in my big double bed – well surrounded by a mosquito net! They don't often bite the people who live here and Bob never uses a net, but they like new blood and if I dawdle too long round my dressing table they chew my legs to bits. The beds here are always stuck more or less in the middle of the room, to get more air. They all sleep with their doors open, but I don't 'cos I'd wake too early as they get up long before Bob and I do.

The Old Man had his first egg today for over 2 weeks. Apart from that he now has a teaspoonful of cream in a gill of milk every two hours. He is now to go to the hospital next week. Did I tell you they want him to go to England for an overhaul? Possibly though he would go to Canada instead. Mrs Arthur is an incredible person. She's 70 and does all the housekeeping etc., looks after her ducks and chickens and at the moment is forever attending to the Old Man, in spite of the fact that there's a nurse here every day. Even here it is difficult to get good servants. Easy enough to get someone, but very few are much good now. They all want to be needlewomen or something that they think is more superior. They are slow and I doubt if anything short of dynamite would hurry them. It always makes me laugh to watch them walking, for its usually slow and with a terrific bottom waggle!

There's been quite a wind today, but it's been nice and fresh. Too blowy for the tennis matches though. Bob just managed to win his first round of the Open mixed. He's playing with a youngish married girl who he's played in one or two tournaments before with. We aren't really good enough for the open, but are in for the handicap and ought to do fairly well if we can beat George and Hilda Challenor in the 1st round. They've given us quite a nice handicap of + ½ 15. Actually if we met one certain couple they would be owing us points and we always beat them level! So we're not fussing.

Yesterday we had a busy day. Up at 7.30 (after getting to bed after 4am) and went to early service with Bob and Mrs King. I really rather like going to church out here. After that we went straight on to the Yacht Club for a Breakfast Party. It was Jill Hodson's birthday. She is much the same age as June Curry. Had a bathe first then an egg and rum flip then breakfast on the beach. Flying fish pie, salad rice and beans, followed by sausages and Heinz baked beans – followed by a banana. Others had breakfast cake and marmalade, but I could go no further. At one point I was sitting on a seat next to Bob and juggling with a boiled egg. Unfortunately I juggled it into my cup of coffee which was in my other hand and most of it went all over my nice clean dress, and only a very little over Bob's trousers and shirt! It wouldn't wash out so I shall have to have it cleaned blast it. We'd eaten too much at too late an hour to want any lunch so after a game of cricket with the kids we went back home and slept till it was time to go down to Jack and Sister's for tennis. Had several sets there and stayed for dinner, after which another couple came in and we played cards. On Saturday Mrs King and I went to an exhibition of flowers and fruit and veg. The orchids were really magnificent – lovely big cattleyas and huge sprays of dendrobiums and many other kinds. What struck me was that they were all very pretty blooms, not like those sinister looking things you see at the Chelsea Flower Show. There were lots of roses and a lovely show of hibiscus and bowls of cut flowers and some beautiful ferns. There were different competitions too for table decoration, buttonholes and bouquets. I saw the Governor there and David in attendance hob-knobbing with the CID policeman over the nasturtiums! The Governor by the way has gone to Demerara today to be acting Gov. There for 6 months while their own man goes on sick leave. The Colonial Secretary will be Acting Gov here and David is staying on for a bit longer. The new ADC will go to Demerara with HE.

One wonders what would happen here if there was war, or if the majority of white people left, the locals would play the devil with the Island, and I doubt if as many of them would go this time. Well, to get back to the Exhibition! – the fruit and veg were most interesting to me. I saw raw ginger locally grown, and all the veg I've been eating since I came. Government House produced some beautiful cabbages, but we never eat many greens here except for squash and okras. The fruit looked lovely too. Plantains, bananas, ordinary, red, and fig – paw-paw, oranges lemons, limes, guavas, grapefruit, shaddock (like an enormous grapefruit) melons etc etc. After that we watched a little tennis and then went home and changed. Had dinner with Denise before going on to a 'games' party. There were about 30 of us and we each had a number which was the table we were to start from. 15 tables (2 people at each) and the winning one moved one up. Played dotty things like picking up shoe buttons with a thin hook on a string, and changing about 15 peas into another saucer with only a straw and smelling different smells, and cutting crinkly paper and making words out of one big word and adding up vast sums very quickly (I won the 2nd time please note!) Oh! and Darts. After that some people played Poker and 9 of us played Tripoley. It's an American Gambling game and very good fun. I lost 1/6. Afterwards 6 of us went on to the Morgan and danced for a while. Johnnie Manning (you don't know him do you? Went to school with Bob – Manager of an estate – married – very nice) bumped his toe against a stone block which he afterwards decided would make a very good anchor for his boat. So after dancing with me we went to view the said block, which was at the time being very useful in keeping a door open. He thought he'd like to get it to the car and the see about paying them something for it afterwards. Well we found it weighted about 75-100 lbs and it was not easy matter to pick it up walk around with it without drawing some attention to ourselves. We did get it along to the table where the others were, but there it stayed for eggs and bacon had arrived and we were hungry! Did I tell you that one night when we got home late there was an enormous big spider on my sponge? It was a hen spider and had laid its egg there too and when we got in my sponge was swarming with many little spiders. You know my feelings towards that particular insect – well Bob's are much the same. However he got the flit and flitted them till the big one sunk to the bottom of the basin. Mrs King had to boil my sponge for me after that! The other night at dinner a forty–leg came in. They really do bite badly and are about the worst thing here.

Oh I've heard from Bunty Wrigley and am going on the 3rd. She said come before, but I don't want to cut short one day of my time here – there's too little left as it is. Another family have asked me to stay for a week – they say stay on in T'dad a bit more, then come back here to the Hodsons and then to them – Dr and Mrs Hutson and Betty. Very nice. But it would mean another month and I can't make up my mind anyhow if I would like staying on and yet not being here at Upton. I wouldn't see so much of Bob, or be so independent. You ask am I happy Mum. Darling I've not been so happy for a long time – not consistently like this. Don't worry, I'm not changing my mind, but I shall hate leaving Bob all the same.

Must go to sleep now as it's late. Best of love to you both. From Bunny.

Have only had one letter from Lil since I've been away. Write here as I'll get them on the 11th. Wrigley's address Bungalow 21, Pointe à Pierre, Trinidad but I doubt if an answer to this will reach me.

Darlings,

Only a very short letter as I have just 10 mins before Bob goes and this will have to go late fee. There is a boat out on Sunday which may take mail, if so, you'll get two together as they should arrive the same date.

Since your last letter came I've made some different plans! I just can't leave this Island yet, as I've now got two invitations to stay, and the idea now is to get the Costa Rica on May 9th! You said don't come back till you want to, and there's nothing on till May and the weather is bad still. So altogether I think it's a pity not to stay for another month as I have the chance. I haven't actually cancelled my passage in the Columbia yet, but have booked provisionally for the Costa Rica. If you don't get a cable from me on the 10th or 11th saying I'm sailing, you'll know I'm staying. The only thing I have in mind is that if by any chance there should be a war I would naturally come on the Columbia otherwise its definite I stay. I shall stay on a bit with the Wrigley's, probably till the 15th or so, then back here to the Hodsons for a week (or nearly) (c/o Capt Hodson, Roumaika, POB 26 Barbados) then to the Huston's for a week or 10 days (21st – 30th about) c/o Dr Lionel Hutson, Wakefield, Bridgetown, Barbados, and then back here till I sail on the 9th. If you get muddled with addresses send it to the usual one for John Hodson is in the office and all letters go to Box 26 for this family and his. If you really want me home for any reason, cable, see! c/o Arthur Barbados for any of the time I'm here and not T'dad. By the way I'm flying to T'dad on the 3rd instead of boat. $22 simple and it takes 1 hr 15 mins as compared with 12 hours and it lands me at 5.15pm nearer the Wrigley's instead of 7am and further away for them to fetch me. The planes are very good now – Dutch ones and run 3 times a week. However if on this occasion one should find reason to crash you will doubtless hear about it, otherwise you won't, see? Can't possibly spend money saying 'arrived safely' after a little hop of 200 miles! Oh yes your little daughter is the very devil when she's away from home – flying here and there without her parents leave!

By the way I wonder if the said parents could see fit to lending the said daughter a small sum of money, say £10 or perhaps £15 just in case I run out which I doubt as I still have £20. Send it c/o Barclays please.

Must stop, Bob going.

All love, Bunny

Darling Pop and Mumsie,

Another rotten letter as I never had time to write it yesterday. The last one was probably somewhat incoherent as I didn't have much time then either, but I expect you have gathered from it that I am staying on till May 9th arriving home May 19th. How's that? Suits me well, in spite of the fact that I shan't be seeing my beloved family for another month. If I came home I know I would curse myself after a week or so for not accepting a damn good offer and another month of sunshine – so I have accepted it. Although please understand that should you feel I've been away from the fold too long, all you have to do is send a cable and I'll see about catching the Columbia. Now about that little question of money! It's not urgent, and if there is a mail leaving soon after this arrives, it could be sent by post I should think. Otherwise cable it to Barclays. It is only for safety sake and I may not touch it, but I'm not sure how expensive T'dad will turn out and I may want to buy some things there and then find I'm short for the trip home. Whoever meets me at Victoria (if anyone remembers me by then) had better come armed with much cash to pay customs duties with! Oh no, my mistake, that's all done at Plymouth.

Yesterday Robert and I played our handicap tournament match against George and Hilda Challenor. He used to be about the best singles player in the WI and always has won the doubles for years in the tournaments. No one thought we would beat them even with a handicap but we did – in 3 sets 7-5, 2-6, 6-2. It was very brilliant tennis and not the sort I like – she hits a soft ball and a bit screwy and they both rely entirely on court craft. Bob was serving well and playing well at the net, but couldn't get his other shots at all. They said I was the only one who played well, but I didn't feel I did as I hate a soft game – as Bob says – I like to take the cover off the ball! We have to play again today – against a rather good couple – the boy has just been in the final of the singles. After that we go to a huge cocktail party and then on to a dinner and then dance at the Yacht. We were at the Yacht last night after tennis. Bob played Bridge – I sit and watch sometimes in the hopes of learning a little about it but I don't really want to play much. Yesterday being Friday was Planters Day. They all come in from the country on Fridays to do a little business and get money from the Bank to pay the estate men with. The last 2 Fridays I've run into Johnnie Manning a friend of Bob's. Last week he took me to the Manhattan Club for a drink and yesterday we had one in the Flying Fish Club! He's very very right and as wicked as the devil. He's the one who wanted that weight thing at the Morgan – he tells me his toe is still very sore! I got some lovely pictures from the Flying Fish windows the other day - and the owner, Bob Yerkes, an American, gave me 2 very nice ones he had taken. He lent me his light meter and says I can have it anytime I want when he's away. He sailed for the States yesterday.

On Wednesday Bob took me over a fairly large Sugar Factory. It's one that the Old Man is a Director of and has shares in. Of course I tasted all the different kinds of sugar and saw the whole works. It is very interesting seeing it all right from the start where mule carts bring in the cane and dump it on a huge platform with a crane overhead. This is electrically worked (most of them work by steam) and swings round and picks up a big bunch of cane and drops it in a moving stairway. A man is there to help shovel the cane along and through a collection of very strong knives which chip it up and pass it on into the factory – where it starts the whole process. It goes through squeezers and when milk of lime has been added it is ready for the different boiling. Can't explain it all now as it takes too long. That one factory produces from 3700-4000 ton of sugar p.a.

The next morning Mrs K and I were up early for my breakfast party at Freshwater Beach. There were 10 of us altogether. 7 of my particular girl friends, Mrs K a friend of hers and myself. It's a lovely place, again with trees overhanging the beach and the Club just behind. Had an enormous breakfast – flying fish pie, savoury egg thing with ham and about 5 veg! Bob is here and going – must stop. All love darlings, from Bunny.

Upton
March 28th

Darlings,

I seem to have been writing a letter to you every other day just lately and here we go again. Bob tells me it's the last mail for about 10 days so I mustn't miss it. I had a lovely lot of letters by the boat that came in on Saturday. Your two, Rhoda's, Tony's, Neville's and one from Jimmie G. Also had one from Stevie a little while ago – I'd promised to send him a PC of a Flying Fish – now he wants a real one!

Hope by now your hands are better Mum – It's horrid to have a continual itch like that. However, "Greg's" beautiful cool hands must have a very soothing effect I feel sure! Can hardly wait till May to see his new 'pearlies' – I think you might get Santer out again with his camera, then I could get some idea of how really ravishing he must look now. I hope your tusk came out without too much trouble Gilbert, and that it healed up quickly. They don't have gas here so people have to have injections whether they like them or not.

The Old Man is still in bed, and it seems to me they are just working in the dark, for they haven't yet decided for certain that it's duodenal. They got him up onto the sofa one evening, and the next day he had a lot of giddiness and the day after the tests were very slightly positive. They are going to England in July, and Bob will have to go to John and Kitty which he won't like too much.

I'm very thrilled about my new car! It really sounds lovely Mum and I'm longing to see it. Can't think that a 10 h.p. will do 70 mph very easily though. Can't make out now whether Ron is having my old Vauxhall or not, in your first letter you said Jim was selling his car, and in your second you said something about him selling my wireless – well if Ron was having the car I imagine he'd keep the wireless. Yes I most certainly want one in the [Sunbeam] Talbot. That one cost 12 quid second hand and I can't think one costing £3.10 would be much good. You should get quite a lot for mine as it was expensive when new. I must have one with the wave length for Luxemburg, as that's the station that has dance music on at odd times throughout the day. There must be some place it can be fixed without spoiling the leg room. Do send me a photo of the car. Please. Funny Jim selling you that as, up to date, he's always run down Talbots. They are certainly good lookers anyway and it remains to be seen if it lasts well. I'm so glad it has a drop head coupé as it will be lovely in the summer.

Only 5 more days here before I go to T'dad. I shall be interested to see what it's like after here. Most people find it very gay even out at Point à Pierre, which is a little colony just for the oilfields. Bunty says Dick will get a few days off at Easter so they will be able to show me a bit of the Island. I shall take as few clothes as possible so as not to have too much excess luggage for the plane. Think I'll order a case of T'dad grapefruit to be put on the Costa Rica. They are those lovely pink ones and very juicy. Mrs Arthur is going to make up a little box of sweet potatoes and eddoes and things for me, though the nicer kind of sweet potatoes won't travel.

Bob and I are now in the semi-finals of the Handicap. We have to play again on Friday – do so wish we could get into the finals. I don't know who we have to play yet. He got beaten yesterday in the Open – his partner was playing like a drain. Last night we went to a very good film – Dawn Patrol – a flying thing. A little too harrowing and there was a good deal of sniffing going on and even my usual cast-iron control in a cinema didn't quite hold out!

Big row going on at the moment between Mother and Son! Son's tummy has got too fat and Mother is having to let out a pair of flannels and son thinks he knows best how to alter them. So Mother says he can damn well take them down to the tailors and pay for them to be done! Quiet after the storm – she's doing it her own way!

Went to a lovely house on Saturday for a cocktail party. A young couple live there who haven't been out here long. He used to be with Vickers and then his wife was ordered away and they came out here as his people are here. The house is all new, and has a lovely view right down over the sea across the cane fields. They have two swimming pools, one for them and one for the small son and both are flood lit. After that we went on to a dinner of 24 at a fairly big house in the country. Some of these old houses are most attractive with their verandas and open rooms. After dinner we went on to the Yacht Club to dance. It was about 20 mins out of town or more and 5 of us decided to go the long way down to put off time as we didn't think much of the rest of the party! However, when we arrived at 10.30 we found it was still the first dance as no-one but our dinner party had gone! There was a dance at the Marine as well you see. A few more came on afterwards but not many. I didn't enjoy the end of the evening as Bob and I had a fight! I took a remark of his a bit too seriously and later told him to go to hell over something, and he took that too seriously. Unfortunately we slept on it and hardly spoke the next day! A pity as it was a perfect day and we were right over on the other coast (Atlantic side) with some people who have a house there. Marvellous bathing very rough and dangerous. We did some surfing too. Got there about 10 o'c, bathed – had a rum cocktail and a shower bath – then an egg flip and then a huge breakfast at about 12. After that fell asleep – Bob and 3 others tried to play Bridge for a bit but sleep overcame them too – the air is so strong up there. Bathed again after tea and then won 1/6 at Poker Dice! Cocktails again till about 6.45 when we tried to leave but couldn't as the car wouldn't start. Bob took it to bits but it was no good and we were sent back in Mr Bryden's car arriving home 8.30 and late for dinner – still a slightly strained atmosphere but by bed time we were friends again – and it was lots of fun making it up!

Yesterday I went to see an artist woman and bought one of her paintings. I'd seen an exhibition of hers and asked if I could go and see per personally, as she takes orders. Unfortunately the one I really wanted is sold but she's doing me one of a bit called Indian River for $7.00. [*I have this watercolour by May Delamere*]

Tonight we go to a games party at Johnnie McKinstey's. Probably cards and dice. He's a sweet person; in fact I like him the best of the unmarrieds. I think – except for HM of course – who still comes way above anyone else. Bought a little American dress for about 17/- the other day. It really looks quite expensive! Shall wear it tonight. I bought a tie for Jim Curry too, and then found it wasn't a Palm Beach one as I thought but made in England so I've given it to Bob and he wears it to the office with his pale suits.

Am now more tanned than I've ever been. Am also grossly fat – you won't know or own me. Must go and give my long pants to Bob to press as they have no crease now. They are too hot mostly, but I did wear them to Bathsheba on Sunday, as its cooler over there. No more now. You sound anxious about me and the Navy! Don't worry, there wasn't anything in it I assure you and they all left weeks ago! Best love to you. Bunny.

Bungalow 21
Pointe-à-Pièrre Trinidad
April 6th

Darling Mumsie and Poppet,

Sometime since you'll have had a letter, but there hasn't been a mail. Well I don't think an awful lot of this place, and to tell you the truth I'm longing to get back to B'dos. It's horribly sultry weather here, no blue sky and hardly any sun and for the first time since I've been out here, I feel sort of slack. This is quite a nice bungalow, built on the side of a hill overlooking the T'dad Leaseholds Plant. It's all extraordinarily ugly with nothing but large bits of machinery and dozens of oil tanks looking like so many gasometers. Apart from that there are all these nasty little red-roofed bungalows dotted about, with very little tall vegetation in between so that you know exactly what your neighbours are doing. One or two of the houses aren't so bad, but I should loathe to live here. Any sea that is visible is grey and muddy looking – such a change from Barbados. We had a bathe yesterday, but there is no nice shady beach just near here and we had to go in off a jetty thing – of course there are some marvellous beaches in Trinidad, only on the other side of the Island. Had a very good fly down on Monday. Bob, Mrs King, John Hodson and his small daughter all came to see me off, those KLM planes are really lovely, so comfortable, and they supply you with papers and drink and a biscuit all free! Two pilots, a wireless operator and room for 10 passengers. Lav and wash place all with chrome fittings, a lot of rack room for small parcels etc and all big luggage goes in a place up near the engine. Never felt any motion at all except for a bump or two when we were over the hills in the north of T'dad. Flew at about 8000ft and took 1hr 20mins. It's over 200 miles so you see we didn't dawdle! The colouring over Tobago was perfect especially round any odd rocks just off the island – the water was so clear that we could see the formation of the rock many feet below the surface of the water. The first part of T'dad was very thickly vegetated, especially all over the hills, then gradually we could pick out roads and houses as we got over the flatter parts – we landed at a place called Piarco which is south and east of Port of Spain. A perfect landing without a single jolt, in fact I couldn't tell when the wheels touched the ground. Dick and Bunty met me and we went into Port of Spain for dinner. On the way in I suddenly remembered I'd forgotten to post a business letter for Bob at the airport. He had missed the collection and I was to post it this end. It was a special air mail letter to Japan costing 4/7 and would get there via Para, Africa and Europe in something like 5 days. Amazing isn't it? Anyway we caught the mail alright by taking it to the PO and changing the stamps to Trinidad ones.

Bunty and Dick are being very sweet to me and they are good fun. But the people here are very dull on the whole – only met one nice young couple so far who live down the road. They've only been married a couple of months – he's 31 and she's just 18 and they've know each other all their lives. He's a devil with the girls so I hope she'll be able to manage him. He used to be out in Persia when Dick was there. Dick is a kind old soul, quite amusing at times; by no means attractive to look at – in fact pink and very shiny and with funny piggy eyes. Bunty is fast getting a middle-aged spread and doesn't seem to trouble much about her appearance. But she a nice person and insists on bringing me my breakfast in bed at about 8 o'c. The others have theirs at about 7 o'c and then Dick goes off to work. I get up about 9 and have a bath, then we sit about all morning in a sort of veranda place underneath the bungalow. They are all built on white stone pillars, then underneath is all cemented and you have tables and chairs there. Dick comes home at 12 and we have lunch. After that we sleep all afternoon till teatime when Dick comes home again. Last night we went to cocktails with some people near here. Everyone seems to be Scotch here, with ghastly Glasgow accents that you can cut with a knife but very pleasant for all that. The bungalows and the type of people here remind me vaguely of Shoreham-by-Sea – Skinners and one or two others excepted! My God, it's pouring with rain now – what wouldn't I give to be back at Upton. And I'm missing a marvellous weekend at the sea too. Every Easter a whole lot of young people take a house right on the beach on the West Coast of B'dos. Bob was going down and all the people I like best – a pity. They tried to get me to go, but I couldn't very well put Bunty off having asked to come on the 3rd before I knew I was staying on longer. I shall fly back on the 15th and go to Upton for other clothes and so on, then down to the Hodsons. There's a big dance that night at The Marine which I expect we'll all go to.

Tomorrow we are going over to some place on the East Coast for a picnic. About 8 or 10 people I believe. One quite nice lad is coming – a friend of Dicks called Graeme McFadgeon (can't think how you spell it!). He's quiet and rather nice with a soft Scottish voice without too much of an accent. I think he's going to play tennis with me next Wednesday, with a woman called Wendy Thomas who was Lady Champion of the Island and went up to B'dos with the team two years ago. Oh, by the way, Robert and I got into the finals of the handicap – but couldn't pull it off. I should have loved to come back with that little silver pot, but we both played very badly I'm afraid – I couldn't get a thing over in one set. The wind was pretty foul too and anyhow I hate having to play carefully. I think perhaps if I'd disobeyed orders and had a good crack at the ball it would have been better – anyhow we had our money's worth! Unfortunately, I shall only be able to go in for singles and Ladies Doubles in the Yacht Club Tournament as they come off first. It begins two days after I get back. Bunty and Dick don't play, so I shan't get much here. We may go out sailing one day as Dick has a little boat. On Saturday there is a wedding we are going to in Port of Spain – not a big one but it may be quite fun.

Have got very keen on Poker, and Poker Dice tell Ron! Went to one party before I came away (Johnnie McKinstey's) and at one time I was the only girl at a table with 5 men all playing in their shirt sleeves! Actually, that night I lost 2/8 but Bob won about 15/- then another night I won 5/6! And was I thrilled! You can lose a lot at dice though so I go very carefully. The night before I came here we went to dinner with the Hodsons. It was originally intended as a farewell party for me when I was catching the Columbia from here. Anyhow I was the guest of honour and sat on the hosts right and my health was drunk! The party was John and Kitty Hodson, Mrs King, Bob and I, Sandy and Beryl (the ones in the photo I sent) Johnnie and Audrey Manning (Audrey was at Bushey and remembers Jill M-G and Mary West, she was Audrey Austin then), and David Boyle. Johnnie has instructed me to bring him back a pair of cocoa squirrels from here. He says I can smuggle them in in my pocket for they'll sleep, but he says they're just like babies and as they wake they piddle and all I have to do is hold them out! All very nice but I think I prefer to have a little box and declare them! I want to get Bob some orchids too, and someone else wants a brass pot for flowers and Mrs K some T'dad choc. So it seems I'd better charter a special plane!

Dick is going to take me round the works before I go – he is in charge of the power station part. The actual oil fields are about 15 miles from here and all the oil is pumped up in pipes to this refinery. We get a filthy stink sometimes when the wind is blowing this way. The Riley Jim sold them is very nice and they are thoroughly pleased with it. Dick won't let Bunty drive it as she's not very good, so consequently we are stuck here all day till he comes home at teatime. I can't very well offer to drive it when he won't let her. Anyway there's nowhere much to go to, as the town near here, San Fernando, is a dirty hole. It seems funny seeing so many different coloured people here. They are West Indians, Indians and Chinese and mixtures of them all. Bunty has a house-boy butler chap, and a girl that messes about doing odd jobs and an Indian washer who comes in daily and does different things. She wears a funny head dress and has an armful of silver bracelets and big earrings. Saw one woman with a nose ring one day! These Indians have a sinister look with their sharp features and side whiskers – I much prefer the Barbadians. There's one boy in Bridgetown who knows me now and when I leave the car he always seems to be there. Once I left it somewhere while I was in a club and as I came back to it he touched his cap and said "I'sa Mr Bob King's boy an' I'sa bin looking after de car for you Mistress". He had such a nice grin that I gave him 4 cents although I thought he was probably just a beggar. But Bob has one or two regular boys who watch his car for him and I found out later that this was one, but how he knew me I don't know, as I hadn't even got Bob's car with me!

This all seems to be about me and my doings – I'm sorry darlings – but it's difficult to ask much about you, when I don't know where you are or what you're doing. I suppose you'll be at Thorpe for Easter and Ron and Y in the S of France. I hope the change does the old boy good. Also I hope your itches are quite cured now Mum. I wonder if they've found out which flower was causing it.

I must try and write to Lil for her Birthday, but in case I don't, wish her many happies from me. I'll try and post her a letter on Saturday when we're in town, but we'll be out all day tomorrow at this picnic.

There's a breeze getting up now which makes it a little cooler. It's a much damper heat here and they even have hot pipes in the cupboards in the rooms. They have no windows to the rooms, just very fine netting where a window would be and big shutters outside that. So we don't need nets here to sleep under – but I'd sooner have a net and have a proper open window.

Oh, I've not mentioned the kids. Gordon, Lil's godson – is quite a sweet little fellow. Aged 5, slight squint, has to wear glasses most of the time – goes to school every morning. Marie Louise – 2 years yesterday – very fair hair and skin, podgy also quite sweet but a bit of a devil at times and noisy in the early hours of the morning! Gordon loves to get Aunty Bunny in the nursery and pull all his toys out one by one! Will leave a space in case I want to add anything before posting – Best of love to you both. Hope for letters again soon. From Bunny.

Saturday. No time for more, just off to the wedding.
Will write again in a day or two.

My Darling Bunny,

Just a line to let you know that I'm missing you quite a lot. Last night I dined at Sisters and played a little bridge after, Helen was there too. Jack sends messages and they apologised about not giving you a ring to say goodbye, but they didn't think the plane left in the afternoon and were busy in the morning so thought you had gone when they remembered. Betty says she's sorry too as a matter of fact she rang here about 5o'clock she thought you were going by Lady Boat that night.

Great news, Toby Hodson is engaged to the girl they tried their damndest with, out here now they wonder how it will work – what a family.

Was down at the club till 8.45 tonight made about 15/- at dice quite a good night's work? Hope the luck holds for Weymouth. I think everything is all set now, will be taking down John Mc when we leave the office, have been pretty busy the last few days, and I'm definitely coming up to do a little work on Saturday after breakfast- bloody nuisance, anyway there should be a letter from you that morning by the plane.

I've bought a new bathing suit, rather a nice one, and so it should be for $4°° just for a pair of pants.

Darling, must go to sleep now, doubt if you can read this, am lying in bed hence the scrawl. Won't be writing again, as the plane on Sunday week is only the day before you arrive. Let us know what you are doing flying or sailing.

With lots of love Darling, Bob

Bob's Mother reports back to England

Dear Mrs West,

We saw Bunny off by plane to Trinidad on Tuesday afternoon and I cannot tell you how much we miss her. We are looking forward to her coming back to us again before she sails on 9th May. We have made no stranger of her at all and she has fitted in beautifully. It has been most unfortunate having my father ill, as I feel she had had so much illness in the home before she left. Anyway the young people go in and cheer up the 'old man' as we call him and he enjoys seeing them! Bunny complains of having got too fat, but she is just right now, as we thought her much thinner when she arrived than when we were in England.

Things sound rather serious over the wireless today, Italy going into Albania. Oh! I do trust there is no war it can't bear being contemplated.

The young people have been having a very gay season but things are quieting down now – It is also not quite as cool as it was. I tell Bunny she must persuade you and your husband to take a trip out here, but it must be in January or February as that is the coolest time.

With kind regards, Very sincerely yours, Gwenyth M King

You might keep one or two of these letters as I haven't kept a diary and they will remind me of some of the things I've done!

My darling Mummy and Pop,

Had a terrific mail in on Saturday, thanks so much for all your letters – also got an air mail from Bob! Thought I'd finished with letters from him. Well this is the day I should have left B'dos on board the Columbia. She was in here yesterday. We have had quite fun over the holiday and have done things nearly every day. On Good Friday we went for a whole-day picnic right the other side of the Island. Saw some lovely country and a lot of new things growing – such as Cocoa, bamboo, grapefruit and a little bit of rice. The scenery here is much more varied than B'dos and you get quite high mountains as well as long stretches of flat cane fields and coconut groves. Manzanilla Beach where we went was very wild looking, with endless coconut trees and then a wide stretch of sand going on for miles and miles. It is so flat and firm that cars can drive along. I saw one doing it, but apart from that the whole place was deserted except for a few stray locals – it isn't as nice sand as B'dos though for its a horrid dirty colour – it wasn't a very good day either for it poured with rain after lunch and then to add to our troubles Dick's car got a puncture and the wheel wouldn't come off. Some of them motored into the nearest town (about 14 miles away!) and got a couple of men out while the rest of us went home in another car. The next morning I spent washing my hair as I'd bathed without a cap. In the afternoon we went into Port-of-Spain for this wedding – Dick and Bunty and Graeme MacFadyen and I. He is under Dick in the power plant part of the oil refinery. He's a nice person and has only been out here 6 months. He's been engaged to a girl in Cowes for 2 years and is trying to get them here to give him a bungalow so that she can come out. But then he wonders whether she'd be happy for it's not a very exciting place to live and there are very few nice people at all. Anyhow he's spent the weekend pouring out his woes to me! I'm sorry for the boy for they do lead a dog's life here and its desperately lonely for them, especially when they're doing night shift as they have no one to talk to and have 8 hours on duty in charge of the power plant and have to spend the time keeping the workmen awake and seeing that everything is working alright. Then they try and get some sleep during the day in a horrid little room hardly furnished and with no curtains or comfy chair.

After the wedding we went and met another couple and all had dinner at a Chinese restaurant. A priceless place with little rooms all divided off by ½ swing doors you either have one of these or eat in the one big room. We had a room to ourselves and had an enormous dish of some Chinese concoction – bamboo shoots and various peculiar things and a vast amount of rice. You ask for 2 portions and it's enough for all six people! It was very good and was served by a Chinese waitress. Afterwards we went on to the Country Club and danced. Saw 5 different people from Barbados there – evidently down for Easter. The wedding was most peculiar. The people were all very queer and many of them slightly coloured – you get that far more in Trinidad and they mix more with the white people whereas in B'dos it's unheard of. It was a Scotch boy from here marrying a Creole girl. Dick and Bunty knew one or two people but not many. They all got pretty tight and when we'd had as much champagne as we wanted we left. The Bridesmaids were dressed in a foul shade of pink with ghastly little pink hats with a heavy cluster of bright blue forget-me-nots all over the crown! All the men wore ordinary suits and the whole thing became rather humorous. Graeme made impossible remarks to me throughout the service and I nearly had hysteria – two old dames sat in front of us sending back wafts of fustiness – their dresses had, I should think, been in storage trunks for several months or even years. Towards the end of the service (Scotch Church) the parson got up and said "Miss – will now render O promise me" and a very dusky looking damsel got up from the choir and 'rendered'! She wasn't too bad except that she made the most appalling faces all the time – the organist was a fat black woman – also dressed in bright pink, and she never knew when to stop! However we got some champagne which was what we went for! The reception was in a house in the town. Very hot and much too full of sweating humanity. The floral decorations were rather cunning for they had long stems of bamboo fixed down the walls at intervals. Then they slit the bamboo at each section and filled it with water and then flowers – something like this. You see each section has a little floor across and holds water. I've never seen such enormous big bamboos as grow out here – I took a photo of some yesterday about 75ft high. The next day Sunday, we were all very sleepy and didn't do anything much. Graeme took me for a drive in the morning all up in the hills round here and I drove the car a two-seater Chevrolet. Yesterday we all four went on a lovely drive right up the Maracas valley where all the Cadbury cocoa estates are. As you may know cocoa grows in a big pod thing on trees with little beans inside. Saw enormous grapefruit plantations too and coffee. Then went up to Macqueripe Bay on the North coast. Nice bathing but a foul lot of people there. Spent some time in the cable hut which I enjoyed as I'd never seen a cable thing here so I should like to see it, and then go back and tell them how to do things in B'dos!

It is after lunch and Bunty is resting and I am sprawling on my bed in next to nothing and am quite sweaty hot even though there is a breeze. And yet there isn't much sun – it must get very sticky here later on I should think. Bunty looks a permanent grease spot as it is! Had a very lengthy epistle from Aunt Cara. I hope Tommy Tucker is getting on alright – it must have been worrying for Jill. Glad to hear Mercy is 'expecting a happy event'. Had a PC from Ron from Cannes – I suppose he'll be home by the time this arrives. Hope you're feeling better Mumsie, you didn't sound just up to the mark in your last letter, but perhaps Thorpe will have done you both good. Hope the Danes enjoyed it and that you all had good weather. I expect we'll all be going there this summer wont we? Or are you letting it again. Perhaps you'll pay Wee Frankie another little visit?!

How is Lil's Dane getting on? Hope she's good. What an awful thing if Hitler walked into Denmark – you'd be lost without Ellen and Sonja now. It's really very worrying all this upheaval everywhere! I would like to know what you think about it all Pop – yes we get news on the wireless and of course papers a fortnight old. We get more news from USA but it's often exaggerated.

Think I'll have a snooze now so bye bye for the moment.

9o'c pm have just come in after being up to the oil fields about 15 miles away. Saw various wells and one of them working. They are mostly in clearances right in the Bush, but have very good roads connecting them. We were lucky to see so much as it's all very hush-hush and as you go near the place you leave your name at a bar with a local. A bar across the road I mean not a drinking place!

The oil comes all the way from there to this refinery in pipes. They had drilled 500 ft in 24hrs where we were and hadn't come to much oil yet. The car petered out on the way home but after ½ hr of fiddling about Dick got it to go again. Something to do with the petrol pump – had a meal at the Cafeteria on the vile plant here and then took an ice cream into Graeme who is on duty till 11o'c in the Power Station. Very good American Ice Creams in cartons are sold everywhere. Would you mind paying the enclosed please – will refund with luck. Shall go to bed now I think so night-night. It's quite nice and cool tonight – can hear the whistling frogs and crickets outside in the garden. Best love darlings from Bunny.

*cut that out as I find I've written 8 pages! Have missed the collection so it will have to go late fee in any case! What a pity about Lil's Dane. Am waiting for more news of Mary. Poor girl I am sorry for her. [*sic*]

Darling,

Don't think this will be a very long letter* as its high time I wrote to some other members of the family. Arrived back on Saturday to find more letters awaiting me, for which very many thanks. Probably I won't get any by the next mail as you didn't know if I was coming back or not. You are naughty Mumsie not to have told me how rotten you'd been feeling – I could tell though that you hadn't been just up to the mark. I hope Thorpe and a tonic has put you right. Gilbert by all accounts is in the pink which is good to know.

Was very glad to be back again, although latterly I rather enjoyed being down in T'dad as I got to know Graeme very well and we had a lot of good times together. Its funny how quickly one gets to know some people for I feel I really know him well – we used to talk for hours and hours on end about every kind of thing and it's strange as usually we are neither of us very good talkers especially with comparative strangers. He's all muddled up about whether to have his fiancée out there even if they can manage to get a Bungalow which is doubtful. I certainly do get let in for everyone else's troubles wherever I go! These poor people here are now in a flat-spin. Kitty had the Dr. up a while ago about a small lump on her chest that she had noticed 10 months ago and he had said then it was nothing at all. Well they decided to operate last week hoping it was only a cyst of some sort, but it turns out it's malignant – it had been decided that she should go over with the old people in June for treatment, but this morning she came back from having the stitches out and two Drs are of the opinion that she should have a radical op. Which means the whole L. Breast would be removed, and after that have treatment which would definitely mean no more trouble. But the third Dr. says no op is necessary only treatment. So she's going to England to get a really expert opinion. She may come with me on the Costa Rica as they want her over as soon as possible. It's really awful for her and so worrying to know what to do with the two children. They suggested jokingly that I should stay for the summer and look after the house, the children and John! But I shouldn't care for that unless Mrs K and Bob were coming too and they will of course stay on at Upton. I am so sorry for them all; it seems one thing on top of another. They took X-rays of the Old Man but there is no radiologist here and no abdominal X-rays have ever been known to be really satisfactory. They send the photos up to Canada or the States to be read.

They're very fed up with me here as I'm not staying long enough, they say they expected me for a least a week and I'm going back to Upton tonight before going to the Hutsons tomorrow for a week. Then back to Upton for two nights before a weekend with Sis and Jack. Bob is coming down there too after office on Saturday (28th or 29th) which will be fun. Not sure where we'll all sleep as they have no spare room! On that Sunday there is a moonlight picnic at some beach or the other and after that I go back to Upton till I sail – and gosh - won't I hate sailing. It really has been a perfect few months and never never will I be able to thank you both enough for it. You must be able to tell I think from my letters how much, or nearly how much, I'm loving it all and how happy I've been. It'll certainly be something to look back on if in the months to come there happens to be war and chaos everywhere else. I get fits of depression about it sometimes, but they can't last long here.

The last few days in T'dad were very full. We went over that big sugar factory I told you about. The head chemist took us round but as the other man who was with us was a chemist in the oil plant they got a bit technical! However, as I was fairly familiar with sugar factories I understood more about it than the other two!

Graeme took me over to see the famous Pitch Lake one morning and we watched them digging it out. It's quite hard and you can take a car over it in parts. In some places it is all soft and bubbly looking. Its extraordinary the way it sort of fills up again however much is taken out. They have a small factory there for refining it, but quite a lot is taken away by Government lorries in crude form. I had a game of golf that day too. Played a 3 ball with two men. At first I was to play a single then the other chap was coming too and they said if I wasn't really keen on playing perhaps I'd like to walk round – so I said not for hell, if I come I play! So off we went and as luck would have it I played pretty well and beat them both!! One of them wasn't bad but the other was very erratic – but it shook them both to be beaten up by a mere girl and they never got over it! In the evening Dick took me all round the entire plant – I got an idea of what happens but it was rather wasted on me as I don't know anything about all the machinery. Jim would have loved it.

We went and saw Graeme who was on duty in the Power Station. It was very interesting and I clambered about amongst boilers and turbines etc. got rather frightened when I got too high up amongst iron ladders and things where I could see right down beneath me. I wouldn't like to spend 8 hours in charge of that place I must say. The next day Dick took Bunty and I and another girl into Port of Spain for some shopping. It was very hot and tiring and we were glad when the shops shut at 4o'c.

Went and saw a man about orchids for Bob. He had a lovely collection and I got a list from him. I couldn't take any back with me by plane on a/c of the customs, but they can be sent when a cert. from the Dept of Agriculture has been signed. After that went and drank at the Queens Park Hotel where Graeme met us. Walked round the Botanical gardens and then had dinner at the Chinese Restaurant again called Kwong Tung. Came away laden with chop-sticks! Drove home soon afterwards and then sat and talked to Graeme till 3.15am (!) about our respective affairs and troubles and worries and whatnot. He's going to tell his mother to come and see me at home when she's staying in Herts so's I can tell her all about him and his work and surroundings which she would like to hear 1st hand I expect. Up at 6.30, packed, and set off for the Piarco airport. It was raining when we got there so I couldn't take a photo. Dick couldn't come as he had to work so Bunty and small Gordon and another little boy and Graeme came all in his car. The plane was full and we had a good fly back. B'dos looked really lovely from the air – so very colourful especially along the coast. Bob met me – some others were there too meeting someone from T'dad so we all went to the Marine for drinks and then B and I went back to Upton for breakfast. Later I came down here.

Had a good sleep in the afternoon then played with the children 12 and 8 and then Bob came to dinner and after he and I and John went off to the Marine for the big Cancer Research Dance. Rather ironical that it should be a Cancer Charity affair. It was one of the best I've been to and a good crowd turned out. Perhaps I enjoyed it so much because we didn't go in a party and I was able to have more time with Bob – they have a huge garden there with paths lit with coloured lights and seats all over the place and you sit out in the cool amongst palms etc and under a star lit sky – 'maist romántic'! it seemed funny not going back with Robert to Upton and coming back here with John instead. Played about the next day and Bob and Ma came to dinner.

Last night we all went to a film – Goldwyn Follies. Very good too. I played my singles in the YC Tournament yesterday and lost badly 6-1, 6-2. Couldn't seem to watch anything or get anything right at all. It was very sunny to begin with and I got a headache but I ought to have done better. Played again later in the evening and was much better. I only played once in T'dad so was out of practice I suppose. Bob plays his today. Had a funny letter from To again the other day. Do hope he gets his destroyer soon. James is a devil, he's never written once to me. Did Santer [the chauffeur] remember to take the spot light off the Vauxhall 'cos its mine? And I want it - see? I do want a photo of the Sunbeam Talbot. No

The Sunbeam Talbot (Anna)

of course I'm not sick of sun yet! It's more stuffy here near town than at Upton though. Must snooze now before going down to the Club. Best of love to both of you.

As ever, your adoring Rabbit.

Wakefield House, Bridgetown, Barbados BWI
23rd April

Darling Mummy and Pop,

Did I ever thank you Pop for cabling the 20 quid? Anyway I do now – it will enable me to get just one or two more little things that I couldn't have got otherwise. If you remind me no doubt I'll pay you back when I see you!

Got your two letters yesterday Mum. One written April 2nd and one Easter Monday. You'd written "Fast Mail" on one, but I wasn't sure how it was going to get here any quicker than all the rest of the mail! I am wondering if Acheson is doing you any good with these new injections. What will Colin say? Do hope it will make a difference.

Came here to the Huston's on Thursday. Am quite happy but shall be glad to get back to Upton again. Have seen Bob every day since I've been away, though of course not for long. I am feeling very fed up today for I sprained my ankle yesterday playing tennis. It swelled up a lot and today I can see a gorgeous shade of bright purple peeping through the Elastoplast Dr. has produced a pair of crutches on which I try to manoeuvre much to the amusement of everyone else! It really is a damn nuisance as he doubts if I'll be able to play tennis again before I sail. It's only a sprain and there's definitely nothing broken but that doesn't stop it being very annoying. Mrs King rang up last night and I had a letter from her this morning saying I'd better go home to them and they'd send the car for me tomorrow! But I'm not going till wed. eve when Bob comes to dinner here. I can hop about quite well and went down to the beach this morning – its hot work hopping though I can tell you. There was another girl down there who has done just the same thing a few days ago – on the same court in fact – so now they call it the Suicide Court! Bob took a photo of us each hanging on to a crutch and with our bandaged ankles propped up on a heap of sand!

This weekend Bob and I are going down to Jack and Sister's, did I tell you? I can't remember! Another young couple asked me to stay the other day – Julian and Molly Mahon – only there won't be time as I must have the last 10 days at Upton. Molly used to be very much in love with Bob I believe before she was married!

They've just had the cable from the States about the Old Man. They say "X-rays suggest duodenal, writing". They are now coming home on the Costa Rica with Kitty H and me. Mrs King is staying to keep house for Bob as he can't possibly get away for one of the other directors has to go up to Canada and that only leaves John and Bob in the office so he'll be hard–worked poor darling. John tells me he's never known Bob work so hard as he has done this last year! He also says he's sorry I'm not staying out here and says the old people are too. I've never talked to them about it really, or even to Mrs King! Don't go and write to them will you? Not till I get home anyway. Please. It's funny but I've just never got started. It's difficult as I know Bob doesn't say much and I don't know how much they think about it. Maybe next week I'll have a chat with Mrs. King, but there's really nothing to chat about for they obviously know we're very fond of each other and that's all there is to tell them. The first month wasn't so good you know, and I think we both thought the other had changed far more than we actually had – I must say I was very surprised to find that he still loved me and was in a flat-spin about it all. Anyway the fact that we neither of us really know our own minds seems to me proof enough that it's better left alone and I'm keeping to that. See? I tell him he's never loved anyone enough yet to marry them, and it's probably the same with me – but I love him enough to hate the thought of leaving him on the 9th. Don't repeat all that to Ma will you and don't take it too seriously either, its only cos I've nothing to do at the moment but sit and think – and sometimes I think this war will come and bust up everything for everybody.

Went to a funny little cinema near here 2 nights ago. I think we were the only white people there. They all make a terrific noise and get very excited and have sort of attendants running up and down the aisles trying to keep them quiet! An enormous cockroach ran up the wall beside me in the middle of it! Haven't met any more spiders lately thank goodness – they aren't dangerous anyway but I still dislike them.

How are your legs Poppet? Don't go and walk too much yet will you? Ma said they still ache a bit now and again. I am sorry to hear Ellen has not been feeling too good. Please remember me to them both. I can't send another round of PCs it's too darned expensive. My love to Di if you see her, I don't think I'll have time to write this mail, and to Ursula and the Gregs when you see them and Allan and Dot. I sent Lil some grapefruit from T'dad for her birthday. Nearly sent you some only I don't think you like them enough.

Yes, I liked that son of the Lawrence's very much. I got the Bowler Hat boy to introduce me to him. They should be home by now. Had a nice letter from Jim F [Fasson] the other day. He might come down to Bovingdon for a night or so in May if I'm back in time as he wants to go to Cirencester. Don't mention it to Lily tho' in case they don't know! Heard from Sheena too – she called me Public Wrecker of Hearts No. 1 – seems to me you've been gossiping to Lilly Blair about my doings Mrs West. And Jim Curry tells me I should write articles for the Daily Express!

Had a sweet letter from my little Graeme in Trinidad the other day! He's missing me such a lot!! I told Bob about him and he laughed a lot and said he'd quite expected it!

Gilbert West (GLW)

Lucky Yvonne making all that money. Bob made about $6.00 at dice last night at a men's dinner at the Bridgetown Club. I'm glad he went cos it's good for him to get off on a men's party I think and he missed the big dinner there.

This is quite a big house – stone on top and wood in the front and huge rooms, and masses of servants about. A lovely garden with tall cabbage palms, frangipane of every colour, 36 varieties of hibiscus and a huge tree outside my bedroom window called a cassia grandee which has a mass of pink flowers like cherry blossom all down the stems.

Glad you've given Phyllis a pup, she'll love it. How you'd love the Airedales at Upton. They are father and son and are perfectly sweet. I bought a new rubber ball for one of them as he'd lost his. He sleeps in Bob's room and always had great games with the ball up there. Until he loses it. Most of the dogs out here are mongrel looking things and very thin.

No more now darlings – thank you for your sweet letter Mumsie and all the things you said. Take care of yourselves, best love, as ever from Bunny.

Helen West (HJW)

At The Mare Cottage, Bovingdon

Bunny left Barbados on the 9th May and returned to England just as Basil Brown and Edith Pretty were uncovering the unprecedented finds of an Anglo-Saxon King's burial site at Sutton Hoo, barely half an hour from Thorpeness. War was looming.

Upton 14th May

My Darling Bunny,

By this time you are probably dancing and having a grand time. Anyway I've not long finished the helpings of stewed guava, very nice you can believe me.

The house seems very empty and I do miss you – at times!!!! Very glad to get the cable to say the weather was good, hope you didn't feed the fish?

Have got to play tournament tomorrow will have to work awful hard to win as Willy is playing very well even better than he was in T'dad!

The theatrical people have arrived and the manager is a friend of mine so have met most of the nice girls already. They want me to play a part in Rookery Nook, quite impossible as there is too much work to do and I wouldn't have any time for rehearsals. Johnnie Mac, David, Henry and I had the producer manager and the three leading girls out on Saturday – quite a stir when four bachelors arrived in the theatre on Sat: as Johnnie said – we couldn't have had more flashy glances if we had four ravishing dames with us when we walked to our seats. You don't have to worry Darling its quite OK.

Today I have been up at Mavis' we went to Chancery Lane to bathe and breakfast with the Hanschells, then when we got back Len and I slept till 5o'clock. Mummie came down for a cocktail and so home.

Oh! The dance at the Lacocks was a hell of a show about 150 people and when I arrived about 9.10 all the people that I would have danced with were booked up, people must have arrived from about 8.45 so I danced only three dances for the night. Hollie Shinner was there with her sprained ankle so we called for a bridge table and played, people cutting in as they weren't dancing: you can imagine this caused quite a stir, still I liked that.

Romeo has had his springs tightened up, and I am having the free wheel fixed this week, then for another 20,000 miles I hope? You might ask Jim [*Bunny's brother in law*] what he is doing about the MG for John Skinner.

By the way no squirrels came up with the tennis team, you better tell me who the man was and I will write and tell him to send you the money, perhaps you had better write yourself or he may think that I want to swipe the money!

My Darling, I must go to bed, there is really not much news, although time since you left seems at least two weeks.

With all my love, and give my love to your family,

Yours ever, Bob

Mummie sends her love and says she may not get the time for a line to you this mail. B.

Upton 22nd May 1939

My Darling Bunny,

I have just got in from taking the dogs for their walk. Prince went off last night and returned this morning looking well the worse for wear; he is nicely bitten up round the head. The house is very lonely Darling, although I have been lucky and have been out quite a lot, I have been to three shows in all. "Room for Two" on Friday and "Yes my Darling Daughter" on Saturday. I haven't seen any more of the actresses, so you don't have to worry. There are quite a few T'dad people up here now and I have been to a few parties for them, on Sunday I played tennis at Peggy Chandler's except for that I haven't played much lately. Holly and Willie had to scratch and so Mollie and I played the Bancrofts, they are quite good, but we should have won quite easily. Mollie wasn't too good, but in the first set I was 100% above my usual form and we won 6/4. In the second set we changed over after my serve at 4/1 then we started the rot and lost that set 7/5 and the next 6/4!! Very disappointing. Len and Bert won the open, and Lu and Jack are in the finals for the handicap. Laddie and George won the men's so again they have won the three club men's.

We heard that you had arrived about 2pm then got the wire saying all very well, we rather pictured you spending the night at Plymouth with your cousins or Ron?

We have had a good shuffle in the office, and now things are really beginning to take shape, anyway I seem to have drawn a little more work, but it's on the side I like so we will see what can be done. The free wheel knob came apart in my hands so to speak, so I have detached all the wires and now it can only be in fixed gear! By the way, John Skinner rang me and said that by this time he had hoped to have heard from Jim about his MG.

Wed: is a holiday I'm going down to Sister, then on Friday Mummie and I go off to The Crane till Tuesday morning, a real lazy weekend.

Can't think of any more news, give my love to your people and be good, your first letter will be here on the 6th. With tons of love my Darling.
Yours ever,
Bob.

Upton 6th June 1939 (letter 60)

My Darling Bunny,

Thanks so much for your letters which I got today – I was rather afraid the people on board didn't look too grand, anyway perhaps it's just as well?!!

So good of you to give the family the help you have, they do appreciate it awfully, I hope that the worst is definitely over now.

Its ages since the last mail so must see what's been happening. Have not been playing much tennis - am working rather hard. Seale flew down to T'dad to get the "Good Neighbourly" boat for New York so John and I hold the fort. On the 31st went to a grand dance at the Woods – relations of Greta and Lawrence. It was quite the best that I have been to for some time they didn't draw it out and we were home by 1.30, sorry at the time but greatly appreciating it next morning!! Last Sunday I was down at Sister's Robert and I did some nudist bathing during the day then played bridge. Of course I forgot that the weekend before I was at The Crane. The hotel was full with people like Anne and Robin Robinson, so it was rather nice.

Played a little poker and lost, then lost badly at the 1/- in the slot machine. On Sunday I was about £1 up but eventually managed to lose about $12 - not so good. Was up at Johnnie Mac's the other night and lost again so now that you have gone I seem to have lost my luck. Darling, I do miss you terribly, it would have been grand if you could have stayed on when the family went, but of course one couldn't foresee what was to happen.

Have been to a few good films, last night we went to Snow White, quite good, the Mikado is on next week then the Prisoner of Zenda soon after that.

Audie and Johnnie are off to the seaside, she isn't at all well, I will probably be going down to stay with them on the 24th for the weekend. The 26th is a holiday, the tercentenary of the "House", I suppose Doll will be coming up to stay with Mummie, if not Auntie.

Thursday is a holiday and Di and Robert are having a crowd of us down to Bathsheba for the day. Was up at Beach House with Betty Connell for a bathe this afternoon, quite fun although the sea was not too good. By the way, did I tell you that Laughton Taylor hit me for 17/- and costs = 1/- for speeding in Bay Street, dirty dog, anyway my licence is intact.

We are now beginning to get hot, and very little rain, we had 49 centimetres last night which was more than we have had for all last month.

Went round to Lionel today and although there is still albumen, he thinks I may live a few months more, told me to come and see him in about three months time.

They have shut up the house and I am stifling, anyway there is no more news so will go to bed my sweet. With all my love, Darling,

Yours Ever, Bob

Upton 12th June 1939

My Darling Bunny,

Mummie begs to thank you for your letter, I for your message!! Darling, thanks ever so much for the orchids, they arrived quite safely on Friday all looking grand, I spent some time on Sunday planting them, or rather getting others transplanted so that I would get places for them. I told you to get one orchid not three, and they are expensive ones too.

I actually played tennis on Saturday, the first time for three years that I went down to the club on a Saturday. On Saturday night Bert, David, Johnnie and Robert came up and we had a poker session, I lost about 2/6 and the others taking David's money about 25/- I think, if not more.

Flying is going apace now the Flying Club's plane is proving a great success, and soon we will have experienced Bajan fliers.

Was at a tennis party this afternoon of Lucie Mestier (Miss Muffet) we have been getting a little longed for rain, so the courts were not any too good.

Everyone has refused to do the Bazaar show, rather think I may have to do it, hope to hell not, anyway if I do, you will have to go round and get some short plays, one act, and some low comic songs, and anyway I hope not to have to bother you with that.

Can't think of any news have not been doing much of late, and meant to be dining with Plunks on Wed: night. Hope to hear from you tomorrow, all my love my sweet and again thanks so much for the orchids.

Heaps of love Darling, Bob

My Darling Bunny,

Thanks so much for your last letter, poor you it doesn't sound any too exciting, and of course not bathing in England now makes time even longer.

John Skinner's car arrived yesterday and although he hasn't driven it far yet, he is very pleased indeed with it, you might tell Jim for me. The idea of calling a little midge like yours Juliette II – you have to have a car before you can come into that category!! No next time we go on the continent we must have at least another Bentley, I still have pangs after a "Merk" nothing like thinking big darling.

"The Rains Came" and are still here, no tennis for ages, this afternoon Holly had a party which was reduced to scramble practice! Pretty bloody just between you and me, anyway I won 2nd – colossal what?

Well the news of the family is very cheering; I hope they progress apace now. Mummie is not too well anyway Lionel is looking after her so I hope she will be OK. Don't think she has mentioned any of this in her letters, so don't say anything if you see the family.

We are still getting the business going with lots of changes, so far all the changes seem to be definitely for the better and I think as time goes on we shall see how much we were harming the business with the now dismissed and pensioned staff.

Well I have put my head in the noose, I am being made responsible for the Bazaar show to be held on Dec: 2nd - now Darling that means that I am going to worry you!! Will you get hold of lists of one act plays, modern, funny or detective, with not too big a cast. When you think of all these things it is really asking quite a lot of any playwright. Any expenses that you may have get the money from Grannie that will save me getting it from the committee and sending it to you.

It looks as though the Flying Fish Club is going to come to an end. Nothing definitely yet has been given out, but I think that the rumour might be right.

Am meant to be playing tennis at GH tomorrow, but there isn't a chance of any with the rain, then we are going to see the Mikado, they say it's very good. On Sat: was the sub: dance for Lucille at the RYBC, very disappointing they played far too many encores for the first few dances and we didn't get supper till 1am that being the 8th dance, eventually we stopped before the end.

Monica Partin - you will remember her name!! passed through here with her fiancé, not the same one that she had when she was last out here!

Darling, can't think of any more news, Mummie sends her best love and says she will write in a mail or two. She also asks for the negative of that photo of me taken in the south of France for Fanny. No hurry really. With all my love Darling, yours ever, Bob

My Darling Bunny,

Many thanks for your letter which was the first for over two weeks. Grannie said something about not getting letters from Mummie, we were wondering if the letter business was not being done properly?

Darling thanks so much for your pen, I like the engraving and its grand having it back. So glad you are going to Butch's wedding that was on Sat. They sent a cable from the RBYC. Afraid the hieroglyphics meaning sniff are too complicated for me, or it may be that my mathematical brain makes too much of them!! By the way the KLM plane had to stay up here tonight as there is bad weather in T'dad. We were up at Bert's place practicing a men's sing song for Lu's party on Sat: night it's all in Tyrolean, and we are getting some wild songs ready to give the effect, when they rang Plunks to ask if he could stay. He is now acting 2nd as Dickens is on leave in England.

Well, Romeo has gone again this time two big ends! So once more she has been taken to bits and this time we hope she will stand up for a bit longer. Was driving one of the new Studies – they are grand, and really I was very tempted to borrow the money and say to hell with Romeo. On Sunday went to a picnic at Chancery Lane, it was a show of Lizzie's, nominally breakfast we arrived about 9.15 and bathed for ages in a terrific sea then fed and played poker at which I won 4/5 and then home 4.20pm very little sleep I'm afraid.

Seale, the other director, arrives back from his visit to USA & Canada on business, on Wed morning, he has done the whole thing in four weeks, somehow don't think he will ever go again. It's no use rushing things like that - he should go around with the buyers and Hokers more, but is such a blasted fusser.

There are a few people coming in for pot luck tomorrow and then going on to the flicks - it's a sort of farewell for Peggy Chandler who leaves next week, or may be on Thursday. Talking of that won't be writing again then as after all Darling, it's only a day later.

Did I ever tell you that you and Lyle Sealy and I had both drawn horses in the sweep at the RBYC? The horses only had three legs between them though so no luck – Henry won it - $70°°. Mummie had Lionel up to overhaul her and he says she is very fit, so that's fine, I was rather worried as I thought she may be in for some trouble.

Things are going fine at the office, such a different atmosphere now with the change over, it is really very pleasant working now, and I like the job that I have got now, it's more responsibility and I don't intend to let any of it be taken over by Seale on his return, he is really rather a lazy person too, so shouldn't mind except that he likes to have a say once there is no decision to make.

Mummie sends her love and says that she hasn't been able to write this mail but will do so soon. All my love Darling, Yours ever, Bob

Upton 10th July 1939
(Envelope marked 65)

Thanks for your letter, and the solution to the puzzle, I'm afraid that none of us got it; I showed it to Mr Allan (Collymore) and even the brain of the C.J. did not think of that idea.

Chancery Lane Beach

Yes, that was the girl we went to stay with - she is now in New York seeing the world's fair and staying with friends, it's a 21st present. Hugh and I were at Sherbourne with her brother.

There hasn't been much doing lately, quite a lot of rain and except for bridge time hangs rather. On Sat: was the show in fancy dress for Lu, a very good do, I believe we go through some 40 odd cartons of tinned beer, not bad between 7.30 and 12.30! If no rain I hope to get tennis tomorrow and Wed: at the Savannah. Last night Mummie and I dined at Sister's and played bridge. On Wed: Laurie and Greta, Jack and Sister are having 'pot luck' here then we are going on to the flicks.

Agatha goes off to T'dad tonight for a short holiday. Tom Paton is going the round trip to B.G. [British Guyana] and back with old Dr Alleyne his drinking friend – should be a funny trip.

Darling can't get going with this letter there isn't really any news, and I don't feel in the writing mood, had rather a miserable day, very busy then spent the afternoon just reading the papers at the club, perhaps that accounts for it.

Kitty seems to have had a very disappointing time with her arm, rotten luck, I had hoped that the Old Man would have had his eye done before he went off to Scotland. They wrote to say that Jim had been round about a car and it sounds very cheap to me, what's wrong with the car!! Don't tell Jim that I said that!

Darling I must end and go to bed, longing for your letter which should be here on Thursday.

With lots and lots of love my sweet, Yours ever – Bob

Royal Barbados Yacht Club
Barbados BWI   17th July 1939

My Darling Bunny,

Lord knows how I will be able to get together any news at all as things have been too dull for words. Thanks awfully for your last letter, I'm looking forward to the photos of Butch's wedding, I quite imagine that she would make a very pretty bride. Mummie has not been too bright, and I have actually got her to stay in bed as much as possible. Lionel was up to see her and says she is quite fit and that it is probably due to her age that she is having these haemorrhages for such long periods, anyway it has her looking very badly and of course feeling rotten.

I continue to work much too hard for my liking, this afternoon I got up here at 5.30 and then to add to the depression there was only Dunks in the club, so we chatted for a bit then as he had begun to read I thought I would write, so you see Darling I am not writing under very excellent conditions.

George Clarke and his wife, Lu's mother, are off to England tomorrow with young Trevor who is going to Blundell's. Some people think that they are quite mad going near Europe at this time, but personally I don't think there is going to be war, anyhow not in Europe, maybe in the East.

I played tennis almost every day last week, and not too badly either, looks as though I may again this week if the weather is kind, even on Saturday, can't think what has come over me!

Went to two films last week "The Great Garrick" and "The Little Princess" both very good, on Sat: night I saw the latter then went of to the club but didn't dance, it was a dance for the Aero Club. A friend of mine with whom I was at school out here years ago has just returned, he is an engineer; he has a car exactly like Hugh's Riley, and although it's done 51,000 miles sounds very nice.

Have got to have the orchid house pulled down, some beetle has got into lots of the wood and eaten it out.

Anyway I will enlarge it now that I have got to pull down some. They look very nice, I am sending down to the fellow in T'dad for another type of Dendrobium. Have been recommended it as quite the prettiest of that species.

Darling don't think I have anything more I could scrape up, not that I have done too badly, now have I?? Darling I do miss you awfully and I believe I still love you!! All my love my sweet. Yours Bob

HMS Hostile
Sunday [no date - Tony was on HMS Hostile from July 1939 until July 1940. Hostile was sunk on 23rd August 1940]

Bunny my beautiful,

Well "little coz" I enjoyed last night more than somewhat, and I think we both behaved "splendidly"; I like that word – it smacks of a duchess at a Red X meeting!

And what with all those people, just pay no attention m' dear! And we didn't, or I don't remember doing so. I learnt two things – a) that to say is just "nobody's business" – how has it taken me all these years to find out? b) that the Gargoyle has distinct possibilities – wasn't the pianist evil?

I feel slightly depressed today. As the ship has become unbelievably filthy since I left, and it appals me to think I have the job of getting her clean again.

Don't know what you think of it, but I'm all for a repeat party if I can manage it next weekend. 'Cos the VAD, bless her little heart, can only get matinee leave. But I think it were wiser nobody knew of it, as I can imagine "they're seeing far too much of each other" being a fairly common remark. Which may be true, but what harm can it do gal?

As you know John Mannatt has just married and damn my wig if the Gunner didn't announce at lunch, "I got engaged early this morning!" More champagne! Versa grave.

I got rid of the dozen 2/6 oysters this am without a hitch m'dear! But then we did take a lot of exercise last night!!

I'll let you know about next week-end in code! Sundays are hellish days! Especially in dockyard. This is not all remorse for yesterday – for frankly Bun I liked it.

Some love to you my sweet.

Tony

Upton
22nd July 1939

My Darling Bunny,

You can't say a thing to me about missing mails!! You missed the Dutch, an unpardonable sin my Darling. There isn't much news since last Tuesday's mail, the weather has got rotten I think, but there hasn't been much rain.

On Wed: I went down to Bathsheba to see Johnnie and Audie, she is looking much better. I am off there tomorrow. Oh Thursday I went down to the north point on insurance, I took Dick Challenor as he is now out of work after the crop, awaiting a new appointment at some other estate. We got back about 3.45 then after changing I went off again to Mollie's where after dinner we played Bridge. We played again at the RBYC this afternoon.

Haven't had Romeo done yet, the lights don't dip now but the engine is doing quite nicely.

The orchids are looking very nice, yours are lovely. I saw a beauty this morning, a lovely cattleya, white and dark wine lip.

My sweet there isn't much in this but things are fairly quiet. Longing for your letter.
With all my love. Your Bob

Upton
24th July 1939
forwarded on to Reedlands,
Thorpeness, Suffolk

My Darling Bunny,

This will be a really short line as what with one thing and another there isn't much news. I'm writing this in Mummie's room, she I'm afraid isn't much better, and it's now over three weeks that it's been going on. She isn't looking too badly but of course is feeling pretty bloody. I think she will be going down to Cave's nursing home on Wed: anyway I will be seeing Lionel tomorrow and then see John and see what about coming up to his place, I mean for myself.

Thanks so much Darling for your letter and the photos of the wedding, I gave Sister the other one and she liked it very much.

Have played a little tennis but hit quite a bad patch in the middle of the week. Sorry to hear that the Old Man is not going to have his eye done over there, we are writing to try and persuade him to have it done early in October.

Well the test match seems to be spoiled again, although Grant had a very nice knock today at the beginning of the innings. Hope that the wicket will be much better tomorrow.

On Sunday I rearranged the orchid house. I have enlarged it as some of the wood got attacked by some sort of wood ant, it looks very nice now, much more roomy.

Darling I must close down now, remember we have not told Grannie anything about Mummie going to the nursing home, we shall see, Lionel may prefer to have a nurse up here, we have only just said that she is in bed. Mummie sends her love and says she will write soon again.

All my love my sweet, sorry this isn't too good this time, but I still love you.
With best love, Bob

My Darling Bun,

What a change to write to you my dear when you owe me a letter, instead of me owing you one.

Well darling how are you, I hope you have recovered from the repercussions of the West. You must have had a wonderful time – and it must have been very flat coming back to the old country again.

I have just come back from camp at Stols six miles from here, such a good holiday! This year we had to work very hard up at six most mornings and not finished until 5.30 at night. Then alcohol until the early hours of the morning – so there was not much time for sleep. It rained most of the time which did not improve matters. The only bright spot was I managed to win the jumping – for which I get a handsome jerry!

I am jumping the same horse at Hawick Show on Saturday so hope she does well as the Duchess of Gloucester is going to be there – and I should loath to fall off!!

I am really going to come South my dear when I get the hay finished, so may I come and stay with you part of time. It seems years since I saw you. It will be probably about the end of August, but may be earlier if we get some good weather.

I am not in a mood for writing in fact I have not been for some time – so do not mind if this is not very interesting.

My affair has seemed to frizzle away because of the usual complaint – lack of the necessary – hellish to say the least of it. Which is even worse because it was very genuine on both sides – so we are more than good friends still.

Still Bun darling do write and tell me your news. Tony is very pleased with his new job: I think he will really settle down again.

Looking forward to seeing you again, darling, soon.

With my very best love, Jim

Roumailai 27th July 1939

My Darling Bunny,

Thanks so much for your last letter; it was a bright spot in quite a lot of fog. Mummie is safely at Cave's Nursing Home, and I think looking a little better already, she isn't much better really, but I think that she will soon improve now that she is really quiet and nothing to worry about. As you will see I'm down with John, he is very kind, in fact everyone has been, Lionel offered that I stayed there and Mrs Mack wanted to know if she could do anything or if I could come and stay with her – very kind of her.

Have been working quite hard lately, didn't get much time to stay with Mummie today, anyway she has had lots of people in, even in the morning.

Sorry to have given you all this trouble about choosing plays Darling, but it is most difficult to choose from catalogues. If you could get R. Seames on the subject he could probably give you names of ½ doz plays that we may never have heard of. Anyway I'm sure that you will get the right stuff.

Haven't done a thing since my last letter, hope to get some tennis on Friday, tomorrow the first this week, then I'm going to Dolls for cocktails, it's her birthday. I might go to a flick after, for we told John not to expect me for dinner, he rather likes his dinner about 7.30 and shouldn't think that I will get away from Dolls till long after that.

Darling, every time I go into my room here I think of you, not that I ever saw you in that room, the night I came in for you, you were having your dress done up in Kitty's room, but still it is quite nice thinking of you – Hell, John's influence must be catching, I don't generally write like that.

I'm afraid I have left your letter up at Upton so haven't got your Thorp address, so will send this to Bovingdon.

You go careful with these Navy, they are very quick off the mark, don't take this seriously but what I mean is not too seriously, just a little flirting is quite OK – sorry I can't report any, these T'dad girls that have been up here were here when Mummie was ill so couldn't keep in my hand. Such a pity, must be losing my technique.

Marco Polo is on this weekend must try and go on Sat: or Sunday.

Now that I'm finishing John has just begun to write anyway can't think of any more news so must close – I still love you.

With lots of love, Bob

Roumailia 31st July 1939
forward on from Mare Cottage to Reedlands, Thorpeness

My Darling Bunny,

Lordy, these boats are one on top of the other; it's just a couple of days ago that I wrote so not much news in this. Mummie I'm glad to say is much better, and although I will try and keep her in the home as long as possible, is already talking of when she can get up and move out.

On Sat: night dined with Johnnie Mac and then went to see Marco Polo, quite good – last night I dined at Yorkshire with the Arthurs, quite a nice but quiet dinner. Romeo is giving trouble again, rather fear that it may be a little end, but hope that it's not. Think I will have to get rid of him if anything more goes wrong.

On Thursday is the first day of the races, I'm going down to Mollie's in the afternoon and play bridge before and after dinner. Sister said something about coming down for next weekend, it's the August bank holiday, but I'll wait and see how Mummie is.

Oh! By the way forgot I have got a letter from you since Friday. Thanks for the French's Catalogue (Samuel French Ltd publishers of plays and musicals) have been wading through it, it is damn hard to find from a catalogue – you say something about songs but Darling I'm not putting on a musical show, I won't want any music. I think the best thing would be to tell them the type of thing I want and see what they recommend. Or better still let them send me three or four plays. I will write to them and let them send out the books then when I choose I will be reading the actual plays. If however, you could get Ronald Jean to give you a couple of good snappy sketches for charity shows they would be most appreciated!!

Darling sweet can't think of any more news so will close.

With all my love. Yours ever,

Bob

Bob and Johnny McKinstry

My Darling Bunny,

Thanks so much for your last letters with the play and monologue advertisements, and the one from Thorp. Think you said something about answering questions must get up and get it. I, by the way, as you might guess from the writing, am in bed. John is dining out somewhere so have come up to write this.

Mummie was to have gone to Dolls this afternoon, but she had a bilious attack on Sat: night so I have got her to stay till Thursday – she is much better though and I hope she will be strong enough to get home in a couple of weeks.

I went off to Sister yesterday morning and came up this afternoon for tennis at the YC. We have had races today, and I believe a huge crowd. The weather has been grand, we are having a drought, and the planters are getting very depressed.

Have quite a good week ahead of me – tomorrow going for a bathe and cocktails at the Leacocks, wed: bathe and dinner and bridge between Mollie and Sister, Friday dine with Plunks and poker. We may be opening a branch in Broad Street, it's all in the air just now, and don't say anything about it even to Kitty. Goddards are buying out Johnson and Redman, so they look like taking too much control.

Darling, am getting sleepy must see what questions I have to answer – yes Darling the pen is fine, but as you probably remember I keep it at the office so never write letters with it. Why of course I would sooner know who you are going around with, I told you that before you left. I don't expect you not to have a spot of flirting now and then; wish I could get a little myself. Johnnie Mac and I were only saying a few Sat: ago it's about time something nice came to the island, things have been so dull!! Can't help feeling that Gimson has too much money though; tell him to buy you the orchids with the plants then you could give them to the family to bring out when they are coming!!

Darling sweet, must go to bed, or rather to sleep seeing how I'm in bed now.

With all my love. Bob

Fairhaven Elie, Fife, Scotland
12th August 1939

Bunny Dearest,

Life was very unpleasant this morning. It wasn't for quite some minutes after waking up that I realised there was no good morning kiss to come, and even then it only filtered through slowly. O Tempora! O mores! However, I haven't yet committed suicide.

There are some things for which I can't and wouldn't thank you; they are quite above that; but there are a whole heap of things for which I do want to thank you.

Yesterday ended one of the happiest two weeks I have had in my life, and even this morning's nasty emptiness somewhere amidships has a little sweetness hidden it, and what Celtic there is in my make-up well appreciates that better – sweetness, so thank you for everything.

I got across to Marylebone at 6.25 and the Ricky Train went at 6.32 so I got the 6.55, but it wasn't very good scotch and I had to split the difference between the station clock, which said 6.46 and the Refreshment Room clock, which said 6.44: "at about 6.45pm".

I've told your Mama how I haven't been able to write except from the car which is at this moment parked in a certain spot on the Inner Circle, Regents Park.

The last two News Items add up to 2 minus 1, and no rain, and the whole thing, I suppose, equals "sentimental Ass". However, that's better than "little old mouldy pig" and anyway, there it is.

I daresay you have, or will, read my letter to your Mama. The job mentioned is to an experimental Gas Warfare Station down Salisbury Plain way, which should be very interesting and rather informal. I was very afraid it meant that I would be rushed off right away, but they calmed me down this morning, and Scotland can rest as a possibility.

We are pushing off sometime on Monday morning and I suppose will make a two day trip of it in this car, which – by the way, doesn't seem at all so good after FLR and the Humber. Coming up the Bye-pass in a hurry this morning was really pathetic.

I've just been having a think (very exhausting) about asking you to get someone to take a good photo of you and to send me the negative so that I can get it enlarged up. I want it alright, but the thing I want most is a certain light in your eyes which is there from time to time, won't come out in any photograph. However, if you would like to be nice to me again, that negative is one way in which you can be.

Well: I guess I must push off now and collect Gladys and take her down home, so Au Revoir, Bunny dearest, soie sàge et prendre gaide de toi-mème, céder en effet tu n'est pas maintenant toi-mème suil; et pourtant, j'attendrai. [*Good bye, be good and look after yourself, give in as you are not yourself anymore, and however I will wait*].

With my love Attie

My Darling Bunny,

I have just heard that the KLM did not come up this afternoon, of course it would happen like that the first time I send you an airmail letter.

Went to a bathing picnic at Chancery Lane on Saturday then on to the cinema and the Aquatic Club. Then yesterday went home and picked breadfruit and later had supper with Doll. Nothing on till Wed: when I go up to The Crane for a bathe and dinner with the Hutsons - they are up there for two weeks. Had a good night on Friday, a bachelor dinner with Plunks. We played vingt-et-un after a large dinner only 1/2d a chip but I managed to collect about 14/- not at all bad?

Lord, afraid this letter is terribly written, but am writing in my lap in front of the wireless. Afraid anyway this letter will be very short, but my sweet I just don't seem to be able to collect any news, must be too sleepy, and another tough day tomorrow. We are going to modernise the grocery, the business about having a branch in Broad Street has not materialised although we have new ideas for that now but really want the Old Man out here, he is so peculiar he wants to go in for new ventures, but likes to think about it for so long by which time someone else has got it.

Darling sweet, must go to bed. I love you – Bob.

p.s. just remembered about the Talbot [*Bunny's Sunbeam Talbot*] so sorry to hear about it, hope it won't be much more than the wings.

Love Bob.

My Darling Bunny,

Thanks ever so much for your air mail letter which arrived here in 6 days, also the ordinary mail, a lovely long letter. Now if I write to you by air mail today it will seem like ages between my letters as there is a mail tomorrow to England – so this is almost without news, just to see how quick I can get a letter to England. Please check the time and let me know for future time.

If you see Ronald Jeans I want a one act play for about 5 people, funny, lasting about 30 minutes. Must be off now.
With all my love
Bob.

Bunny dearest, I thoroughly enjoyed myself in town. It's a nice experience to be met, dealt kindly with and seen off by a lady. I must try it again, if possible omitting the "seeing-off", which doesn't sound so good anyway, come to think of it.

This is the most crazy situation. Reid, whom I relieved, has been getting "hurry-up-the-situation's-getting-worse" telegrams ever since I got here and the whole station is suffering from combined Naval, Military Air Force and Home Office Panics, as it can be kicked from all four quarters at once. The result is that nobody bothers a hoot about me except to desire me to get on with the job and produce the answer without bothering them any more than is absolutely necessary. I personally find that there are two very good reasons why this is a little difficult; the first, domestic; the second, official.

I have nowhere to settle down and no transport. The Hotel (The Mill Race), in which the Reid's have existed, is quite nice and very reasonable financially: small, rather olde worlde and quite pleasantly situated in Salisbury, distant about seven miles from Porton. It's probably grand for the married couple but no damned good to me. It is very full, entirely of elderly and perennial dames and young Army Officers and Army spouses. (With the exception of one temporary civil couple whom I strongly suspect of being illicit honeymooners and at whom, as a result, I have cast alternate glances of mundane interest and envious hatred). Also, it has no LICENSE.

In any case, I am "slept out" down the road in the house of a refrained she-dragon, who has so far insinuatingly ordered me to bed, bath, shave, etc. at appropriate times. However, I have managed to snoop a room in the camp until Monday or Tuesday which will give me a chance.

The transport question, I haven't settled yet. This morning, I bought Reid's open Morris 8 from him, and then at 5.0pm (he having left the camp at noon and Salisbury at 4.0pm), I got back to find a quite separate deal via his wife to the local garage and no car for me. Very irritating, as it was quite a reasonable deal.

The official difficulty is large. The job is quite unlike anything in the service. I find myself in charge of a whole set of engineering workshops producing various bits of machinery as called for by the Experimenters. More than that, I'm not going to confide to writing, the whole thing being terribly secret and confidential and anyway, rather complex: life is full of sentries, who pop out at you and say "'Ave you a PASS", and who simply cannot be bounced.

I intend to get home for Saturday night. As you are probably going dancing and I don't suppose I shall get there until after 8.0pm, I won't try ringing you up this time.

It is extraordinary what odd places I have to write letters to you. The only spot I've found here is my room 'down-the-road' on a very rickety table beside the bed, at midnight AND there's a mosquito, blast 'im. Awful, aint it.

I'm still quite dazed as to the situation here and probably shall be until same time next week. I hope you had another pleasant evening in town, and got down to Suffolk safely. I envy you the East Coast Air, all over again. It's pretty sticky down here.

Must close now, Bunny dearest, or I'll never be able to get up tomorrow and go to work, though I think the she-dragon's professional pride will terrify me into leaping out far earlier than necessary, in case she should think me late for work. Oh 'for a morning kiss from the beloved's bed', - and this one 'ere wot I'm asitting on, I can say with full authority, is the worst bed in England. It has its own gradients, and hard – coo, lor luv a duck!! I've been buying your sticking-plaster-for-blisters!   All my love, Bunny dear. Attie

Roumailia 25th August 1939

My Darling Bunny,

There is a French boat going tomorrow so will get a letter off by her. Thanks so much for your long letter, how did you get on with the taxi driving, I mean lorry.   You certainly chose a thing that when you hit you will do much more damage than you can receive!!

Mummie is really looking much better; she is up at Yorkshire and quite enjoying it too. I hope she will go to The Crane for the last long weekend of the month, I may get up there for the Sat: and Sunday, will have to see how things go.

News is pretty bad today, everything seems to point to war, but somehow feel that something will stop it at the last minute. Anyway wont write anymore about it now as all everyone ever talks about is the bloody war!!

Played tennis on Tuesday the first time for ages, haven't been doing much lately, had a little bridge, and out to The Crane with Betty once or twice. The bathing up there has been simply grand.

Whymis bust up his car the other night then two nights later Abe turned his over. Of course it has been hushed up, but not too good for discipline. Oh! I never told you that Bunny Edwards and Suzette were out snooping on the Savannah one night, and were attacked by a local man who said that if Bunny didn't pay him some money, he would expose them. Apparently a row followed in which Suzette got a black eye and Bunny a bit knocked about. A couple of nights later Plunks and Abe went out and caught the fellow and beat him to hell. The latter of course was hushed up and no one knows who beat up the fellows.

John is sleeping peaceably at the radio having got back from Tom Paton's cocktail party properly plastered. I left about 8 o'clock and came home. He never showed up till about 8.30. Not a very good show anyway.

Molly and Julian have been given a trip up to the World's Fair, they are worried now that they won't be able to go, and anyway the American Exchange has jumped to 12% premium, so they will find it a very expensive business.

Haven't seen much of Sister lately, suppose we will be going to a flick tomorrow night. Suez was on this week but somehow I missed it. Agatha returned from T'dad and seems to have had a very grand time indeed.

Darling sweet, must go and wake John and go to bed.

With all my love, Darling Yours ever, Bob

Bunny dearest,

I was very glad to get your letter this morning – I was beginning to be afraid that they were holding up the mail. (No modest fears that you had forgotten me, you notice).

Life is almost exactly the same from my point of view as when I last wrote. I did manage to get home for Saturday night, but only by the skin of my teeth, as all leave for Active Service Personnel had been stopped by then. However, as I spent the Friday between Army Blankets with no sheets or pillow cases, I was rather glad to be able to collect same from home.

I have a room up in the camp for a few days until I can get myself settled down somewhere. The whole place is so full of Army now that this is very difficult. Also, the Transport problem being still unsettled, it's a little awkward. However, to tell you the truth, there is so much work going on that I haven't any time to worry about how I'm going to sleep or get places and still less what Hitler is going to do next. Besides, I still have at least three photos that just have to be examined from time to time.

If the worst occurs, where will you go; Bovingdon, Thorpeness or where? In normal times, I think I shall appreciate this job. It's only 80 miles from Ricky and I don't see why I can't see you at least once a week, which is something. I pack up about 11.00a.m. on Saturday mornings and as long as I'm back on the job by about 9.00a.m. on the Monday, everyone is satisfied, so if things get back to normal, you will probably find yourself writing to me thus "Please don't come over this Saturday, because --- "Heigh-ho! For the piping days of peace".

The real consolation will be that it is undoubtedly better for you and I that war should occur now, if it must, rather than in two or three year's time. It sounds trivial, but whatever may happen, it is really a big thing when you consider it.

I hope to be able to write you a more settled account of self and affairs in a couple of day's time: either that or a telegram, anyway. I hope all the family are flourishing and that J. Fasson Esq. is enjoying himself, though I don't think he can enjoy Thorpeness as much as I did.

My love to your Mama and Papa (a kiss to each, please).

Soie-sâge Cherie.

All my love
Attie

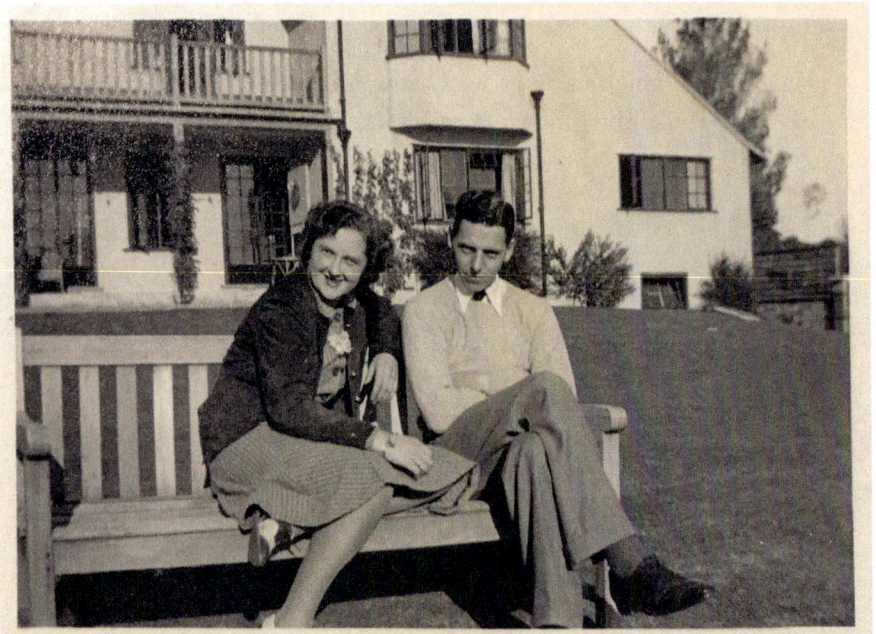

OUTBREAK OF WORLD WAR II

3rd September Neville Chamberlain broadcast to the nation that Britain was at war with Germany. Bunny and her parents were playing tennis at Thorpeness Club when war was declared.

Officers' Mess,
Experimental Station,
Porton, Wilts
Tel. Winterbourne Gunner 262
Sunday am

[Bunny has written in pencil on the letter 3rd September WAR]

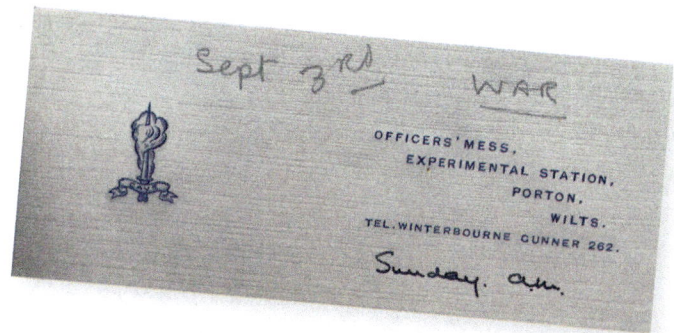

Bunny dearest,

I sat down and wrote off a letter immediately after our telephone conversation last night: a strongly ideological effort which became rather involved, partly owing to the difficulties in putting these things in a readable way and partly owing to the filthy noise produced by an unintelligible radio and an unintelligent bunch of Army Officers. Anyway, the sober light of dawn persuaded me to rewrite said effort.

What little I heard clearly last night seemed to forebode bad tidings in this letter of yours to come, and in my usual charming way I immediately interpreted the gathering gloom as personal to me. However, I perceive that such is not necessarily the case and in any event, cannot refer to the worst or you would have said so. Moreover, an English Sunday is English Sunday anywhere and the intensity of same in the middle of Salisbury Plain, in uniform, in the rain, in the circumstances, will probably create a record depression letter, or no letter, so why worry. Tomorrow will be Monday.

I suppose this war is now inevitable. It is the usual perversity of Fate that I, whose theory of life has been constructed upon the belief in the inevitability of war, should, at the moment it arrives to prove the contention correct, have such excellent reasons for wishing it otherwise.

I ought really to be going into this thing quite ready to be made or finished. I am almost exactly where I planned to be at the critical moment, and about as ready as I ever shall be to seize an opportunity, if it comes my way. I am fairly ambitious, and you can't get the tops without taking a chance.

However, my ambitions are now a good deal less self-centred and what I want are joint results and not single endeavour, and the chances one takes are going to be a little different as a result. Above all, there are two dangers, if war does get going.

The first is militarism. Once a nation is really in the grip of Militarism, Free Will and self-determination are practically speaking at an end, and it will probably be extremely difficult to give one's private affairs any consideration. One becomes first a number in a vast machine and not a human being at all. This tune, I suppose that is liable to occur to you just as much as it is to me.

The second danger is the break-down of civil order. That's rather further away and probably a little pessimistic, but opinions seam to vary so much as to how long this is going to last. If it does go on long enough to bring everyone to a standstill, anything can happen. Anyway, one really must know what one is fighting for and that is why I might have to send you a telegram, and joint strength is far more than twice single strength.

That's about enough of the heavy stuff, Bunny dear. These seem to be rather heavy times.

I suppose I shall be shot off to a ship as soon as things get under way, but one will never get any advance information now. In the meantime, things in this wilderness are about the same, except that I now possess a very fine motorcycle. Accommodation gets more difficult each day, but we shall manage I expect. Also, I've more or less got the hang of this work business.

Bunny, I hope you'll take things easy. This uniform and ATS and so on is all jolly fine and helps the country along and so on, but it ought to be quite secondary. It's nothing to do with your real job of work. However, I'm sure you'll be pretty good at it and anyway, you have enough common sense to win most of your own wars. I haven't been able to get near a golf course down here. So I've taken to squash as about the only available exercise, with an occasional game of hockey thrown in. Now that night driving is practically impossible, the movies are out of the question as there aint none no nearer than Salisbury. Cor! Awful, aint it?

Well! Let's await the letter. This isn't a bad effort, anyway as regards length though whether it makes sense, I don't know. My love to your Mama and Papa. I hope they are both bearing up and in the best of health. Re-reading this, there doesn't seem to be anything very pleasant in it, but I hope it's covered by the fact that all of it is on account of I love you, my child, See –

Take care of yourself, Bunny dear. All my love Attie

Roumailia 5th September, 1939
(envelope marked no 75)

My Darling,

Thanks so much for your letter, I hope that I will get another one tomorrow by the Dutch boat. Well, here we are just waiting for news, we still get the wireless, but quite naturally the news is very censored. America gives us some very sensational stuff. Don't know yet what will be happening John has received no orders yet, and don't see that many people will be allowed to leave here for overseas. In fact the Governor has said that many who may want to go will not be allowed to. If this war lasts any time I think we will have our hands full with these people here. Naturally they have appointed food control boards, and things are being arranged daily, I have offered my services with the police, but like so many others have been told that just now there is nothing to do.

Mummie is still up at Yorkshire, she was not so well at the end of the week, but I think she is getting on slowly, am going to ring as the news is over. Have not been doing much lately, was down with Mollie and

Sister on Sunday didn't do much except a lovely bathe during the morning.

So far we have no news of the family; we presume that they will be leaving about the end of the month.

Afraid this is a terrible letter but you can't write much with everything in the world is such a hell of a mess, it seems quite untrue still. Don't know when this will get to England, anyway will try and get this off just in case the Harrison boat will be leaving tomorrow.

Must end off now, this letter may be opened by censurers, anyway write soon.

All my love, Bob

Officers' Mess,
Experimental Station, Porton, Wilts
Tel. Winterbourne Gunner 262
Tuesday Undated [12th September]

Bunny dearest.

That was swell. Just how lucky I was to get those two days and how nearly it didn't work wont bear thinking about. It did come off, and it has made an enormous difference, and that's quite enough to get on with.

It was very sweet to see you again, and that was one of the nicest morning awakenings I've ever had. You must do that again sometime.

Attie at Reedlands, Thorpeness

I found your letter waiting for me when I got back on Monday morning, which was very pleasant. I think your Mr. Cousins must have had it in his pocket for some little time, blast him, as the Post mark was most distinctly Friday evening. However, your Sunday note arrived here this morning and that was very nice too.

I had a trouble free run home on Sunday at about the same speed as the one to you. It's really very odd, for though I can remember every bit of the road, the whole thing seemed to happen in a flash, rather as if the Time Factor stood still and one moved in space only. Perhaps it has some significance, but I expect it's quite a usual sign. Also passed a very pleasant night at home and was infuriated to find that I'd turned out too early at 5.30a.m. I finally got under way at about 6.30 and as the road was quite empty and mostly very straight, I got here in under two hours. That bike can certainly move a deal quieter than I want at present. Perhaps we shall have a chance of demonstrating same.

You didn't mention the Euan-Smith – Marlborough idea to me at Thorpeness. I think it sounds excellent. It's quite a long way down to Marlborough from Suffolk and one should really spend a night at this end, what with all this difficulty about night driving, etc. It's the obvious thing to do, 'aint it.

The only chance of getting a letter off in this wilderness is to post it at lunch-time. As the place fills up with a shouting, drinking mob, I snooped out of the shops as early as I could to get one off today, but I'm afraid I didn't get away quite early enough to write a reasonable letter. The jacquerie are already upon me.

I did enjoy the few hours at Thorpeness so much. I only hope I get a chance to snatch them again, or better still, to hear that you've gone to Bovingdon (you're sure to do that the day before I get sent to Harwich).

I talk to you far too much, and you not enough to me, so I hope you manage to sift the grain from the cockle. Anyway everything is swell and I'm very happy.

Au revoir, my lady, All my love Attie

HMS Hostile
At Sea
18th September 1939

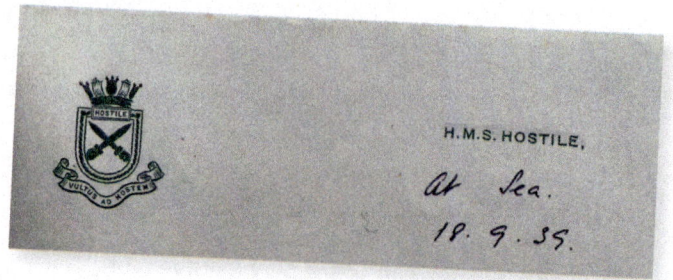

M'dearest Bun,

Doch! What a thing – now writing to thank you for
your sweet birthday wish long long ago. But as always, I have my excuses. And "this 'ld war", or the feverish
preparations to get the good ship Hostile ready for it – has had a lot to do with my late thanks. It's all very
tragic – but I suppose for the best in the long run. For if ever there was a Holy war – surely this must be
it – there could never have been two more benighted governments than the Bolshie and the Bosh. So we're
bound to win in the end, tho' that won't be just yet I'm thinking.

Most of the free going tripe, propaganda, and what not, is merely to hood wink these wartime attractions –
the censors, for altho' life has been pretty full since we commissioned two months ago – and it has all been
great fun really, tho' a bit warring, I'm not allowed to say anything of a service nature.

I've not heard from the family since James was down with you, I wonder where "the ?Jian-tos" are stationed
now?

Petty will have great difficulty choosing which of her many regiments "to follow"! But as a VAD she'll be
fairly busy by now I expect.

Faint whisperings have been heard round the clubs, of a flying type called Turner – as always we are awaiting
confirmation before issuing comment. For the news agency thro' whom I got this piece of information – was
that notoriously unreliable source, the Blair Sisters! *[Their respective mothers]*

Hope all are well at the Mare.

Love Tony

Letter on Alleyne Arthur & Co Ltd airmail paper
18th September 1939

My Darling,

Thanks so much for your letters it seems ages since I wrote, but what with boats not going, then others
turning up out of the blue its most difficult. I decided I would write airmail and then again soon.

Things are being got under control gradually and except for the women of the island who have gone quite
mad forming Red X units – for what, God knows. Things are being fixed by Government control, and so
far there is nothing given to the young men. The Governor has told everyone that they probably will not
be allowed to leave the island – you see we will have to look after ourselves internally and apparently the
Government realise that the few men that could go would not be any real help to GBs forces just now and
the same men will be most useful out here. The volunteers are being called up for a month at a time just to
keep in training and to keep the machine guns and gunners in practice.

Things don't look any too good, but the news is so little that really one can hardly tell what is really
happening.

Darling things are naturally very quiet out here and that alone makes one wish to get something to do –
hope that I will be allowed in the police when they appoint jobs, as then I should get some more interesting

work than just in charge of some pumping station or electric works.

Darling must end off now – don't know what the family are doing – expect they will come out as soon as possible. Mummie is as well as could be expected.   All love Darling. Yours Ever, Bob.

Upton 29th September 1939

My Darling Bunny,

Thanks ever so much for your lovely long letter, I should have got it answered by the mail that left on Sunday, but no-one knew that the boat was going till Saturday night, anyway, I will send this air mail. Mummie will enclose a letter to Grannie so please forward it if they are still in England. We are rather in the dark as to their movements as they said that they may be sailing on the 4th to America, but so far no word if they have a passage or not, I can't see why they don't go over to Holland and come direct, it would be much cheaper too.

Well Darling, Lu and Plunks are engaged, what do you think of that? A very good couple, but no one thought that she would ever have gone for him.   Dickens has been appointed to Mauritius, so don't know if Plunks will get a move up, but anyway Lu has about £700 a year so that should keep them for a bit anyway.

Have been playing lots of tennis, it's the only thing to do, have at last got a job for a few days, it's on the allotment of petrol, rather simple but still feel that have got something that will help, do wish I could get something in the Police – George Challenor spoke over the wireless the other night about the local defences. We have all sorts of arrangements made for prices of food stuffs, so as to keep the price as low as possible for the working classes.

We have had a couple of black-outs, pretty foolish personally, but still it gives the people the impressions of war.

Mummie is ever so much better again, and I do hope is really on her way to recovery, she is so glad to be home again. Jack and Sister go off to Bathsheba with Bert and Den tomorrow for a month, hope to go down for a long weekend sometime; I could do with a little holiday just now, especially as the weather has got most awfully hot. Last Sunday in the sea was the first time I have ever known it too warm to cool you.

Darling I must close now, longing to hear how you are, I would give anything to have you out here now, anyway may see you over there, who knows.

All my love my sweet, Yours ever, Bob

This letter numbered 1   *[new numbering system due to unpredictable war time mail]*
Upton 8th October 1939

My Darling Bunny,

Thanks so much for your last letter -1- that idea is a very good one, I must remember to number all mine. I also received another letter from you by the Harrison boat which only arrived here on Thursday. They don't know where they went but where ever it was they were fired at and the 'fish' missed them by 15 yds! I knew three people on board, and they didn't enjoy it any.

Well at last I have got some work to do, apart from being on the Petrol rationing. I have now become an

ARP warden, and drive around with a W on the unshaded part of my lights and have to go round whenever there's a blackout and see that the locals put out their lights. Thursday will be the first time that we put in an appearance, so will tell you what it's like wandering round the tenantries in the dark in No. 2.

I have begun the rehearsals for the Bazaar show or rather begin tomorrow, so will have quite a lot to do now. The B'dos Government wireless which broadcasts every evening at about 6.30 our time definitely stated that no-one was wanted either in the volunteer force or for service overseas, and that no one would be allowed to leave the island. Things are still quite calm here, although we have got to raise wages soon, too many people not getting enough to live on with the advance in prices of food stuffs.

We wait for news, which is very limited, but that is not to be complained about. Have had very little tennis lately, and won't have an afternoon off this week, I make up for it over the weekends when I bathe a lot. I'm just off to Bathsheba to Sister.

My Darling very many happy returns of the 21st. Mummie joins in this. This is the time for birthdays, for we can't send presents!!! Funny Ha Ha.

All my love, Darling.

Yours ever, Bob

Upton 9th October 1939 – from Gwen King

Bunny Dear,

This is not a letter, only a note in Bob's to wish you very many happy returns of 21st. No one will have very happy ones at present, Mollie's is tomorrow. Not getting regular letters is too awful and I shall be more than thankful when I get Grannie and Granddad back. John has called Kitty today to return with Pam. I wonder what she will do, she seems to forget that her 'war work' is here. I am feeling fine now once I do not try to do too much, but it is terribly hot. It is hopeless trying to send presents from here so we have written to ask Grannie to get one for us. Forgive me – in great haste. Very best love and take care of yourself, yours very affectionately, Gwen King

Officers' Mess,
Experimental Station, Porton, Wilts.
Tel: Winterbourne Gunner 262
9th October 1939

Bunny dearest,

I recon Friday night as another of those memorable oases in the desert of life, and by no means the least pleasant at that. I had the suspicion of an idea that it might be rather nice to see you again, not to say to dance and generally enjoy things, but it was much nicer than even I thought it might be. It was a grand evening from beginning to end. May there be many more of them.

I met up with soldiering type who came up to town with me, and he slept on one seat and I on the other. To carry the coincidence a bit further, he must have left the Café de Paris just before we arrived there. The Porton air must be pretty good, for I felt on top of the world all next day, despite the absence of sleep, and reeled off 18 holes of golf in the afternoon. I'm afraid it cost me another six balls, owing to the continued tendency of my drives to leave the tees like rockets and whistle out of sight to the right of the fairway. The grass in the rough is shockingly long. However, the next day I got the loss down to four balls and collected three or four bogies and a birdie (we won't talk about the three or four holes that netted something like sixteen a piece), so there may be hope of getting below the hundred one day. Who knows!

I'm going to give my phoney ankles a try out tonight with a game of squash. The exercise may just possibly do it some good, though I don't think much marked improvement will take place until I can live down in Salisbury and get some more X-Ray stuff. Not that it is annoying or messy or anything at all, as a matter of fact. It just looks red and gets irritable if rubbed against or with much sweating, and so it is stopping me taking violent exercise and therefore getting a good deal fitter. The Rugger side, and a very occasionally hockey side, are functioning here and I could get quite a lot of fun with them if it were not for these damned ankles.

If the preceding items can be called News, then that concludes same. I could give you a word (perfect) picture of the surroundings, which are rain-ridden at the minute, but it wouldn't do you any good; nor me neither.

There are also several very personal remarks which I could make about, to and at you, but to tell you the truth, there are one or two memories from Friday evening which were hard to realise at the time, and which, though already at some indeterminate point in time, are still sweet enough and strong enough to be left alone. I hope that whatever you wanted from that evening, you got sufficiently to feel, like I do, that the memory doesn't want jogging just yet, because it wouldn't improve on it.

Well, I must away to my squash. My respects to your family. You may tell your Mama that she has nothing to fear for at least two weeks as I have informed the enemy that I am liable to be about between now and then. They wouldn't dare to offend me.

The gramophone record follows almost immediately. Take care of yourself, Bunny my lady.
All my love.
Attie

Officers' Mess,
Experimental Station, Porton, Wilts.
Tel: Winterbourne Gunner 262
Wednesday pm 13th October

Bunny darling,

Friday was a good thing. I am not in any way surprised that we both enjoyed it, but I was a little startled to find that in our letters which crossed we had almost identical final words. Mine were, as usual rather more ornate and verbose than yours, but the idea seemed to me to be exactly the same. Quite why I should be startled at all, I don't know, for we have always known that there was that certain something, with which a thing done together is terrific and without which, it is nothing out of the ordinary - whatever else there may or may not be, that can exist quite independently.

I suppose it is just another of those things that one knows, but which still come as such pleasant surprises when presented to you yourself. Good Lord: It's amazing how much the value of things is doubled by sharing them with someone instead of simply by yourself. (If you examine that last sentence you will also be amazed at the bad English there in: however, if you can find a second or so to examine also what it means and think of the one or two occasions we have had, I hope the said English won't matter to you, my lady).

If you remember, I told you that I was expecting to have to go North for some machinery tests. That was rather in the air. I do seem to be the chap down to go but 'when' is as vague as ever: sometime soon is the nearest estimate. I mention it because it is one of two things which may interfere with the following suggestions. The other is, of course, that for one reason or another, I may be refused leave at the critical moment.

Re. Friday week, October 20th, I intend to ask for a week-end leave from Friday evening, and I shall probably be unable to catch the train I took last week. The next one gets up at 8.5pm. you will be having dinner with the Arthurs then, I suppose, and so I shall see if I can get my dear Father, whom I haven't seen or heard from since before the war, to give me dinner at his club. I also suppose that the Arthurs, having somewhat of a voyage next day, will retire to bed fairly early, so I thought that if I called for you at whatever time you say, - 11.00. 11.30, midnight: in fact when my lady commands – we might get in a few dances, and possibly finish a bottle of scotch. (I shall be surprised if that's still there). Next day we can proceed Suffolkwards when convenient and the sooner the better.

I shall have to return to Town on Sunday afternoon in any case, but that won't interfere, and if we can get down there by lunch-time on Saturday, I might even be able to show you what a good golfer I am (I should think from what I remember, I'd be playing well above form if I lost less than 18 balls on the Thorpe course). Anyway, the weather won't permit, 10 to 1, as I have not yet arrived at the stage of golfing-and-damn- the-elements.

Tant pis, Voilà mes ideas *[So much for that, here are my ideas]*. I mention them so that you will know where you are and have something to work on, but make whatever arrangements you like, for I know that it isn't altogether an easy position, or rather may not be on the 20th and 21st. Just let me know what you arrange and that will be OK.

The squash game completely exhausted me. I'm so unfit it isn't true. It didn't appear to do me any serious damage, so I'm starting to play games in a quiet way, and hope for the best. A good crack with a hockey stick across one of these 'ere ankles won't do it any lasting good but I suppose I can get some reasonable pads for protecting said vulnerable points.

I haven't sent the record back as yet because efficient servant threw away the box. Another is being obtained when I shall despatch both, and order ?..... in lieu. I think they ought to play ball with me in this matter. If they don't, I certainly shan't pay for the other two.

By the way, there is one other possibility re. Friday. I suppose it is possible that you may not go up to Town at all. In that case, if the trains permit, I'll get down to Thorpe some time on Friday night. This seems to me to be a very businesslike letter, but it is quite something to be businesslike about.

Besides, I say "Good-morning" and "Hullo" to a snapshot in my cabin, and it smiles back at me, and I'm sure it says "Hullo" too, and that makes me smile, and it's altogether a good thing. But you can't fix business like that; hence the business like letter. It's nice business this time, so it fits in well with the "Hullo – smile", and I hope we'll all be satisfied; you me and the snapshot.

I think we had better organise a phone call on tomorrow (Thursday) week. It's a good idea anyway, and I suppose we are both liable to last minute alterations.

A bientôt, Cherie. Sleep well and look after yourself. Love to the family, and hope that they are all well and cheery.

All my love,

Attie.

My Darling,

Have just returned from Mollie's - I was there for the day and slept here last night as Mummie was asked to The Crane for Sunday and Monday – we had a very quiet time and didn't even bathe. I have been having a fairly hectic time, what with the blackout and then petrol rationing and rehearsals, I only went out on Saturday night to see "Drums", otherwise any night that I have been at home I have been to bed very early, I would like to have a short holiday, but of course that is quite out of the question, I will get a nice weekend on the 28th when I go down to Sister, and am looking forward to it.

Things go on and on its very monotonous and people seem to be getting more and more nervy, anyway in the case of our directors, I shall be very glad to see the "Old Man" back again. Things will have to be re-arranged, as I am not satisfied with the way things are being handled, and John seems to adopt an attitude of being on his own, anyway when a decision has to be made.

Darling, must go and do some more work. With all my love, Bob

Upton
22nd October 1939
No. 2 went last week but forgot to number it - No. 3

My Darling Bunny,

Thought of you yesterday and wondered what you were doing, don't expect you had a very good birthday, anyway by the next one we hope that there won't be any war. You must excuse this scrawl but am writing in bed.

I got a letter by mail from you posted on the 14th Sept; it arrived here on Oct 26th. In Gran's last letter she said they were missing quite a few letters no doubt by this time they will have come to light somewhat late with the news. Well the family should be in Holland today, the trip out will be somewhat of an ordeal from all accounts of people who have arrived back. The sea is no place to hang around on just now.

Have just woken up its now just about 6 o'clock, you know the way I sleep on Sundays? Barrett has gone ill, so Mummie has a lot more to do, hope she won't overdo it, anyway we hope Barrett will be out again by the weekend: this is the one that I'm going down to Sister. Mrs Clarke – Little Auntie - was coming over, of course if Barrett is ill we won't be able to have her and Mummie will have to go and sleep with Doll, such a pity as I know she doesn't want to leave home again but I do need this week's rest.

John and Elizabeth were to dine here today so we are taking them to the Aquatic Court Hotel instead. This is her half term, or some sort of exeat. I'm wondering what John and Kitty will do with Pam when they come back, really the more I see of that family the more peculiar I find them. I'm very determined that the Old Man makes some changes at the office when he returns, not in the staff, they are very good now, but with John and Seale, they draw their salaries and are not earning them. Seale does have a bit of work to do during crop, he is with the sugar account, but he will not take any responsibility and although he likes to have a say in things will never do anything on his own, he will always give too much chatter once someone else starts the thing going.

The rehearsals are going quite nicely for the Bazaar show, I think it should be a great success; anyway, I shall work like hell to make it so.

Went down to see Jack and Sister on Monday. They are looking fine, Jack is burned and looks like a local: they seem to be having a great time. There is very little on and with the rain haven't had any tennis except yesterday for weeks. Never seem to get to a cinema except on Sat: then Johnnie Mac, Mollie, Julian and I seem to arrive together.

They are overdoing this Red X business, God knows I want to give as much as possible but like all "Bajans" everyone in the parishes want to outdo the other and so if you aren't very careful you find that you are spending more than you have. Mummie has begun to keep an account, and has decided that as it reaches so much she will refuse everything for that month. I think it's the only way; I would much sooner give so much to the bank and not have all these odd people begging for things. The latest is that every time you go out to the Savannah it costs you 1d. Funny seeing everyone paying a penny as they are about to play tennis!!?!!

Darling, I must close as Mummie is going down so will have to rush. With all my love Darling sweet, Yours Ever – Bob

P.S. Very doubtful if the airmail will be here today as the weather is bad, anyway it may, so will post. Love –B

Upton 27th

My Darling Sweet,

Don't know what the number is, I notice your last one is not numbered either, rather think this must be my III or is it II? Rather hopeless aren't I. Anyway to begin with ever so many thanks for that lovely shirt, I do like it tremendously. You old soaker you, every time you go up to town you seem to a-bibe different mixtures, don't blame you really, you must find the hours of nursing rather long, or at least they sound so to me. So sorry to hear that Hugh has been moved to another camp, let me have the new address, I never got a letter off to the old address, rather difficult to find things to say, without saying things that one shouldn't. No, I've no necking to report, I've been living rather a quiet life, and reading a lot – I still get fits of war mania, the latest being a local naval defence scheme in T'dad, but honestly don't feel that if I were in a motor boat patrol in the ?Bocus, or along the Venezuelan coast that I would be doing any more good to the war effort than I'm doing now. For a young fellow who has just gone out to work it has its attractions with a moderate salary. Do wish you would write exactly what you think about my position with the war. I keep feeling that I'm shirking a job of work and then one hears from Officials how they only want lads for the RAF of course that's out for me.

Your last letters only took about 11 days to get here, quite the best time so far. Thanks for the jokes; I hadn't heard either of them. Can't say that I know any new ones that would be any too nice for you! What's the difference between Hitler and a dog? Hitler raises his right hand, the dog ...well you know.

Mummie sends her love and says that she will write soon. She has been having teeth out and so has a new plate. We have had to put away old Toby, and so now I have bought a little puppy. Don't know what he is exactly, but he is well marked – brown and white – with a longish tail.

The tennis tournament at the Sav: [Savannah Club] is just coming to a close; there was a big entry and very good crowds. The team to go to T'dad is about to be picked, don't think I will go down to see it, T'dad is so full that you cannot get any reservations, most of the team will have to stay scattered around, or with people – not such fun that way. Quite apart from that I don't honestly feel that I could get away. Have been rather busy the last month or two, and even more so as John is away on holiday, down on the St James coast.

Talking of that, we are going about 14 of us, to The Crane for Easter weekend. To-date not quite sure who will be going but think probably about 14. Will write and tell you all about it, Darling I do wish you could be there, wouldn't that be grand.

There have been lots of new legislations lately: one thing is income tax which has gone up pretty high. Unfortunately the proceeds are for various local things, mostly for the locals. I can see that even if we do not get bombed we will see hard [times?] with getting stuff here, and when it's over I'm sure we will have another show down as in 1937. We have had a lot of press at our estates this year, although I don't think it's the labourers fault, so often it's the whites to blame, someone so damn silly.

There should be a boat going to England in another month or so, will try and get off some stuff for you, not rum I'm afraid there is some difficulties about that.

Well Darling, must go to bed now, I think I've done pretty well with this letter, but I should have written last week, so I've made up by an extra special effort. I still love you, and please don't get too fat!!! Ha! Ha! Longing to hear from you, with lots and lots of love my sweet, Your loving Bob.

p.s. Mollie Mahon tells me that she had a letter written to you which was returned – "address insufficient" – cant think why, thought you were well known at Hemel. Love B

In November and December Bunny completed instruction with the Aldeburgh Branch of The St John Ambulance Association and qualified to render "First aid to the injured"

RN Hospital
Stonehouse Plymouth
Tuesday undated Nov 39

PS My Gawd! Did I write all this?

Bunny darling.

Thanks very much for the letter and the photos. The latter aren't bad: for once, I don't think I look like a half-witted half-caste. Talking of photos, I now realise that one of the very few clever things I have done in my life was to catch you so well in the snap I took of you; the one you sent me an enlargement of. I told you before that it quite definitely said 'Hullo' to me. It's really quite uncanny, for there is no more life in that snap than in any other I've ever seen and no matter how good a portrait you have taken, I'm certain it will never be as alive as that. It's a good thing I have it now, for the rest of this place is dead from the neck up and down. I'm beginning to get the same way; downwards anyway.

There are still the two letters due to you of which I wrote in my last epistle. The last two weeks disruption has rather interrupted the flow of our exchanges – from my side, at least. However, although the sensible thing to do might be to forget the points until I see you again, I'm too sure that I'll forget them altogether when I do see you.

You know, one of your remarks produced a snort of indignant denial when it reached my end: of those occasions when you have shed a little tear. You declared that that was only after a certain amount of alcohol. Well, I hadn't thought about it, but when I did, I came to the conclusion that you were probably right, to some extent. Alcohol always loosens one's control to some degree but in general it only means a slackening of one's confounded conventional limits and things begin to go with an easier swing. If they turn out as they did on the few occasions you speak of, it's only because there is a reason for that unhappiness which is normally bottled up. Fundamentally, I'm bound to be dissatisfied with the present state of affairs, as you know, because I haven't got as much as I might have. We've discussed that pretty thoroughly, and are both as satisfied as we can be about it. You are fundamentally dissatisfied, I suppose because you haven't yet found a real object for your existence. We talked about that a bit too, last time and I suspect you realise it very well for yourself. The point is that at moments when those dissatisfactions become a bit too much for us, it is the very best thing in the world that we should have each other to help us with them. Continued bottling up can only make it far worse. I'll bet you felt much happier in yourself after any of these very few occasions. I did, anyway.

It hurts to feel you cry, but in those moments, Bunny, we have almost certainly been much closer to one another than at any other time, and that makes them something rather valuable: valuable to you as much as to me, for they don't at all depend on what may or may not happen. So don't regret them, Bunny dear, and if you do "never forget" an evening on the Meare, at least remember it as something which helps to make up the whole picture.

Now the thread of my impassioned discourse has been quite broken by one of the "gorgeous" nurses. They have a wonderful variety here. Most of the work is done by Naval Ratings – Sick Bay Staff – but they are mostly young and just out of training classes, so they have three or four of the R.N. Nurses wandering about to see that everything is O.K. They are quite pleasant, but believe me, they don't classify as gorgeous: not by streets.

This particular one is a V.A.D. for the duration stationed here. She's a great talker, and very early on told me all about her "sweetie", a sergeant in the Army. I insist on pitying her for wanting to marry into the Brutal and Licentious, and she never quite knows when I'm being serious. Anyway, I'm always careful to be suitably impressed and she brings me illicit cups of tea at odd times. But I simply could not help laughing just now when she came in. She asked if she could help me write this letter, so I said "Certainly not. It's to my girl friend". When she said "which one?" I showed her the photo you sent me, and she immediately became very technical: clearly an enthusiastic photographer, for she finally said "Last time my sweetie was abroad, I sent him over a hundred photos". "What! All of you". "Of course" Dead serious: but if you could just see her, the thought of Sergeant Sweetie getting over a hundred photos – Ah! Well! That's love, I guess.

Right now, I'm in the bored stage. This damn thing is never quick and if you are with it the whole time, it certainly seems quite stationary. Also, the bed is beginning to feel very uncomfortable. Between the war and the stupidity of the Sick Berth Staff, I haven't yet succeeded in organising myself a private radio, and all the magazines and cigarettes and things that I think I want, but I'll have that all straightened out by the end of the week. It's very sweet of you to ask what I want, and thank you very much for doing so. I really have most of what I want or can get it, which comes to the same thing. Of course, it's always very nice to get things from you, but I shouldn't worry about sending anything, Honey.

I suppose that Jimmie will have gone long before this gets to you. If he hasn't, say "Cheerio" for me. I'm not a bit jealous on that score from here. I accept your word for it that Jimmie is very good friend of yours and I like him myself. I might very reasonably envy him for being where I'm not. The same applies to any other friend of yours. But as long as you remain to me what you are now, I'll always be extremely "jealous" of anyone who makes you forget about me. And on that score, let me tell you that if you ever fall for someone who isn't that way, then either he's not worthy of you or you're not worthy of him.

There is one thing I would like. I can't play a gramophone here but if you would go on sending me the names and/or Record Numbers of any songs or tunes that strike you as being nicer than usual. I haven't sung for some time now (May the Lord forgive me for writing "sung"), but I think I shall feel like making a lot of noise in a few weeks time. And talking about a few weeks time, you may remember we had a rather elastic date for sometime towards the end of November or the beginning of December. You thought you would be going up to Town sometime then for Christmas Shopping or some such feminine wile. If you can postpone same until December, I may yet have the good luck to see you there.

You know, Honey, I'll soon be writing as much as I talk and that's too much. I'm afraid I still love you very much, so will you kindly remember to continue as you finished your last letter.

S'il faut attendre longtemps, n'oubliez jamais que c'est à cause de ça que les reunion, on pourra dire quélle soit, au meme temps, chic et sauvage. Et pourtaut – À bientôt, Honey. *[One has to wait a long time, and do not forget that because of our reunions, whatever they are, at the same time, chic and wild. And yet - See you soon, Honey].* All my love   Attie

RN Hospital
Stonehouse Plymouth
Saturday 11th (& possibly Sunday 12th) November 1939

Bunny, my darling.

I am still in bed and still being punctured at odd intervals, and I'm well into the extremely bored and fed-up-with-the-damn-thing stage. Like you in your last letter, I intended to write you tomorrow, but instead, or possibly as well, I just think how very satisfactory it will be to simply write to you. At the minute, I am lying on my side holding the writing pad in one hand and scrawling with the other. The scrawl is commendably readable thus far, but I've no doubt I shall have to get up and settle down to it in a minute, as yet might say.

Also, as I previously explained to you, this room is on the ground floor and so the entire bottom half of the window is permanently covered with steel plate, while rather more than half the top is painted black. The minute portion which remains is uncovered during daylight, it is true, but the answer is that I have existed by artificial light for ten whole days, and the eyes are definitely weakening under the strain. Ah! This blessed age of advanced civilisation!   (I simply must write this in a MORE REASONABLE POSITION.)

I must say that I am more than glad to find that we both tend to share things more and more. It isn't just the things that we do and the incidents that happened to mean something to us and no one else, but it's the other things that aren't so pleasant. Things are always cropping up which are just a little too heavy for the ordinary person to carry by themselves. Those are things which require to be shared, if life is to be reasonable. Remember that when you share something that is worrying or annoying or just getting you down a bit, it can be more than simply getting it off your chest – to do that is in itself a jolly good thing for you – for if the person with whom you share it understands and cares, he is bound to take a real share, and that's bound to lighten the load.

Of course, there are big things and small things; funny, and not so funny, and not funny at all things. And it's much easier to share completely when you are together. But big or small, together or apart, they are all part of the main theme, and the difference in circumstances is negligible beside the difference between being able to share at all and not be able to.

We progress, Bunny darling; not that any of the preceding is news to you, my lady, for it is obvious from your last letter that it 'aint, but merely to complete a contact between us. When anyone is as fond of you as I am, or as you are of me, for that matter, when we are together, it is nearly always sufficient to simply feel things. I mean, one feels things are right or wrong, the things that happen around us strike the same note; it isn't necessary to say so: we both know. I say "nearly always", because of course wherever the emotions are concerned there is always liable to be a strain when they get too worked up one way or the other, and one gets a clash between sense and sensibility, instead of the two clicking nicely as per usual.

I reckon that is also a thing we both know, now. The more you have to be shared, the bigger my shoulder becomes. That's automatic, my sweet. The more I have to share, the bigger your heart ought to become. That might be automatic, but I think I told you the story of the Scotsman who, going into a telephone box, said to the Scotsman coming out, "Is that phone automatic" "Naw. It's a' ta-" Heigh Ho!

Your Papa sent me a letter. A very pleasant one, surprisingly – for him – serious, which I liked even more than I would have pages of abuse. As a matter of fact I had the day previous to its arrival sent him off the book I borrowed, accompanied by a few words of stilted abuse, so I have no doubt he will have ample opportunity for more talk of "pearls before swine" and so on. Will you please thank him very kindly for his wishes. You might even give him a kiss from me. The reaction should be funny: in fact, I wouldn't mind betting that if you kiss him first and tell him afterwards, one of his reactions will be to wipe it off with a handkerchief (or even to spit, depending upon where you kiss same).

Your Mama, I have replied to, as I've no doubt you know. I tried to be rather reassuring without being obvious but I'm afraid I wasn't very clever about it. I couldn't be really, because in addition to what I've always said about aeroplanes, I think that if the Germans go into Holland or Belgium, the East Coast might have more than planes to contend with.

They couldn't possibly keep up a supply of troops and material across the North Sea, but if they could time one large landing to coincide with a big push for Calais or Dunkirk, I suppose it would have a tremendous effect. However, I can't think that it could be anything more than a rather remote chance. The only nasty thought I have is that anything like that would have to be very quick and a complete surprise show, and there you are, absolutely the first thing in the way. On which though, I packed up for the night and still managed to sleep well, so I guess it must be a fairly remote chance in my opinion. Don't let that stop you getting back to Bovingdon le plus tôt possible.

Well, Funny face, I wish I thought I was going to see that funny fact of yours next week-end or even the week-end after that. Anything beyond that is too horribly far away to contemplate. I shall just have to live in hopes that the time will go as quickly as it has done on several other occasions that I can think of.

Now I've been interrupted again and I'm afraid this is going to miss the only collection of the day. This isn't a well planned letter at all, honey. As a matter of fact, I'm just writing what comes into my head and that, as you know, is usually nonsense. However, it isn't much good trying to get down to facts and figures about when and how I shall see you next. I haven't much idea yet when I shall get out of here, as I certainly don't want to spoil the cure for a ha'porth of tar. If things continue as well as they have begun, I don't see why I shouldn't be home by December 1st or thereabouts.

Stupid language, English. "Not quite true" might mean anything from "very, very nearly true" to "90% a black lie". But I'm not trying to solve that one, for so long as you can even sign yourself with "very much love", it's quite a lot to get along with, my lady. If the endings from this end make you feel lopsided, well I'll be a bit more circumspect about them, though I hope you won't have to rely on the written word to know what I mean.

Anyway, if you don't have literally all my love or all my thoughts, you have quite enough of them to make a little world into which you can slip away when the rest of the universe gets a bit out of joint. I'll be waiting for you, and we won't bother about the others. Best wishes to everyone at Reedlands. You might tell my spies that I am still waiting for their reports. It seems to me that their discipline is slipping.

À bientôt, Bunny dearest. Take care of yourself for this comes to you with quite most of my love. Attie

6	6
6	6

Not sure but think this is No. 5 or 6, have forgotten to number the last few - any way let's say 6

My Darling Bunny,

Thanks so much for your air letter no. 7 don't think it can be 7, or else I have missed one. Mummie thanks you for her letter and sends her love. Glad the family got a nice broach for you, we wrote and told them to get you something, as then it was very difficult to get anything away from here. They now say that parcels may be sent, rather think only under examination.

Well the family arrived safely on 11th at about 6am: they were ashore by 7.45 all looking very well, but somehow Kitty must have been a bit of a strain and Pam on board none too pleasing. Do wish I could understand John and Kitty, as you know they rather annoy me and I cannot ever be natural with the.

Two days before the family arrived Medford in the Grocery (Manager) announced that he was going to start business on his own. He has no capital, but thinks that he will be able to do very well just on credit. He has also got the best counter hand going with him. Can't imagine how he will get along especially with the war on and high prices. Rotten happening just as the "O' Man" has returned, anyway I think that we will do OK – damn well got to.

We have been having lots of rain, and so very little tennis played last Friday at the Savannah, first time in weeks. Pretty busy with the play, things are going nicely though and I do hope that it will be a great success. We anyhow work without any quarrels and things are so much easier.

Tom Wilkinson and Hilda Messiah have announced their engagement perfect epidemic. I spent the day with the Stokes' they are at the sea side, and of course Molly and Julian are up for every weekend. Just heard Winston's speech, he "sure hotted" it up what. My Darling can't think when you will get this as the KLM don't run any more. Anyway I will just write and post, you may get it sometime. All my love, my sweet, Yours ever. Bob

My Darling Bunny,

Many thanks for your last letter, it got here quite quickly as it was posted on the 5th and of course now that the KLM don't come here it has to come up by boat from T'dad.

The Harrison boat left here at the end of last week and they say it's the Xmas mail, some of us wrote by it as there was hardly any notice of it, and anyway it will arrive rather early if it arrives at all. Nasty business that "Simon Bolivar", *[SS Simon Bolivar struck mines off Harwich on 18th November 84 lives lost]* so far there is no definite news as to who was missing from here, but we think the Manager of B Bank was on board, and so far no one can hear of his rescue.

The show progresses slowly, have called rehearsals for Tuesday Wed and Friday this week. The real hard work now begins, I do hope it will be a great success. Have had very little tennis of late, not so much rain as this show, anyway Theo Gittens, (wasn't out here when you were) has got a court for Thursday, it's the second Race day and so if fine should get some good tennis. Sorry the pen's run dry. Last Saturday went up to the Morgan, think I told you they have built a new place very nice indeed, ultra modern. Then on Sunday morning went to church with Mummie and later to the club where I found Greta and Laurie Bancroft. Mollie Mahon rang me and asked if I would like to come up to the sea side (they are up every weekend with the Stokes' on the south coast) for a bathe and dinner, well somehow I got to sleep in the afternoon so never arrived up there till about 5.30, anyway it was quite a pleasant evening and not too late. Di and Robert Bryden are back again, they were up in Canada and then New York. Robert has not been very well and had an operation so you can imagine how worried all the girls are, as most of the things are American. Have been having long chats with the 'O Man' and telling him a few home truths.

Darling sweet I must go to bed, there really isn't any more news, except I love you.

Be good, with all my love, Bob

Upton
Dec 8th
No 8

My Darling Bunny,

Thanks so much for your lovely long letter No. 9. Darling it seems ages since I wrote last, but there have been very few boats, and then last week I missed a mail, I'm really sorry, but I was working really hard on that Bazaar show – that came off on Sat: with great success, although the crowd was not as good as usual, but still the gates were some 160 people short, so the show would naturally suffer as the cheapest seats were 2/- if I had got even 60 of the 160 short the show would have done better than usual so I think I got a very fare share of the people who were there. You said something about paper cuttings – wont sent them by air mail; anyway they just have the usual polite things.

Your nursing exams sound very frightening – I don't think they are taking it so seriously out here, should hate to think that any of these girls had to keep me alive for even 10 minutes!!

Poor old Hugh, he must be very fed up doing nothing, yet I bet Rhoda is much happier that way.

Afraid we are going very hard with the new Grocery Manager – so far we have not been able to find anyone who would do. The only people who would, don't want to leave their present jobs. Anyway can't help feeling that we will eventually get the right man – fatalism again Darling!

I'm awfully afraid I haven't got an Xmas present for you yet, most difficult to think of something, anyway Mummie's and mine will come sometime before next Xmas, and anyway my sweet I shall think about you on Xmas day, will be a very different Xmas this year wont it. Mummie is in bed again, this time with a type of flu, a nasty cold and running a temperature of about 101 & 2, rotten luck for her as "Pygmalion" was on this week and she had set her heart on going – a damn good film too isn't it.

Am going to a huge dinner tomorrow night at the 'Ocean View' Hotel, a Dutch affair got up by the Wilkinsons then on to the Poppy dance, it's so big I feel that there should some funny things happening as with all those people there will be some people who are not too friendly to one another, perhaps I may be rude to someone! Everyone is debating when they are to have the New Years dance, seems fairly obvious to me – 31st – but then they say about being Sunday evening, I think we are having a party at the Leacocks then on to the Marine, should be much nicer than being at the Marine.

I have bought a new racquet, another Dunlop, this time the 'Max Ply', my other one was cracked in the shoulder and although not bad I thought I had better get one before they became scarce.

My sweet there doesn't seem much more to write about, so will go to bed. All my love Darling, and as happy a Xmas as possible, and a grand 1940, we hope for the reestablishment of a worldwide peace. That sounds most ministerial, but you know what I mean. When I don't write Darling don't worry, I still love you. All my love, Bob.

Officers' Mess,
Experimental Station, Porton, Wilts.
Tel: Winterbourne Gunner 262
undated

Bunny darling.

It does hurt. But nothing that is worthwhile was ever achieved easily, and this is more than worthwhile.

It hurts more than it should. When you say that the present state of affairs is liable to be the end of England that you and I have known, I'm afraid you are nearer the truth than you know. To have had a different answer from you would have given me something very real and very strong for which to live and live right, and I think my courage and yours may need all the support it can get.

You have evidently felt that blank futility of it all. That is what requires something strong and live against it. I've had it rather worse than I should because lately I've been tasting some of the rarer sweets of this world, that have been living and real, and the dead, bitter ones are the worse in consequence. That thing which I might have had would have been strong enough to make these and future difficulties secondary: so its absence hurts the more.

That's that, my lady and I wrote it because I want to go on knowing you. Your letter shows two different wishes, alternating: one to continue as we have been up to now: the other, to exist a lot further apart. I know that you are fond of me, so I presume that the second is only an account of this question of it's being "unfair to me".

Please believe me when I say that, no matter what has or does happen, there is no question of anything being fair or unfair to me. There is nothing unselfish about that. On the contrary, to cut away, in any way, the companionship which we have so far had, would be cruel. As a matter of fact, as you know, I didn't want to marry for a long time yet. It's only this bloody war which has necessitated a bit more information, because one is always liable to have to take a chance. So from the unselfish viewpoint, I'm glad you feel as you do. What may happen doesn't matter so much.

Now that I've relaxed somewhat, I can see that your letter, Bunny my lady, is an extremely good thing. It would be most unlike you to rush into saying 'yes' for any reason other than the right one, and I don't honestly think you have known me long enough for that. On the other hand, I judge from it that you love me more than I have any right to expect. Further, you have been very honest.

Between these things and what we have already had, we have a lot to share, Bunny. Don't let's throw them away. Let's go straight on. I'm not suggesting any platonic friendship, nor am I labouring under the delusion that two more trips to town will induce you to say yes. I simply don't want to stop or to throw away something very rare in this mundane existence.

I'm more than happy to know your mind and to know you and treat you as I have done so far, and I can't ask more than that, but I need it. All that has been written on the assumption that your second wish is on account of the 'unfairness' question only. If there should be any reason of your own for our not continuing as before, then you must decide for yourself, for everything I have said is exactly what I really mean and feel: on that I will state my oath. But if there should be some such reason, I would like to know, for to cease now would be bad, as well as hurtful. From what I know of you and from your letter, I can't conceive of any reason but I'm not you, so I don't know.

You know, Bunny dear, that bloody letter you sent me was one of the best and sweetest things you have ever done. I only hope this one shows you me as that one displays something of you, for you see I, and I think you, have written these in a time of pretty high emotional tension, and it's what you really mean that comes through. However, I thoroughly agree with you about the awfulness of putting these things to paper and I want like anything to see you, if only for a short time. I've done my best to put it to paper because I'm afraid that I may not get a chance to see you for some time.

Aldeburgh is a hell of a way from here, but if the Admiralty spare me as long as next Sunday, I can get away from here by about 10a.m. so if you have any ideas and can manage anything, please let me know. I can't get as far as Aldeburgh and back before dark, but I can get quite a way. There are lots of other ordinary things I really want to write about, but not in this letter. In any case, we may both be taking a blacker view of this war than necessary. It may be only a short one. Who knows? So cheer up my lady. If this does nothing else, may it prevent you from ever saying, let alone thinking, anything so awful as that you would "prefer me to forget you a little" Cor! Chasemeroundtheduckpond!

If you refer just once again to my first lines, you may also remember that strength only comes through sorrow, because it has to be tested to be proved.

All my love, Attie

HMS HOSTILE
c/o GPO
London postmark December 12 1939

Bun, m' dear,

I enjoyed your letter a lot – firstly, I think you're damn right to "ca' canny" *[Scots expression: go cautiously]* with the N.O. cos' as I think we agreed years ago; it either is, or it isn't, the real thing. And there can be no half way house. In family gossip I have heard it said that "wee Janie" rather pushed Lily-loo and Jim together! It turned out well I should say, but it might just as well have flopped! Men family gossip and therefore not to be taken seriously – but there you are.

Well, this war soldiers on, and still appears quite fantastic to me. We sit tight on the Maginot and just wait for the blockade to be sufficiently felt "behind" the German lines – which the unfortunate 'boch' unless he goes thro' Holland and Belgium can't land an offensive till the spring! Out here we do about a fortnight at sea, doing 22 kts in all seas looking for a non-existent German. We have made one capture and a rich one at that so far! Simply because there are no Germans to capture, or so it appears.

A lot of my old "flight" were working with us for a while, but they've gone now. I quite wished I was back in the air again. But after a rather too thrilling a downturn in the North Sea, they have settled down to hundreds of hours flying time and damn all to show for it, so perhaps I'm well off!

The Germans gave away a band of Iron Crosses for sinking Robert Everett's ship! *[probably HMS Courageous, Aircraft Carrier, sunk on 17th September 1939]* Which was entirely untrue – but Robert said something fell unbelievably close, and went off like an ammunition dump!!

I hear tales of big things in the marriage market from "the Country". But the Pet has so far put work before play!! I wonder in more senses than one! For her letters don't seem frightfully disinterested or uninteresting for that matter either.

Glad to say my ailments are gone, knowing, as you say, that I can't go sick – one does snap out of it.

A sweet thing wrote to me the other day and besides some 'goodies' (too fattening m'dear) sent the following unclear, but amusing story.

A "lovely boy" decided to volunteer, so asked if he could join the WRENS, on being told it was only for the fair sex, he said "Oh dear, I did so want to join a crack regiment! "Filthy" but funny I thought!

If this should fall into the hands of the enemy, it won't matter a great deal – as they won't be able to read it. Neither will you, but you can imagine all the nice things I probably have said – if only you could read it! But 22 knots does shake a bit.

As you see, there is precious little front page noos, but I seem to have rambled on about something.

I'm playing some pretty hot tennis these days on the concrete courts they have out here. But as I say three days in port and a fortnight out, does leave a good deal of energy to be worked off – and the shore side people are all very black! Dear, Dear, there I go again.

Best love to you Bun, and the family. Tony

If you write send it by Air Mail – costs 1/- I think!

HMS Courageous leaving Spithead for exercises at sea on 2nd October 1930. Illustrated by Tony Fasson

Officers' Mess,
Experimental Station, Porton, Wilts.
Tel: Winterbourne Gunner 262
Wednesday pm – *no date – first day of winter ? 22st December*

Bunny darling.

Enclosed herewith is the haversack for your gas-mask which I promised to send. I suppose your cardboard box is the same size as the ones issued locally here. At any rate, the whole box should just fit in, and all you have to do is to open the cover, open the lid of the box and withdraw mask. The stuff is waterproof and should be strong enough to withstand the strain of this war anyway.

Today has been the first day of winter. Do you remember an afternoon half an age ago, when we sat outside the 'Plough' at Spean, and the trees were heavy with blossom and the next field thick with buttercups? I've never really seen England in spring before, and from then until now, I've had the same thought of sunny, scented existence, with a variety of warmth and colour, and the same frame of mind, for the most part. This afternoon, I am in the middle of open bleak spaces. The grey clouds came up, and the rain drops alternated with icy gusts of wind, and everything looked one colour, grey and cold.

When one looked back to the lights and fires, on for the first time in the shops, from that far afternoon to this seemed like one picture, that is very lovely and complete, but which is back over the page in the album.

I didn't think about it. Today was so much a change that the picture simply presented itself to me. I was rather depressed to start with. It's so difficult to make oneself stronger than the circumstances around one, and when anything so intrinsically valuable as these last few months have been to me, suddenly presents itself to you, as a little block of time which is past and done with, it does depress you.

I suppose it's because it's easier to miss the good things you have had, than to visualise the good things you may have. But there – "Hope springs eternal" and the sun's gone and come out (if that is good English I'll east my gasmask, but it feels very expressive).

I've had no news of any sort, except that Gieves sent me a reply from which I see that their Head Office have evacuated Portsmouth and moved to Sussex. Considering that Gieves haven't left The Hard, Portsmouth since 1785 or some date near there, it gave rise to some merriment. I hope they lost my account in the process.

I've had some experience of night driving as per regulations since I saw you, and it's not too bad really, with the headlights on. We managed to average about 20 mph without undue danger to the surrounding countryside. It's pretty awkward in a town the size of Salisbury, and cyclists without rear lights are a something menace, but otherwise I was pleasantly surprised. Perhaps one is already adjusting to suit these cave-dwelling times and that reminds me, I must fill that Tank up to the brim with juice today.

Well. I must say again that I enjoyed my weekend and that I'm so very thankful for it. If this is winter now and if the spring and summer are past and done with it, it doesn't matter anymore. No matter how grand or important they were, the main things don't stop, and it's the other springs and summers that we exist for. (More bad English, but I'm afraid this sounds like, and probably is, a lot of nonsense anyway). All the same, the springs and summers will probably come in very handy, as you might say, by the time the winter of this little show is over.

I forgot to say that owing to 'panic-stations' and pressure of business, I couldn't give my "sail makers" department time to do more than one of these haversacks, and so I can't sent Papa and Mama one at the moment; I will do so when the chap gets some spare time. I thought you would probably need yours, or at least, find it useful.

My respects to your family, and to Langers when you see her.

Au revoir, Bunny dear.
All my love. Attie

Greenfield, Chorley Wood
(Christmas 1939)

Bunny darling,

Herewith the present, with all my love and very best wishes. Late as usual, but none the less sincere for that.

I hope you have a roaring good time, thought I don't think it will be as good as the week for which I have to thank you. I think its best left with just "thank you". All my love, darling, Attie

Letter from Grannie King

Upton
Thursday December 28th 1939

My Dear Bunny,

You are a wicked little thing, you have never written one line since I came back and I long to hear what you are doing in these dark dismal days. First of all, I must thank you for the greetings telegram which we got quite safely on the Friday before Xmas, and then I must send every good wish for the coming year. And how I hope and trust we will have peace in the very near future. Also I have to thank you for the pretty card to the Old Man which we got yesterday morning. Well, Xmas is over, and I wasn't sorry as I had such a lot to do for at least a week or ten days before. I had the whole family here, 18 of us, I never thought the dining room would hold so many and I meant to put the three youngest children at a table by themselves but Bob said how much nicer it would be to have everyone together at one table, so we racked our brains to find out how it could be done. I finally borrowed a round table from Hilda and put half at each end of our table and so got everyone in at one table. Bob's idea!! I was pretty busy as Gwen had to go to bed for three or four days, and I had all the milk etc to see after, as well as all my own work, anyway I got through and they all seemed to enjoy themselves and ate a very good dinner. Kitty carved the turkey for me, thank goodness, as it was one of my own raising and weighed 16lbs and I didn't want it hacked up, and Bob carved the beef for me and you can believe me John sent back for a second helping before either Kitty or Bob had quite finished helping, or even sat down to their dinner. I had a huge plum pudding, and they made it look exceedingly foolish I can tell you, and the jug too. The poor Old Man, of course, could have no plum pudding, but he did very well, and had soup and fish and turkey and ham so he didn't fare badly. The heat on Xmas day nearly killed me, as to in church I thought I would have suffocated. It is so dry, that is why we have these hot days, tho' today there is a fairly nice breeze, but am scorching some. We are now digging our yams and I think of you a lot, for I know how you would enjoy them and I wish I could get some over to you. The eddoes are not ripe yet. The old man spends every morning out on the land, but he stays in town much too late. The Friday before Xmas he and Bob never left the store till nearly 6 and the Sat: before the two of them came home at 7. The Old Man was just all in that night, but he won't hear of course. John was laid up for the better part of last week, so the others or some of them, had more to do. The hotels out here are going to see pretty hard times this year, I hear there is hardly anyone at The Marine and no bookings and they have just done it up beautifully and they say The Balmoral is the same, no bookings at all. English people can't get down and I suppose the Americans are afraid too. A party of young people are dining Dutch fashion at the young Leacocks on New Year's Eve and then going on to The Marine. Dancing doesn't begin there till after 12 and I heard of another big party of young people dining somewhere else so The Marine loses them, and people are not dining and seeing the New Year in this year as they generally do. Personally I shall be glad to see the end of this year, it hasn't been a very good one for us, but I always feel the New Year may hold something worse. One never knows. I think the Old Man is going to have his eye done early next month, he is to go to Dr Gibbons on the 5th and then he will decide. I do hope it will be a success, if only he will keep quiet that is of vital importance for at least the first five days and he still has those spasms of coughing. Again I am going to get you to forward the two enclosed letters for me. Hilda tells me old Mrs Brewer is very worried to know if we got home all right so I must send her a line, and also our faithful old Archdeacon. You know he started for The Gambia in a coudy and somewhere in the bay his steamer collided in the darkness with one of the others and they had to return and took three days to reach England in the dark. My old Capt. on the Costa Rica must be on their way back out here now, poor old fellow, I think of them a lot. Now, my darling little child, I must be off and write another letter so good bye.

With heaps of love from the Old Man and myself and the best of luck in the New Year also kindest remembrances to your people. I am Ever your loving Grannie.

My Darling Bunny,

My sweet it has been almost two weeks since I last wrote, I am sorry, but have been really rather busy and somehow have been to lots of cinemas and cocktail parties, thus no writing at nights. First of all many thanks for your letters, card and present have not played yet but may over the weekend, as I am staying with Mollie. Saw Johnnie this afternoon, he begs to thank you for your card and says he was going to send you one then didn't – the thought is better than the deed!

We are having a Dutch dinner at The Leacocks on Sunday night, and then on to The Marine, dancing starts at midnight. Last Saturday dined with Jack and Sister at the RBYC their brother William Sisnett is up for Xmas, he is an Engineer in T'dad. There were lucky tickets and four of our party of twelve got one each, Lu, sister, Helen and yours truly. Very acceptable as it saves 5/- for dancing.

We had a quiet Xmas, I went bathing each day, and on the Tuesday at Cattle Wash where the sea was extra good. We had the family here on Xmas night 18 of us all together, not too exciting, but better than usual. We had a very busy Xmas at the office, or rather at the grocery. The locals had more money than ever before and everyone seemed to break their former records. We did by about $200°°. I never got away till 5 to 7 and had to be at the RBYC by 7.40. One new grocery manager – Bobby Edgehill, don't know if you met him, has been round quite a lot and at last we have a gentleman as head of the grocery, he is young and will have to learn, but should do very well.

The 'Nazi Spy' was here this week, gad what a good film, the best propaganda I've seen. Now for 'The Lion has Wings'. Am thinking of having Romeo painted, just thinking mind you, but as I shall have to keep Romeo for some time yet, think I had better paint him while there is any paint to be had!!

Darling do hope you won't be selling The Mare Cottage, that would be rotten, it's such a grand place, and anyway Reedlands is so much further from town, and I should think cold as hell. I have a hunch that this war won't be as bad as we fear, hope to see the end of it by the middle of 1940. Here's to it.

Afraid I have a little necking to report nothing serious as you should well know. But still you know me and it's a pleasant recreation!! Anyway you reported some the other day too. The New Year dance doesn't sound like anything much, nothing at all interesting will be there, but still you know what New Year "gives" as the Bajans say?

Mummie is up and about again, do hope she will be fit again now, the flu pulled her down a lot. We will be having fun in the New Year, as I think I shall be made a Director, in which case I shall insist on the Directors – John and Seale – being given some real work. John being the worst offender, even the Old Man has begun to realise that.

Darling I must close now, as there doesn't seem to be any more news.

All my love, my sweet, and the very best of everything for 1940. Will make an effort and write soon again!!! Tell your mother she can't know you, if she really sent that message about thinking you were being a good girl, and what's that about getting fat, and no flying fish either.

All my love,

Bob

Porton
In my OFFICE
Monday afternoon – undated

Bunny Dearest. I loved all of it. Another complete picture painted and put away in a joint-stock album. Exactly the same as the others have been in its pleasantness, the laughs and suites and contentment; the hopes and sighs and even a tear. But for all that, something new and quite different. Its rather wonderful and not a little disturbing in its combination of contentment and dissatisfaction. I suppose that that is how these things should be in the ideal conception, and in any case it always leaves me feeling that I rate the whole thing higher and not lower:- futile or not. Anyhow, Bun, I enjoyed the whole weekend very much and rightly or wrongly I felt a good deal closer to you than I have at some times.

There was a moment for which I am sorry. The war and this bloody skin disease seem to have lowered my self-confidence and self-control as well as my vitality, or I would have held my lop-sided tongue and stopped moaning. The words were true enough, for the feelings are there. But they are bound to be, under the circumstances, as I guess you know very well, for that is a large part of what you meant when you said and wrote that "it wouldn't be fair" to me. At any rate, that is what I accepted and asked for, so I regret to say that on Saturday night I failed to keep my part of the bargain. Forgive me, Bun. There are a lot of things I don't know about, and I was punished on the spot.

I'm not sorry about the whole sequence, for if it began with a bad moment it ended later with a moment which can only be bettered once. It meant a lot, Bun, that moment: more than you know or than I could show then. From what I know of you, I am a little afraid that you may think about these things and either get to worrying about me again or else be afraid that I am putting a wrong value on them. Don't do either, Bun. There is one thing of which I shall never lose sight and that is that things only mean what you mean them to mean. I've told you that before but I do so want you to realise it and act accordingly, so please don't be afraid of leading me up a path or any other nonsense like that. Believe me, before I alter course to port or starboard you will have been so explicit that there won't be any possibility of a wrong tack. So please stay "happy about the whole thing" better still, happier.

One of the curses of this war business is that our meetings tend to be a little blinded by emotion, but I should say that on the whole you are having a pretty fair chance of seeing my weaknesses at least. Dammit! That almost calls for a cliché about there being some good in everything or something.

I still love you very much Bun, so I don't want my stupidity to either spoil a very perfect thing or upset you. I hope this has helped to stop that. If you were going to read this at the same time as I write it: i.e. the day after, I think it might have clicked into place. As it is, it will probably sound like nonsense by the time it does reach you. Maybe it is anyway.

A proper letter should reach you tomorrow. All my love, Bunny dear, and thank you for everything. Attie

---

Early January Bletchley Park get their first break with Enigma. Winston Churchill becomes Prime Minister. Hitler invades Denmark, Netherlands, Belgium, France and Luxembourg. 10th May first German bombs fall on Kent. End of May/June Dunkirk evacuation: Operation Dynamo a 'miracle of deliverance' 300,000 troops evacuated. 4th June Winston's 'We shall fight on the beaches' speech and 18 June 'This was their finest hour'. Battle of Britain – first major campaign by the Air Force. Palaeolithic art discovered in Lascaux Caves, France. No Wimbledon due to the war. July German air raids start on London- The Blitz. Colour TV first demo in New York. First McDonald Hamburger stand in Pasadena. UK Dig for Victory campaign, Home Guard, Air Raid Wardens.

Upton
12th January

My Darling Bunny,

Many thanks for your letter (Dec 8th) which is the only one I have had for ages, there were two boats in from England this week, but still there is no telling how long they were at sea. Anyway I hope you will have sent off an air mail which should arrive soon. Darling perhaps it's a little guilty conscience, but are you holding back from writing because I have not been writing so frequently? You know it's partly laziness and a good lot of extra work – please my sweet if you aren't too busy write as soon as possible, and as often as you can. I will be writing more often now in the New Year.

Well since my last letter we had our New Year's party at the Leacock's a very good show, but I do not think much of the idea of waiting till 12 pm to start the dancing, rather tends to damp the spirits which one has got after dinner. We arrived at The Marine at about 11.40 and the judging of the costumes had not finished yet – Julian and Den were the only two who got prizes in our party, not many left in time to go in for it, anyway the Wilkinsons were the judges, so don't think I would have had any chance even if I had gone in for it.

I was staying with Mollie and Julian for the weekend, so we left about 4.20 and were in bed about 5am and never turned till around 10am. Dick came down then and we went off to Sandy Lane for a bathe, Jack and Sis hadn't got home till after 6am. They went on to The Morgan and were still asleep when we left down there. After breakfast we went to sleep again and so we broke up the party that night.

There hasn't been much doing since then, I have been playing lots of tennis, and damn badly too. This afternoon we had the meeting of the tennis committee and arranged for the tournament at the Savannah, the tournament at The Belle Ville Club is starting first. Do wish you were here to play with me again this year think I will play one of the mixed with Helen.

Tomorrow I am playing tennis with Pat Hartford at Sandy Lane (Jack's sister) don't know if I will go on to The Marine after that, there is a "not-outs" dance there before the next term starts, should be quite good fun, they only have dances there every two weeks now, as people can't afford every Saturday.

Have been to a few good films lately, also been playing bridge. Was asked out to bridge the other night, but had rotten luck and lost badly. They have been having racing in T'dad. Bunny Edward's horse won the cup and champion horse, Florence Smith, didn't get any 1st but seems to have had a very good time. David Boyle is ADC to Sir Hubert Young in T'dad now, and from Florence's account doing quite well, and has a fair following of the fairer, or not so fair, sex, you know T'dad!! The others think he is not quite sane!!

Well my sweet must go to bed – and please write soon, what were you doing yesterday? Thought about you several times during the day – probably flirting! All my love my sweet,

Your loving Bob.

My Darling Bunny,

Many thanks for your letters, little note book and also the very nice ties, pretty good choice for a girl, that's as good a compliment as you could want my sweet!! Funny thing the letter with the note book was cut at the corner, they are doing their inspections very well, so glad to hear that they have collected so much money from those Germans in America, damn brutes, trying to get money and jewellery through to Germany and the Americans saying that they will not have their cargoes stopped.

Lovely that joke re the chocolate, told Lu and others, very much appreciated. Darling you know I'm not jealous about your boyfriends, life would be too boring if one never looked at another girl, sorry there won't be any tourists for me this year, anyway something may turn up, although so far life has been very scarce of flirtations. We'll done, fancy passing the nursing business, lord help the patients!!

As to your remark about the prices of Air Mails, they have now put up the price again, a darn shame, as it's the only way to get mails quickly. How funny meeting Lyall, we hear that he will probably be getting his commission in March so should be in France about April/May.

As to the photo, you know it's rather difficult I can't just go and stand next to a lorry and let Fitz snap me, anyway will see what can be done, probably will be able to get one at Easter, anyway it will be difficult to send, can't think of any more excuses just now.

The Old Man gets out of hospital on Saturday. The op. has been a great success, and he is longing to be home again. While he has been in hospital we have been rebuilding, quite unknown to him. We have knocked another door in the wall and divided the kitchen, which was too large, into two thus putting the pantry next to the buttery. We have put in water in both and now with an extra window it looks awfully nice. The old pantry was really nothing more than the continuation of the passage, is now open.

Have been losing regularly at Bridge, and on Friday am going to a poker party, hope my luck changes. Had a very quiet birthday played tennis at Sandy Lane with Pat, then came up and saw a flick last Saturday. We had an impromptu party, dinner and flick, Johnnie Mac was in great form, very funny all night. We can't get a house for Easter this year, all the places are taken, anyway I am hoping for a repeat of a sailing show down the Grenadines – the small islands, uninhabited between St Vincent and Grenada – there is grand fishing and shooting, and of course should we stop in at Grenada again there are lots of very pretty girls, rather sunburnt, but still they all are! Have been talking to Johnnie about it don't know that anything will ever materialize.

Well must go to sleep now, as you will have realised I'm writing in bed. Goodnight darling, and be good. With all my love. Bob

Bun dearest.

I opened the right letter first, so the second one had the desired effect. One can't help feeling a bit depressed from time to time these days, so I don't suppose that it did you any harm. At any rate, I envy you your spell of the Night Life. I haven't had much time to think about it, but a few evenings ago I was feeling just in the mood and then the radio produced a magnificent selection of dance tunes for at least half-an-hour. I would have given a lot to have been on one of our London parties that evening.

Plymouth is incredible. It's a poor enough place in the piping times of peace, but in these days of black-outs, it can only be described as appalling, or worse. I think I told you that the college produced a Cocktail Dance every fortnight which was quite fun in any case, but which under these conditions was quite terrific. Well! The German Measles epidemic packed that up. We aren't exactly in quarantine but what functions there were, have practically disappeared as a result of the outbreak. I did go to one (tee-total) W.R.N.S. Dance and am due to go to another with a W.R.N.S who is engaged to a Warrant Officer I know very well. (I don't know if I told you that I had promised to be the Best Man in a month or so. Awful, ain't it). But there you have the limit of my social activities, so it's no good complaining that my letters tell you nothing, 'cause there 'aint nothing to tell, funny face.

I should be off for the mid-term weekend, the week-end after next, but I see singularly little chance of taking it. If I do manage to get up, I see equally little chance of having a large scale party on the approved lines, as so far, no one will give me any pay. The Accountant Branch are always pretty poor about changing over accounts from one branch to another, but this war is providing them with an opportunity to excel themselves. The last time I got any pay was at the beginning of December, may the Saints preserve them. However, as I say, I'm afraid that it's extremely unlikely that I shall get away at all so tant pis.

I have my Poles pretty well settled in now and all talk some kind of English which is, from time to time, intelligible. I'm still never quite sure whether they have understood the importance of anything I try to impress on them.

It must seem a little odd to be in residence at Bovingdon again. It made me think of "Violets", "South of the Border" "J'attendrai" and all the other tunes that went with evenings that occurred half an age ago. They were good days those, when the air was warm and there was always a light, quite often moonlight, and one could do what one wanted. They were more than "good" days; they were happy days. Ah! Well! I dare say we shall see their like again, albeit not for some little time, mais il vaudra mieux pour ça, comique visage (si que –) *[but it will be better for this comical face - if that]*

Still, if they have gone beyond recall, and temporarily beyond imitation, I don't think they were altogether wasted.

The weather trap is in operation again down here. It went all cold on us after the trial warm spell and with everything in sight iced yesterday, today turned out to be beautiful and quite warm. About Sunday I suppose the next violent freeze-up will occur, and some more will be caught in the 'flu trap. Your sweater is performing yeoman service and keeping me very nicely warm, thank you kindly. It has also defeated the Enemy Measles, so far.

I hope you enjoy your stay in the Home County, Bun dear, and have a good time. Let me know any dates of leaving etc as soon as you can, for there is always a chance that I may get up after all. I hope so.

My respects to your parents. And a whole lot of love to you.
Attie

Letter addressed to Reedlands, Thorpeness and redirected to The Mare Cottage, Bovingdon

Upton
February 12th

My Darling Bunny,

Haven't heard from you for ages, the last letter we had, the ones with letter for Grannie and Mummie is dated Jan 1st. Anyway, hope to hear soon. Perhaps it is that you have at last moved home to Bovingdon.

Well we have begun crop at last, and gradually everywhere is getting going, a pretty poor crop this year, or rather nothing up to average. Have been playing a lot of tennis getting going for the tournament; don't think I will get anywhere as far as we did last year.

We have been in the throes of elections, the last of which were today, and although I haven't heard all the results we have got a few more black vagabonds in the house, anyway it's just a chance that once in the house we hope that they will quieten down, we don't want any more trouble just now.

Darling all three of your orchids are just about to bear, I'm very excited to see what they are going to be. I've also got a few of the others bearing too, about the best collection all at one time I've ever had.

Mummie has been laid up again, nothing too bad this time, but still she has been so fit lately I think she has probably been doing too much, the family think that it's because she played tennis last week, don't know but it may be a coincidence. The 'Old Man' is getting on fine and last week the doctor let him look through a lens - he is awfully thrilled because he said he hasn't been able to see so much for years.

Lu's wedding invitations are out today, rather strange to think of a big show in Lent, its March 16th. I hear Plunks has got special dispensation to drink for a few days!! Anyway it's sure to be a wild show.

Have got a little necking to report, do you remember Mrs Miles (Canadian Bank of Commerce's Manager's wife) her daughter used to be down here and has just come down on leave, she is a nurse now, she has brought down a friend so Johnnie Mac and I have been taking them around, anyway Darling nothing really and you probably aren't interested, you should know that I love you, and after all haven't had a chance of any flirting for ages!!

Had a weird dream last night that I had joined up and that I had met Hugh, he didn't look the same and I thought he was someone else. Can't help feeling that I would be glad in a way if they did let some of us go over, one feels that one is shirking, don't know, just struck a morbid patch I suppose.

Must close my Darling, write soon please.

All my love to you, sweet,

Yours ever, Bob.

My Darling Bunny,

Thanks ever so much for your two letters received by air this morning – Jan 29th and Feb 8th. I will begin by answering any questions there are. Funny you should have dreamt about David Boyle, he has had rotten luck in T'dad. He lost his job suddenly, and not, I understand, his fault. Evidently Sir Hubert is a very hot headed man, and found a guest of his bringing down his own suitcase, David being on another job, he called up David and fired him there and then. He has now got a job with the Navy business down there. He also thought of getting into the oil fields. Poor David, he doesn't seem to have any luck and of course his manner is rather against him.

No, so far have not painted 'Romeo'. But think I will be doing so this week. Have decided to paint him black with silver wheels and a fine silver line round his sides. I think black will look very smart and should last well longer than a pastel shade. No Darling, as to the remarks about necking, can't remember who it was, but definitely not Helen, never tried that and somehow don't think ever will. Have more to report now with the girl I told you about last letter, after all she is down here for a couple of months with her boy in Canada so it's really quite a good chance. Johnnie Mac is looking after her friend and as we have been going round together am looking out for gossip, anyway my sweet, you know exactly what it is, you ain't jealous I don't think, there is no need to be, just some good clean fun, to keep my hand in!!

Glad you feel that way about Kitty and John, they have never been able to get anything out of me. They are very dangerous people, and say the most amazing things, so I have gradually got further and further away. John at the office is of no help, and in lots of cases quite the opposite. I often wonder how things will go when the Old Man dies. It will be rather a difficult business believe me.

So you've changed to the Army now? And married ones at that!!! Well my sweet be good, you know the rest? You must have had a hell of a time with this cold spell, the old Arch Deacon arrived back this morning and told the family how terribly cold it has been.

Bunny Edwards has cleaned up the races up here, which were last week, so if he goes on like this he will make a packet. No he hasn't been seen with Suzette for ages, don't know what has happened, perhaps Tom has been a little fierce.

So sorry to hear that you have not been well, do hope that you weren't laid up long. By this time I hope you have got back to Bovingdon, it would be much nicer for you and nearer town too.

The Savannah tournament started on Monday, I have not had much luck in the draw, I play on Thursday against Jack Johnson, and with any luck should win, I then play Johnnie Mac! Went to dinner with Clifton Wright on Saturday, a very good show, then onto The Morgan where I won the bottle of champagne. They draw on the ticket numbers, very nice to end up the show with free champagne!!

On Sunday went down to Bath with the Simpsons then back to 'Verdun' where Mrs Simpson lives. There I heard the most lovely selections of jokes from a Trinidad lad. We then played 'Red Dog' do you know it? A good gambling game, but unfortunately I got rash and lost about $3 again, and anyway I have been winning a little at Bridge.

Have got the wedding invitations to Lu and Hilda's – the former is March 16th the latter April 10th – weddings. Lu and Plunks, Audie and Johnnie, Mollie and Julian, Dick and Edna are dining here on Tuesday, we shall go on to a flick if there's a good one if not I shall try and take some money off them!

My sweet I must go to bed, do write soon again.
All my love, my love, I love you still. Bob   Rather good what?

HMS Hostile
c/o GPO
2nd March 1940
[Departed Portsmouth for The Clyde and onward to Scapa Flow]

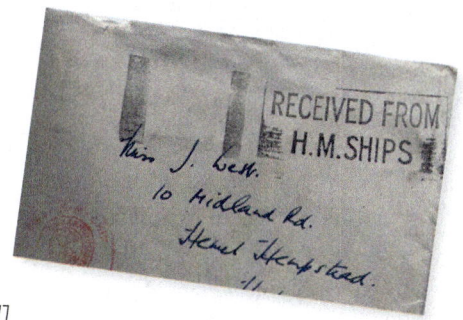

Bun Dear, *[typed letter top and tailed – he must have sent it to everyone!]*

I apologies for this rather impersonal appeal, but it saves valuable time, so please excuse.

The one garment which keeps the sailor warm is a polo sweater. The Admiralty provide them with scarves, gloves and helmets galore, but have apparently not thought a roll top sweater was necessary.

If you could possibly knit one, or even more if you are quick with needles and things, we would be terribly grateful, for we need 80 in all.

Neck sizes 15 ½" - 18" and chest in proportion.

Yours very sincerely, Tony

Thanks for the quid m'dear – as for you assisting, I would not have let you anyway. I don't think you can have enjoyed it more than I.

Royal Naval Engineering College,
Devonport.
(?March 1940)

Bun dear:

You sound somewhat depressed. I was hoping the change and a bit of London world would have brought you back to the top of the world. I hope it was only temporary. I must say I can sympathise with you, for I feel very much the same way: particularly this afternoon.

I thought I had almost reached the limit of my work periods here but no! I've had five extra periods already this week and its only Wednesday. As a crowning blow, I've just been instructed to learn how to build aircraft, about which I know nothing. It always amazes me why they fly, anyhow. Well! Maybe I will learn something, but I'm much more likely to go crazy.

Anyway, all I really want right now is one of our London evenings. It would just about set me up and I certainly want it. It's a great pity you haven't got some reasonable relatives in this part of the world, funny face. I suppose one just waits patiently and knows that it will be all the nicer when it does come.

Our leave period seems to be from April 17th to May 7th, for half of which I shall be on duty. I hope it will be the first half but as the division of labour includes certain senior types also, the final answers will rest with their wishes and so I don't know as yet: probably start on 27 April: what a hell of a time away.

These last couple of weeks have been a bit stiff, as already indicated. I've been working up the Hockey also, as the first of the big games, which I think I mentioned to you, happens tomorrow. I feel it's going to be somewhat above my head but should be fun anyway. I haven't dared to play any squash yet but the skin still seems to be happy on Hockey. I think I'd better stick to that and give the more strenuous things a bisque until after the summer; if we are allowed to have a summer.

These cursed golf courses are so far away that I've had precisely one game since I joined, and that was only about fourteen holes.

I don't seem to be able to mention anything without working it into a moan today, and that's just about what I feel like. "Run off with a Wren", says you. Cor! Chase me round the Hoe! What a chance! I had the first even reasonable dance since New Year last week. I did go to two Wrens dances in a party last month. They operated in the Plymouth Co-operative Society's Hall: all "operative" and no "Co". I couldn't take any more of that but the Lord Mayor produced a Guildhall Charity Ball, which the R.N.E. Staff Officers supported en masse last Friday. One of the Lieuts (E) produced a sister-in-law aged 17. She is learning ballet dancing and was staying with him for the week-end. She had learnt some plain dancing as well, and I quite enjoyed the evening. I mixed up some of your Planters Punch to start with, but only with Jamaican Rum. Still, they weren't too bad. Altogether, a tremendous evening for wartime Plymouth.

Thorpe should be getting pleasanter now I suppose (quite apart from the advent of the Brutal and Licentious, from whom the Lord preserve you). Better weather and longer days will make an enormous difference, I suppose.

I spent yesterday forenoon working in a destroyer. Whatever this place becomes, I'm quite certain I'd rather be here than in one of those boats at present. Later on in the war it will be a bit more settled and organised; at least, I sincerely hope it will, for that is almost certainly where I shall go when I finish here. On the whole, perhaps it would be safer if we finished off this war first.

Well, Bun, I hope my moans have cheered you up. Don't go and become a Wren or W.A.T. or anything else like that. Not yet, anyway. As regards suggesting any alternative, well, of course the essence of the argument prevents one's being able to do that. It is the spontaneous affairs that occur from time to time that I am in favour of, and one can't 'suggest' them. They just happen. I don't believe you are going to be nearly as much use to the country or anyone in particular washing dishes or driving a car as one of a number in a section, as you could be with your own initiative unhindered. Besides, I've never seen a woman's looks improved by uniform.

Heigh-ho! Lets both pretend that we are having an evening in town, with you in uniform and me in plain clothes and then we'll both be happy. Well! You can spend an evening in my uniform next time we get together, and I'll see how I disguise as you: but I don't think we'd better go out comme ça [like that]. Dear old Bun. I wish I were meeting you this week. Love to the family and as always to you. Attie.

Office (Alleyne Arthur & Co Ltd)
General Merchants
Barbados
March 18th

My Darling Bunny,

Many thanks for your lovely long letter of 19th Feb. I should have written last week, but thought I would wait till after Lu's wedding so as to give you the news. Before I get on to that let's see what has been happening.

Got beaten in the open with Helen, and two people who played for the island last year, not too bad though 6-4/6-3 and anyway we had great fun. Have been to one or two dinners and gambling afterwards, haven't been doing badly. First I started at home when Lu and Plunks, Johnnie and Audrie, Dick and Edna (Leacock) Mollie and Julian came up for a dinner to here. We were meant to be going on to the flicks, but you can imagine with that crowd what time we finished dinner – 9.30 – so they said they would like to play vinght et un, well you know I never lose at that game so I managed to clean up about $2 at ½ d a chip – quite nice going. (It's too hard to read on both sides so will carry on here). Last Sunday played a kind of Red Dog at Mrs da Costa's and got about $2 again. Last night dined at Florence's – David Boyle was up from T'dad for the wedding and is staying there. We played Bridge and I managed to end up 1/9 up. Have got to play men's doubles this afternoon with Kenneth Hunt, but alas it's against Dr Shute and Sandy so we don't expect to win!!

Now for the wedding – of course it had to be at the RC church, but it was a very nice short service, then on to Francia. Plunks had Abe for best man, Den, Agatha and Betty Clarke being the Matron of Honour. Of course they all looked lovely, and once at Francia with drink running like water the show went on till almost 9 o'clock. Lu and Plunks have gone to some small house in St James till Wed: when they will go to St. Lucia where Plunks was born. After they left we went down to the Marine where eggs and ham and bacon were greatly appreciated – Audrie and Edna were in grand form, don't believe I was in too bad form myself. And so ended a good show, and only about two kisses darling, Mollie Mahon being one, bad business that Julian may be a little sore if he was to know. Apart from the wedding very little necking to report with Buddie, haven't seen her for some time, so you can see how serious I am my sweet!!

Now for some surprising news, I'm off on a trip to Dutch Guiana on Sunday (24th)!! Dick and Edna thought of it, it's on the Aluminium line from here to some place in Venezuela – Viera de la Cranzia, there we have two days, then T'dad for 2 days – B.S. for 1 day Paramaribo for 1 or 2 days then up the Suriname River to the American Bosite works about 100 miles up through the jungle. They say this is the most wonderful part of the trip all the natives are wild and use arrows to kill snakes, crocks or us if we go the wrong way!! From there we go to a port called Port Amsterdam then back to T'dad. It will take about 2 weeks and here is the real joy – costs only $7150. I will fly back from T'dad on Wed: 18th just in time to usher at Tom & Hilda's wedding that afternoon. Have tried out the camera and hope to get some really good stuff, not to mention a few orchids. Oh! The Old Man and I wore two different flowers of two of your orchids to the wedding.

My sweet must close now, hope to get Romeo back today really looks awfully smart now.

All my love, darling, Yours ever – Bob.

HMS HOSTILE
19th March 1940

You sweet little Bunny-boo,

I did enjoy "the magic" – nearly made myself sick in the first half hour! But I've survived, also an air raid, so all is well!

The sweater is dandy, but if you can manage another – a bit larger next time - because most of the sailors are a bit larger than the Weevil. Who sends his love and thanks you a lot – under pain of death he says I'm to tell you he's very well and finds that Surman's embrocation is invaluable for his bruises after I've been cross with him.

I've just heard Lord Haw Haw telling you about an air raid!! As usual he was too exaggerated for words. We always put on that record "Let's have a damn good laugh" after listening to him. D'you know it "Ein Reich, ein volke, ein fuhrer, I thank you!" [sic] [Nazi slogan meaning 'One people, one realm, one leader'].

James is no longer in these parts, but training somewhere in Wales – He's to be a Captain soon, but has to pass an exam or two first poor dear!

Thanks a lot Bun for the goodies and comforts. The sweater was just the thing. I've made a gift of "an apple for the teacher" to the ships radio-gram so can now hear it "Ad lib ad nauseam". Best Love, Tony. "To" to you my poppet!!

Royal Naval Engineering College,
Devonport
Telephone Dev 740 Ext 451
Telegrams College Devonport
Monday

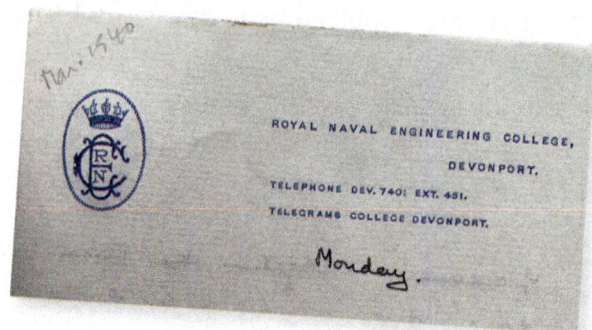

My dear Bun.

It's an enormous time since I wrote to you; over a week! I'm afraid it feels like no time at all.

I got down to Cornwall for Saturday and Sunday and was eventually able to spend Monday there as well, much to my surprise. I did absolutely nothing, drank practically nothing, took very little exercise and eat terrific quantities of cream. Altogether, the three days did me a power of good, and I immediately wrecked it by returning to a very old-fashioned evening indeed. More West Indian types were just in and one thing led to another in a very swift manner. Next day, the other watch pushed of on their week-end and of course, the few survivors have been hard worked ever since. I did have Saturday afternoon and got inveigled into the above order; name your price.

Must beat it now, Funny face, but I'll write again in a couple of days time, on account of this one is way over due. Let me know how our various dates for leaving Bovingdon, going to Yorkshire, Leicester and so on go. I'm as vague as ever; but I reckon that I should get ten days leave in about 8 weeks from next Friday. That's a hell of a way away, 'ain't?

À bientot, comique V. Sois sage, [goodbye funny face be good] but enjoy yourself just the same. My love to your fond parents and just a tiny bit to you: about so much. (Now figure out how much that "so" is). Attie

Copy of a letter, written in Bunny's hand, from Tony to his mother and father, Lil and Frank Fasson, just before and after the First Battle of Narvik after which Tony was mentioned in dispatches.

4th April 1940

… They had captured a German ship and put a prize crew on board and brought back 7 prisoners. When told they were going to England they said "Ach that iss goot – meat".

When we passed them on to a bigger ship today (4th April) they seemed sorry to have to go and insisted on shaking hands – "Danke schoen – war is a stupid business!"

11th April 1940 Well, well, well! Things never come singly, do they? The BBC will have told you of the Battle of Narvik – but here is a firsthand account! I can quite honestly say, that except when a torpedo passed directly under us without hitting, I enjoyed every moment of it. At last to be able to have a smack at the b-boche!

We had taken another prize and were escorting her home when we were ordered to rejoin the flotilla, or half of it. We therefore arrived off Narvik at dusk – landed at the mouth of the fiord to learn the Germans were in occupation in considerably stronger forces than we had thought!

So Captain "D" (Hardy) [HMS Hardy] decided to attack early yesterday morning. All that night we cruised off the fiord in a snowstorm with no lights, having great difficulty to keep in touch as of course no lights were used or wireless allowed. Then at midnight we entered, all hands at Action Stations, - still black as night, no lights, and tons of snow. One of the boys ran aground but got off, and about 4.30am we arrived. The Fiord is very wide at the mouth and we nearly lost all when two Norwegian steamers ran slap thro' our line in the pitch black night and cut the five of us in half, however we eventually got together again, which in itself was a miracle as visibility was so bad, and as I say arrived off the Port of Narvik.

It was intensely cold and we could see about 800' only as we entered the harbour dead slow – final signal from Captain D – "Good luck, hit 'em hard and often!" was well received by a half frozen Hostile!

I could see dimly about 6 ships in the harbour, it was quite light thro' a drizzle of snow. And then all of a sudden we were "in action". Leading ship fired a torpedo and opened fire with her guns – and up went a transport blown clean in half. I could see a destroyer vaguely, a little back from the Merchantman. I could not get a range for altho' it had cleared the range taker could not see her clearly. So I did a bit of rapid guesswork and the Lord being with me I'm damned if my very first shots, two as only forward group would bear, gained direct hits and set her on fire! Not bad at 8000 yards, which was the range on my gun sights!! A prize fluke of course but vastly encouraging to us, and demoralising to the enemy, who were by then waking up! Gun flashes from half a dozen planes began to appear in the mist, and the whine and black blobs of bursting shrapnel from the shore batteries, appeared in the air. All of a sudden I saw five or six torpedo tracks approaching our line – I screamed to the Captain and by going full ahead hard over, the nearest one missed us by only about 10 yds! Shells were falling all around, but the Hostile seemed to bear a charmed life as we steamed up and down. By this time most of the transports had been sunk or sinking – so full speed ahead and we zigzagged away making black smoke to cover our retreat. By this time two of our ships were on fire, tho' all five left together. About 3 or 4 of the big German destroyers had by this time got clear of the harbour and gave chase. When suddenly ahead of us down the fiord appeared two more of the blighters cutting us off!! It was then that a great tragedy occurred. A shot fell in the Hotspur jamming her engine room telegraphs at full speed, so that when the Hunter zigzagged they collided, and one sunk as we dashed past at 32 knots. The Huns were firing much too well by now and their 5.5" guns could do more than our 4.7" and we were caught between two fires, so it was hardly surprising that Hardy's steering gear jammed, and she ran aground. So that left 3 of us one badly hit – but the Huns for some reason failed to follow up fast, altho' concentrating on our luckless lame duck (Hotspur).

They would undoubtedly have sunk her but for the Captain's (Hostile's) gallant effort. He ordered Havoc to turn and together we raced back to her assistance. I thought to myself at the time, well I suppose we have to do this, but was quite convinced that we would all 3 be sunk instead of one! But, why I cannot imagine, the Huns failed to close in on us, and at much reduced speed all 3 of us got clear.

Passing round a corner lower down we sighted a large shape coming towards us – our hearts sank, we thought – "Heavens a German Cruiser". But it was only a large Merchantman, who as we dashed past, looking over our shoulder at the time, we ordered to stop. She was a Nazi, and did not at once obey, so I put a couple of bricks into her, and that settled her.

We left Havoc [HMS Havoc], who was untouched, to get the crew clear and then sink her. Suddenly about ½ hr later I saw an unbelievable burst of flame over one of the mountains and then dense white smoke which rose to about 10,000ft and 30 seconds later a crack like the sound of doom – the Havoc had sunk our 'large Nazi steamer' and she had been filled with mines and torpedoes for the defence of Narvik, and blew up.

So tho' we did loose some ships we had prevented them fortifying and mining the Narvik fiord – which if

Credit: painting of HMS Hostile during the
Battle of Narvik by Tony Fasson
and now owned by his nephew, Roderick d'A Willis.

they had had time to do – would have been well nigh impregnable.

Our lack of damage was due to the Captain's magnificent handling of ship when taking avoiding action, combined with the fact that we were at the rear of the line No 5.

We were hit once forward, but tho' a shrewd crack, luckily no one was hurt. God has indeed answered our prayers and I for one, am deeply thankful. An unforgettable experience.

Best of Love, from an older and wiser Tony

Upton
14th April

My Darling Bunny,

Well here I am back home and a grand holiday all over. I better go into that bit by bit so I will begin at the beginning; I made a note of each day.

We did not get off till the afternoon of the 26th instead of the Sunday as we had been meant to. The boat was small but the food good, I didn't miss a meal. There were twelve of us on board. Dick & Edna being the only other British, the crew being Norwegians, the passengers wild Americans. The other men grew beards, I thought it might be a good idea to grow one too but it was much too hot. All the 27th we were sailing along the Venez: coast then early on the 28th we arrived at the port of Porta de la Cruize, the most wild and barren place you ever saw. All the people were dirty and nothing grew anywhere. All that day we unloaded road making material and except for a short walk we stayed on board. That night I met a few oil people and they said they would come round for us next day 29th and took us for a drive over the desert to some place where one could bathe. The water was very cold but after the heat and dust it was good.

That night I saw a bit of rough stuff, one fellow nearly knifed the other, we sailed about midnight for T'dad, where we arrived at about 3am on the Sunday morning. We went ashore about nine o'clock and took a car for the day. We ran into Jock Hughes and after a drink at the QPH we set off for the Pitch Lake. After a long and tiring day we returned to Port of Spain then on to Macqueripe where we dined and watched the dancing. That is a lovely new hotel out there and I was sorry we were in open neck shirts and could not dance.

Next day April 1st I went round the town and saw a few people, had lunch with David, he's very well and I think likes his new job. Then we went for another drive to the north end of the island. At night we had the Scotts to dinner with us at the Chinese restaurant, it was grand. Next morning we sailed to P of Pierre to load up oil for Morga – we couldn't land. Anyway it didn't take very long. We sailed about noon and had a lovely sail all along the coast. That night we began to roll, boy how she could go over. On the 4th we arrived in BG(Georgetown) where I had to do a little work, anyway that afternoon a fellow we know down there took us to all the clubs including one about 26 miles out of town, again I could act as club correspondent or something. They were loading all night, and till about 9am. We eventually sailed about 11am. It's just about 20-22 hours run to Paramaribo that was the 6th. Here again the town is very dirty and dusty. Dick complained that he was crawling in fleas! We left about 2 o'clock and set off for a place they are building up river called Parinam, there isn't much there just at present, but when they get everything built it should be very nice. We then started on our long river trip that was really most interesting. This huge mass of jungle and narrow rivers and all the time there we were on a steamer going through it. About 80 miles up you come across the Juka villages, they are quite wild, no clothes and bows and arrows. Then at last you come on a model town, its private property and no-one except employees, but they have their own hospital club and playing fields and some 4 miles away you see naked wild men, the contrast is terrific.

We arrived back in T'dad on the 11th the day after Tom Wilkinson's wedding, so I missed that. Was out at Alex for the day of 12th and flew up yesterday, so really I did not have much time in T'dad except for sightseeing. That account of the trip seems somewhat disjointed but it will give you an idea of the places.

When I arrived back I found three letters for me, thank you my sweet. Glad you like the canteen biz: but still you are glad to have something to do. Personally I think they would do well if they conscripted women for jobs instead of letting them join so often the ones with influence – not worth a dam – get the positions. Lyle wrote out to Florence himself and said he had got it in the neck about Lil.

Helen is engaged to that friend of mine Theodore Gittens. Plunks has gastric ulcers so is on a very strict diet and on sick leave. Den is going to have an infant. I have got a snap of myself for you which I will send as soon as Fits gets some paper or something, for a good print.

What a grand do the Navy are putting up!

Darling sweet I must go and get some sleep, as I was at The Marine last night, and was very late home, not exactly necking Darling, just 'sweet nothings' in her ear! Didn't someone say that once!!

Be good, and work hard at the canteen. All my love Darling, yours ever, Bob.

Addressed to Reedlands but forward to Lanton Towers, Jedburgh, Scotland

Upton
May 1st

p.s. have got a rotten photo which I will send soon. Love Bob.

My Darling Bunny,

Thanks ever so much for your lovely long letter. I must admit that I'm very glad you have decided not to see Gimson again. I would never have hinted at it, but although I don't know him I have not formed a very good opinion of him. Lord help the accounts my sweet, do hope you won't be too much out of pocket!! No, the so called girl friend is still here, although I have only taken her out once since I've been back, really quite glad, especially as the tennis team from T'dad (pen run out) *[continues in pencil]* arrived tomorrow, and there should be a nice girl or two amongst them. All this should go to prove how serious these flirtations really are?

Well, my sweet, I am now a Director of Allyne Arthur & CO. Ltd. At £300 a year with twenty five shares which this year nets another £100 odd. Will be able to begin thinking of saving soon and then perhaps even a wife, such hard things to find you know, I mean a really satisfactory one, do you know of any? By the way this is only enquiring!!!!!

Have only played very little tennis since I have been back, and pretty bad tennis at that. Have been making a little money at Bridge. Last Saturday I went to The Marine by myself - it was a 'not-outs and outs' dance, rather enjoy these 'not outs' so gay and like to think I'm still able to fit in with these young girls and boys, not to mention that many of the young girls are most attractive. Oh! I can hear you saying cradle snatching, you should be the last to say anything, they are too young so quite safe.

We thought of getting up a weekend party for Whitsun, but the team will still be up here, and the tennis dinner is on the 11th so Johnnie and I squashed that, Jack and Sister are going to The Crane for the week so think I will go up there on the Sunday and perhaps the Monday too. I'm going to join the Bridgetown Club, you know the men's club in town, think it should be very useful for business purposes.

Elizabeth and Angie Challenor have been staying here for a few days, we all went to see 'That Certain Age', I was a little disappointed with it, nothing as good as her usual things. Did I tell you I had seen 'Babes in Arms' in T'dad? Mickey Rooney and Judy Garland, they are excellent, it's their first musical show. Talking of shows, will have to start thinking of putting on a show soon for the Red X. Wish I could get someone to produce it, I would sooner act. Any good sketches – slightly of the Drawing Room standard – that you see you might write out and give me the ideas, I would write up the words to suit. The thing that was so popular in the last Bazaar show I saw at the 'Windmill".

Well my Darling, there seems to be nothing happening to write about so I will close and go to bed. Am sending this by boat which goes direct and leaves tomorrow so should be as quick as air.

With all my love my sweet.
Your ever-loving Bob.

The Clydesdale Hotel, Lanark
Sunday

[no date no envelope but after 10th April 1940 as First Battle of Narvick mentioned in which Tony saw action in HMS Hostile]

Bun my darling old girl – I have hardly the face to write to you but I think you can guess the reason! How are you, I hope very well. The reason you suggested that I had not written to you was not correct – because as I told you my love towards you would always remain the same dear old girl – as Lil has probably told you I have been to the Leicester family often since I was at Weedon. I wish this damn war was finished as it is no use arranging anything in the present situation, not that I am quite certain of my own convictions as usual. I think that is a sweet child and we get on most awfully well together and seem interested in the same good things in this world – but is all seems so futile at present with the bloody war going on.

Now Bun darling this is all just between ourselves – I know I can trust you not to say anything.

Well since I last talked to you we have been turned into gunners and I have now attained the lofty heights of Capt! I have just returned from a three months gunnery course in Wales. In another 4 months time we shall be out with the rest.

"Old To" had a great battle at Narvik – I expect the old girl has told you all about it by now. They must have done marvellously.

The farm still goes on, I wish to goodness I was back. I hope Diddy and Gillie *[Bunny's parents]* are very well.

Are you coming up North any time - do try as it would be grand to see you again darling. Do write because I love hearing from you although I am not a damn bad writer myself.

With my very best love old girl.
Jim

Bun my darling, what a surprise to hear from you and to hear that you are so near. I am so glad you wrote – funnily enough I wrote to you about 4 days ago saying how things were and hoped I would see you soon. Well darling, come and stay here this weekend there is quite a good pub here which people's wives like – just opposite the station. What about coming on Saturday arriving sometime in the afternoon. I hope you will be able to come – we are allowed no leave otherwise I would come home. Let me know by return and I will book a room for you.

Just off my very best love my dear. Jim

HMS Hostile
c/o GPO 12th May 1940

My sweet Bun,

Your last parcel was very gratefully received – "the sweets of victory"! What fun we do have. We got a couple of days leave after our little effort at Narvik, which was short but extremely good for me, as we put in close to home.

The family were in good form and I managed to get up to see Sheena *[his sister]* for a few minutes.

We have moved again, and you may see us as you look out of your window one day! Actually we've met some "undesirables" a second time – at night on this occasion. Terribly thrilling my dear – but the Hostile's luck still holds good. Quite veterans – my dear!

Sorry this is so short, but time is short as there's much to do before the Bosch is pushed back – but he ain't having it all his own way for once – I don't think I'd care about being a parachute Nazi.

At last! Perhaps I'd agree you're as well out of uniform. Hope Wee Janie and the wicked are well to say nothing of your own beautiful self.

Love. To. Thanks a lot for pullovers – don't worry about them.

Royal Naval Engineering College, Devonport
Telephone Dev 740 Ext 451 Telegrams College Devonport
Wednesday May 1940

Bunny dear.

Hey: Hey: Conman, Cheer up. Things aren't as bad as all that. At least we're off now and I think the whole issue will be over – the sooner for it and that's always an encouraging thought. It may be tough for a bit, and certainly they have tightened up all rules and regulations with a bang, but so long as things keep moving fast I personally don't mind. The quicker this lot is over, the less will this country be disrupted and the easier it will be to return to normal, or at least, to what we have come to call normal. So keep going and don't let it get you down. If I were you, I would set yourself a golf figure for a start and keep at it until you get down to it. How about 11 for a start? That is just about what I'm doing with my bowling and if only this war keeps going long enough. I reckon I shall be a darned good bowler.

The first week of the term finishes today, and a fairly strenuous week it has been. Unfortunately, we are now one day on in four, which means that I spend every fourth day in uniform in the college, all day and half the night. Between getting my lecture schemes under way and sorting out the cricket, I've been pretty well flat out every day. However, daylight can be seen through most of the situations now.

The weather has been terrific: not a cloud in the sky, every day the same. In fact, we need rain badly, and I think we shall get it tomorrow. The trouble about Plymouth is that it very rarely rains good and hard and returns to fine. It usually gets around to drizzling and stays that way for quite a time.

I was very sorry to hear about Hugh. I hope he's alright, and gets back to Rhoda safely *[Flight Lt. Hugh Rowe was shot down in Holland May 1940 ending up in Stalag Luft III]*. Cases as near home as this are bound to happen to all of us but I suppose the knowledge of that fact doesn't help to lessen the shock any. Please give her my best wishes for his quick recovery.

I was hoping that these blue-pencil Poles would have settled down quite happily by this term but not on your life. They have one hell of a list of moans and I'm fed up with at least one section of our Allies. By the way, if we get many more of them, the B.B.C.'s National Anthem item on Sunday will go on all night. As it is, they left out Luxemburg and completely discounted Denmark.

Well. Off like a flash again! Keep your chin, flabbily, and don't let the B&L get you down. My love to Ma West and thank her for the nice letter she sent me. The week's leave seems so long ago that it might never have happened at all. That's the sort of thing that makes this blessed war such a curse.

À Bientôt, Cabbage, lots of love from Attie.

June 7th
Addressed to Reedlands,
Thorpeness but forwarded to c/o Dr Gregory
Hemel Hempstead, Herts.

My Darling Bunny,

It was ages since I had had a letter from you, then I got the one with the news of Hugh. I hope that they will have got him out of Holland before the blasted Germans got there.

Things are very quiet and there is really nothing doing. I have been playing some tennis; the RBYC's tournament has just started. I played men's doubles yesterday, and got beaten by Johnnie 6/0 6/0 6/0 just shows how well I was playing. I was very foolish and have not been playing any tennis at the Yacht, and as you know the difference between the Sav: and Yacht is colossal.

The KLM don't come here anymore now so don't know when you will get this, any way I believe there should be a boat going to T'dad soon. Was up at Johnnie's last night to a poker game, was quite lucky as I made a recovery from down about 24/- to up 14/- at the end of the evening.

Bert goes off to Canada this month on business, rotten luck having to go now as Den is meant to have her baby early August so it will be a near thing if he can get back in time.

There have been a few good films on, I think I have been to about three in the last three weeks. We are wondering if the parcel of guava cheese etc ever got there, as there was some discussion as to the post it got away on.

What a rotten letter, but really there isn't any news. I have joined the Bridgetown Club now, as have written this there as I am breakfasting there this morning. Be good. With lots of love Bob.

My Darling Bunny,

It is ages since I have had a letter from you, no doubt with all the air lines closed it is the cause – and then you must be very busy.

Life goes on much the same; very dull not being able to do anything really useful. We have been collecting money for a 'win the war' fund and now the Government seem to be waking up as they have increased income tax and duties.

There is some talk of a few fellows being allowed to go to Canada to train in the RAF. But then there are rumours that they have not been allowed to go because they can't guarantee to take them in any of the services.

Marion Elliot got married suddenly to Birdie Bradshaw, no-one knew anything about it – very good for B'dos. Birt Sesnett has gone off to Canada on business, rotten luck having to go now as Den is expecting a baby soon.

They still have the Old Man upstairs – he looks fine and feels well, but they know that if they let him come down he will want to go out.

The RBYC tournament is just about at an end, I did hopelessly in it. It wasn't a very good show anyhow, no one seemed satisfied – they ran it very slackly.

There are no dances, and what films there are they are rotten so I have taken to reading and of course spending long times listening to the news.

Hope to hear from you soon and hope that they have been able to get news of Hugh. Got news yesterday of another friend who was killed in an accident after having bombed Norway, Holland, Denmark and Germany, a very funny world.

Write soon.

With lots of love Bob

Royal Naval Engineering College,
Devonport
Telephone Dev 740 Ext 451
Telegrams College Devonport
Thursday – not dated

Bun dear,

It's an enormous time since I've written. I'm not going to go on saying that I'm overworked or had no time or anything else like that, because the repetition of a fact doesn't make it any the more palatable. It might bring it home to a disbeliever, I suppose, but unless I miss my guess, you don't need that kind of faith. In any case, it makes me sick to have to write about it in what spare moments there are.

The present situation is shaking things up even more as you might expect. You needn't worry about the half-term party because there 'aint no half-term or any other week-end leave, and I'll be lucky if I get two weeks in the summer. With luck that will mean three weeks leave by the end of this year, so I guess I'm very lucky to have got in such an enormous amount last year. Seems incredible to think back on it: one week or the next was quite immaterial then. Amazing!

My child, I envy you the Highlands very much. The weather has been so perfect down here, and to think of this hole in uniform while you're wandering around the hills and streams – it is doubly unforgiveable. Enjoy them while you can – No! There's the wrong sentiment creeping in again, the live-for-today attitude of this bloody war. You'll actually enjoy them far better with someone else in more peaceful times to come, so use their aloof calm to soothe your own mind. It's a wonderfully calming place, is a quiet Highland glen on a pleasant afternoon. Even the tumbling waters seem to induce pleasant and soothing images, like pictures in the fire and the wind rustling in the tall trees – heigh ho, a pause here as two buses roar past and the gas works gives its half-hourly invitation of an explosion in the Arsenal. (Bathos) (Don't mistake it for pathos).

Anyway, you can see that I'm not in the right mind to give you any very stable advice. I want to win this war as much as anyone. Indeed, I've believed it inevitable for a long time now as you know. But I bitterly resent a policy which might utterly and irrevocably wreck the future by muddle headedness in the present. Things are pretty sticky now and fantastic efforts must be made, but no matter how fantastic the particular efforts have to be, the whole structure will remain sane and not itself become fantastic if people keep some normality in their life. Certain things in life must go on, war or no war. Whenever anything useful can be done towards winning this war, do it. If it's only a small thing, do it. But if it's a small thing, done at the expense of something greater, the normality and sanity of the nation, don't. This country will win because it is a nation of free individuals, normal but determined. Germany will lose because she is a machine. If we become a machine, we lose; now or later, what's the difference?

Do what you feel you must Bun, but do it with your head as well as your heart.

I hope I get a crack at these Italians sometime. I've always wanted to see what made them tick. Still, I suppose the "Isola Bella" won't be the same for quite some time to come. A pity! That "Fillet of Sole Isola Bella!" What a war!

I hope none of the West Clan got involved in the Flanders business. I haven't heard anything of one of my Derby cousins yet; I hope he's all right.

So long, Flubbily. Please keep writing when you can. Love to Ma West and to Pop when you next write to him, and just a little should be left over for you. From me, Attie.

Clydesdale Hotel,
no date and no clues to year!

Bun Darling, thank you so much for your letter. You must come down next weekend and stay here as I cannot come and see you. Come down on Saturday morning and stay as long as you can. Bethia is coming down so that is all right!

I have just rung up home as I am going to Redesdale and thought it would be a good plan if I borrowed Ma's car while she was away. I do not think she did like it till I said it would be all right! I thought it would be useful for next weekend.

Don't make any plans about going south until you come as you must stay longer than the weekend – as we are now free from 3 in the afternoon as we get up at 4am!

Will write darling again but I long to go out with John to a picket! Tell Ma not to mention you coming down to Father! Very best love to Did and more to yourself darling. Jim.

My Darling Bunny,

The Lord knows when and if this will ever reach you, for today we've heard that the French have "chucked in" – don't blame 'em poor dears! They are absolutely at Hitler's mercy – All I pray, and pretty earnestly at that, is, that the Colonial Governors and Admirals away from home refuse to obey orders! About 50/50 I should say. Anyway it will brace up our Army terrifically to be defending "the home town" in actual fact.

I dare say the family may have given you an idea where we are. Anyway it has been a grand change for altho' pretty busy, when I have got ashore about once every ten days or so – I've enjoyed myself not a little.

D'you remember the Balfour–Pauls? Budge married a Paget, I stung 'em good and proper at Bombay – and now they are at – tut-tut! Nearly gave you the "secret" base! Life is very 'amiable', nice cool cafes after the hot days, quite reasonable prices and the food – "well my dear, really it's awful gudi!" All great, and no worse for being that.

The place abounds with grass-widows, so John Little and I have managed a little relaxation. But I doubt that will last for we have been bombed several times lately. The "Wops" don't come much below the stratosphere when releasing their pills – but as they aim at the bigger ships, it is about evens whether they hit you, if you're anywhere within 6 miles of their target! I am afraid they're palpable inefficiency won't last long as soon as the Huns get amongst them tho'.

I saw Peter Medd the other day for the first time almost since my "bump" – dear old chubby face, just the same as ever and quite as reassuring! Incidentally the Weevil sends his love, and thanks you for all the pullovers you've given him! As soon as we got really stocked up with woollens, we came out here! And of course the last time I went home I took all my whites. They are on their way out now, but when they'll arrive I don't guess.

The reason I write this – I was flopped in a wardroom chair after an exasperating morning watch, when all our plans had to be altered because of the news, when they suddenly put on the ships 'gram' a record "The very thought of you" – I wonder if you know it, a tuneful little ditty played rather nicely by Ray Noble. And so I did fall to thinking – got quite sentimental. We've had some good times way back – it certainly does seem ages! Greenwich, your dance at Shoreham, Pitlochry, Jock Gray and the Queens at Portsmouth ad lib ad nauseam. To say nothing of the Gargoyle!

Well I've decided to finish this little spot of bother as an Angel or an Admiral, preferably the former as the latter's uniform is a shade less blush-making! I expect you're all away from the East coast now – too bracing by far! Love to Wee Janie, the Wicked, and the eenest teeniest bit of love to you m'sweet. To

How's the guardere? You'll have him under your eye now – none of these French troopers to worry him!!

In July 1940 Bunny became a Red Cross nurse and was working at Hemel Hempstead Hospital. She always said one of her very first jobs was in theatre when they were amputating a leg which she was instructed to carry away.

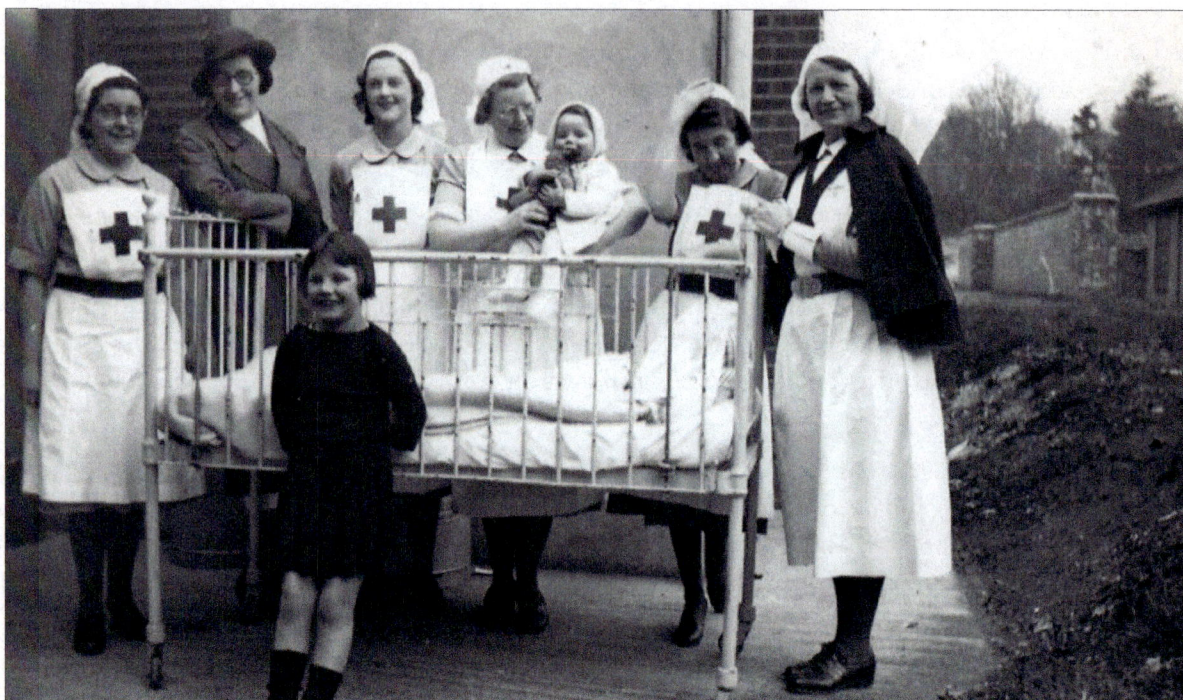

Bunny 3rd from left

Office (Alleyne Arthur)
July 5th

My Darling Bunny,

Many thanks for your last letter which I got last week. Although it was air mail it had taken ages to get here. I am sending this by a Harrison boat which is meant to be sailing today sometime, how long it will take I don't know, but I should imagine it will be about a month, as it has to go to Bermuda, wait there for a convoy, and then ??

There is really no news; an occasional flick is all one can do. The rains have come on in a big way now, and it is only just in time as we were having an awful drought. This means that I will be playing a lot of Bridge, but unfortunately I am playing with rotten luck just now.

Helen and Theo are getting married in Sept: I am to be his best man, which will mean I will have to keep a clear head till I get them away!! The Old Man is much better again, he is allowed down for breakfast, and can go for a drive in the afternoons. Must have been terribly boring being upstairs and only having this rather depressing news to listen to.

John has been at the hospital today having X-rays they think he may have juradinal, (don't know how to spell it). Whatever it is I hope Lionel will make him give up some drinking, as he is very apt to overdo it. Even last night he was at a cocktail party and was quite stupid.

The Colonnade Grocery is likely to be shut down. That's the big one next to Harrisons where Taffy is. It's an English show, and have lost money fairly regularly, so now they are going to shut down or sell out. Will be good for us, hope they do soon.

I hear that Mollie and Julian are leaving Norwood. This is only hearsay, I think they are going to manage his father's two estates, and have to live at the estate with his people, only in a separate bungalow, don't think Mollie won't hate it!

Must close now as there ain't no news.
With lots of love Bob.

Royal Naval Engineering College, Devonport
Telephone Dev 740 Ext 451 Telegrams College Devonport
Undated (?July 1940)

Bun dear, Thanks for the long letter, although this note is not a reply to it, but just to ask if there really is no chance of your being able to come down next weekend. I'd rather you kept it to yourself, but I've just been told off for 48 hours notice for sea. I may not go for months, but on the whole I think I shall be lucky if I get any August leave before they find they want someone for a job.

I don't suppose you can and in any case, I'm not at all sure that this is any place to come to, though you'd be staying some miles in the country if you did. I really just thought you'd like to know how I felt about it, Funny face.

À bientôt and keep out of the Hun's way. Lots of love Attie

Office
19th

My Darling Bunny,

Thanks awfully for your letter received just after I had posted your last airmail. I haven't got it here so won't be answering any questions, in fact this can hardly be called a letter, its only just a note, but I heard that the Costa Rica was going early tomorrow so here goes.

Have been pretty busy lately, the Government want all kinds of records, and business, although not very bright, has lots of other complications. Think I shall be going to Grenada and St Vincent soon on business, no definite arrangements have been made yet, boats are difficult to fit in.

Taffy, Johnnie and I went to The Marine on Saturday night, caused quite a stir three lone men, there were very few people there, and with Jack and Sister we had lots of fun, some low jokes etc.

Darling must be off now with all my love, Yours Ever, Bob

My Darling Bunny,

Thanks very so much for your lovely long letter June 28th. It seems that air mail sometimes takes as long as sea mail; there is no connection between here and Trinidad. The Harrison boat leaves this afternoon so I will get this off by that and you should get this in about three weeks. A couple of friends of mine in the Bank have got leave and are going over to see if they can get into the Army. No member of the local defence is being given permission yet, but I am beginning to think of how it can be arranged to go. Just now John is at home with a bad finger. He has been rather peculiar for some time now, first he thought he had duodenal now the finger. They have nothing they can find, and Lionel, I believe, suggested cutting out some drink. He is really suffering from a bad go of nerves and I think he should go away to the sea for a month or two - complete change. You can imagine that I am working quite hard, and so this alone presents a difficulty as I know the Old Man feels that I should be here to see the business roll on. It is quite difficult really, anyway if things really get tough I will have to do something, I feel rather as though I were putting business before the country, but there are some of the officials who say that anyone who has an important job should stay.

Have been playing a lot of tennis this week, in fact have broken my racquet, so will have to get another one.

Tonight is the big dance and fair at The Marine for war funds, it should be a big show, they hope for at least 1200 people. I have got to sing in a men's chorus, and then run a gambling table afterwards, needless to say I am not looking forward to it. I go to Lu and Plunks first for dinner. Oh! By the way Den has had a son, of course Bert has not returned yet, she had it at her Mother's place, which was not intended, so much have had quite a good time.

Fancy you earning money, how funny ha! ha! Don't kill anyone will you Darling? I think you are probably right about my letters, it's all rather stupid I suppose, but I think you should know me better than anyone else, and that I am apt to be rather like that, I had known the girl for ages and with a tennis team one rather spends ones time going round with someone, must admit that after a week or two I had rather forgotten about it all, or rather looked on it as rather amusing. I am not at all likely to be serious for some time to come so you see that there must be something about you that keeps me wanting to write, and especially hear from you. You know that as far as writing goes we have rather a better understanding and that if I found that by some unfortunate chance I had really fallen in love, you know I take ages to really convince myself of that fact, I could never stand a mistake, I would write and tell you. After all I think that I have been quieter in the last few years than I have ever been in any 6 years before, so you mustn't mind my breaking away occasionally, its seldom that I do with any real trace of seriousness. Johnnie Mac has not been too well, his tummie has been worrying him, and he has been rather out of sorts, do wish we could get a house for the Aug: bank holiday, feel I would like a couple of days at the sea.

Must be off now, be good and good luck in finding a boy in the RAF!!
With lots of love, Bob

H M S LONDON

My Darling Bun,

Your letter and enclosed arrived with the first mail since we left England! Thank you my sweet. It was the first we'd heard about "the fourteen gold medals and other awards!" Our commander has been promoted to post-captain in addition to his DSO so we've not done too badly. I think he's the youngest captain since Bratty, nothing like knowing the types that count!

Well as usual we've got into most that's going, and have been in action with the Italian fleet already* – we left our mark – but they ran too fast and we never really got to grips. We should have been in on that cruiser that was sunk, but just our luck, the only time we've ever missed going out with the flotilla thro' a defect, they ran into a decent glow like that!

However – perhaps we shouldn't complain taking things bye and bye.

We've been bombed fairly assiduously, but the Ity's go in for "stratosphere" bombing which has its limitations even in these clear skies. But we've taken on POWs and I don't think I'll ever fail to be thrilled by a bomber coming down in flames from 5000' or so. And we've seen one or two at that.

War out here is a surprisingly pleasant, tho' wickedly expensive affair. One goes to sea and probably attacks something – a sub, an aeroplane and even sometimes a surface craft. And return to a remarkably civilised existence ashore – lovely weather, lovely lovelies, lovely parties, in fact lovely relaxation at its best. Tho' leave is a bit curtailed. I'm particularly lucky, because the Pagets, old playmates of mine, are both here. And with them as a corner stone I've swiftly got pleasantly enmeshed – which helps to make our life most bearable. John Little, too comes along and we've enjoyed ourselves a hellava lot – and are not completely broke – but what the hell! - I'm afraid is too often the cry.

I'm so glad you've found your role at the right time Bun – after all nursing in one form or another you can do better than a man – I seem to remember saying that before – I believe I've answered this letter before too – never mind.

Nobody but the Pet can work out her salvation unfortunately, but the darling has had a pretty rough deal so far.

I was most interested in what you said about Papa – knowing them both and loving them both equally much. All I can say is God knows why they married. For both are absolutely top witches in their way – and yet candidly both equally "bloody" in other ways if you get me.
Love to you all.

Tony

*9th July 1940 Battle of Calabria – east of Punto Stilo – first engagement for our Mediterranean Fleet` – result indecisive.

Bun Darling.

It's taken a good deal longer to get the second letter off than I thought it would, but even that interval hasn't cleared things up much. We may as well get what facts there are squared off. I hope to be home on Sunday 25th of this month for ten days, and you just don't know how good that sounds.

The present complication is that sometime pretty soon I am being sent on a tour round some establishments, which embraces most districts of England and will take about a week. Quite when, no one seems to know, so I'm all for planning to get over and see you after working hours on Monday 26th. If that comes off, we can talk about the rest then, but I hope you can get a whole day off that week and an evening, (it will have to be the following Monday, I suppose) for a quiet night in town. Nothing like telling you what to do is there?

I have to agree with you that one becomes rather time unconscious at present. I definitely am, but I find I'm very definitely conscious of the length of time since I last heard from you. I hope you are all right, and not finally certified as insane or doing "time" for burglary. It is ridiculous to think that for more than six months we both know practically every movement that the other made although we were wandering about all over the place, and now we are really very much out of touch.

Either way you look at it, those six months were well worth having. May they come again.

I hear that most of the bottle parties have been closed up by the dumb constabulary, though the various reports were rather conflicting as to how many and which of them. Have you been gadding about the Metropolis lately? I don't suppose London will ever be dull, no matter what the Purity League, the Dumb Friends or any other dumb group do. This is 100% opposite to Plymouth, which, believe me, will always be dull, drab and generally disgusting.

Unfortunately, it is rather difficult to telephone you, as the only time you are in – or I have the time, for that matter – is in the evening and as soon as the Air Raid Warning comes into operation, all private calls are washed out. But if I don't hear from you jolly soon, I'll ring up at the most inconvenient hour for the Air Raids, and that will probably be 5 a.m. and a most inconvenient hour for you, my child: so, dear Flubbily, just go into a quiet corner and write me a nice letter.

This is a quiet Wednesday afternoon and I am only stand-by duty, but I've already been interrupted four times, and I loathe having my letters broken into, especially to you, and I'm going to miss this post, and I'm going to stop before I do. At any rate, at long last I can say, I hope to see you soon, Flubbily; I'm afraid to commit to paper a lot of the other things, in these days of censors, but if you think a little, you can probably figure them out. In any case, they'll sound better than they look, so simply

À bientôt, Bun.
Lots of love from Attie

Upton
August 16th

My Darling Bunny,

Many thanks for your letter which I got soon after I had posted yours, as a matter of fact I have the idea that I did not put on 'Air Mail' and I wonder how it eventually got to you. Your last letter took about 18-20 days not sure if it wasn't in the P. Box the afternoon before I got it.

You seem to be getting a very famous nurse, when do you stop emptying bed pans? Sorry Darling.

There isn't much to tell, have had to get a new racquet which I think has improved my tennis a little, have been playing quite a bit between the rains. Except for flicks, and they are only on Saturdays, have been staying strictly at home, thus have only a little harmless necking while depositing a girl home.

Looks as though I will be putting on a show towards the end of the year for local charities, they want help now, as most things are for the war, so I hope to put on a straight play about December. There are a couple of weddings coming off quite soon, have got to get busy about the one I'm to be best man at.

On Sunday I'm going down to Sister's for the day, think Den will be down for a while, the first time out since the arrival of her son. Bert arrived back a couple of days after the happy event – she had a very good time.

The Old Man is being allowed down three times a week for a few hours, makes a great change for him and don't see that it can do any harm. John is getting on nicely and feels fine now the finger is beginning to get better, he will lose the end joint, but still except for picking his ear he won't miss that much.

Well Darling, must close now.
With lots of love. Bob

POB 26 12th September 1940

My Darling Bunny,

I know you will be cursing me, but I have been rather busy lately in the office, and have been far too gay for my liking. I think it is because of Helen's wedding. I have been out almost every evening to some place or other to dine, or bridge or a flick. Nothing at all formal, but still it's sitting up late, and I've got so used to going to bed early I can't take it. We have been having lots of rain, so not much tennis, except the last few days, so I've been making up for it then.

There are a few people coming out here every month to stay for the continuation of the war. Oh! By the way there is a movement on for a battalion for the East, I have passed the doctors tests and given in my name, now have to wait till they start lectures, for with 'Cert A' we will get a commission after a few months lectures, so may be off early next year. So far have not had any news of when we begin, but they have to wait to get the Governor's permission I believe. Lyall Sealy and I are in for that, Johnnie Manning has made arrangements for the RAF rather a bad time if he has to go now as Audie is going to have a baby in Jan I believe – Bruce her brother is acting Staff Officer, and has just got engaged to a nurse at the hospital.

Kitty has not been too fit, she has as usual been doing too much – you know how she loves bossing everything. As to John, I really can't make him out; at times I wonder if he is right in the head!!

Things seem to be moving now, and Churchill seems to think they will try an invasion soon, cant think they will be mad enough to do it, hope they shoot the whole bloody lot of them. Anyway by the time you get this it should be all over as they will probably wait for the moon. God, what a pity one of our lads couldn't drop a bomb on that b- Hitler.

How's the nursing going, by now you must be a highly experienced nurse, don't go and forget to move a bed pan!!!

Darling must close now, hope to hear soon.

With lots of love, Bob

HMS Hyperion
c/o G PO
26th September 1940

My Darling Bun,

So you're a sweet little nurse now – don't be rash with your patients my dear! One does hear such dreadful stories of these libidinous soldiers. Now take a seafaring man like myself: perfectly simple in my tastes, never in the least exacting to anyone, and so clean about the sty – why can't you come out and nurse me?

Anyway it's not "come to Alexandra *[crossed out ? by censors]* and forget the war" but "come and enjoy the war"! In fact, but for a certain amount of hard work, I'd feel a bit of a worm, hearing of all your blasting at home.

For all that – we have been in action once or twice – and one time – Oh my dear, you must have heard – my poor Hostile was sunk! However, I joined this vessel the other day, and paid it all back, by strafing the Italian army at night. Most exhilarating, we went pretty close in, and started some fires "gigantesque" which could be seen after we'd pushed off at a distance of about 30 miles. A petrol or ammunition dump blew up with a lovely glow – I'm afraid I rather hope that a few yellow bellies got singed as well.

Just previously we called at a small place close to the lines and were inundated by soldiers, who proceeded to wallow in our one bath, and consume vast quantities of iced beer!! Most of them were Coldstreams – I'd met some before at our base – all immaculate and some "very precious" too. So it was fun seeing 'em all warlike and grimy. That place was bombed regularly every day, and they'd been there two weeks poor devils. But considered highly desirable compared with this guerrilla war far in front with 4 to 1 against them.

One time a column of tanks got all but round their rear, however they just managed to get clear with fifteen minutes in hand.

This Dakar business seems rather bad – it's so difficult to know what to think of the French. I suppose with them it's just who happens to be in port at the time.

I lost all my gear including military pass etc. so have had to have my photo taken – as I have a few left and there's no great demand!! I'll send you one of a very gallant but overworked sailor!

There is a rather nice Greek girl here – daughter of the Consul. Elle s'appelle Nicholle – you'd like her I think – I do. Love to you all. Tony

Bun dear. I'm sorry to have been so long in sending you a line. Your first either was a good one - probably better than you thought; and I don't much want to answer it in the odd moment. However, the more-than-odd moment doesn't seem to be with us any longer, and in any case, I should have dropped you a line long before now.

Your letter told me a lot of things and so many of them are worth talking about, but really, now that it's all sorted out, when one comes to write it down, there is nothing to say; except perhaps, that I still think it's a pity.

You know, I've known quite a lot of people in a simple way, some better than others, and I've never regretted either knowing them, or not knowing them better. But there is one thing I regret and, I guess, always will regret, and that is that marriage and my first 'Grande Passion' didn't coincide.

Even if that just isn't 100%, and one wouldn't change it for the real one that comes along later, it seems an awful pity that it couldn't be made to last. Things are so new and terrible too, I suppose, that afterwards, the feelings have to be very deep and sure to achieve anything like the same heights.

Now I wouldn't know how you stand with regard to all that, for while you didn't surprise in your letter with regard to me, I don't in the least mind saying that you did surprise me with regard to Bob. Maybe there is a connection, and if so I hope it works out as well for you as I would have like it to do for me. If it doesn't – well, - if all you are prepared to think of at the minute is the finishing of this war, it is liable to be a long time before you find out the answer. I know I'd like something else to help through that question time, so if you think you have the answer, I shouldn't threw it away, lady.

Personally I don't worry much about finishing this war, for we don't live for the victory in war. We live for the ideals which victory will allow us to maintain, and I rather fear that the maintenance is going to be just as difficult to ensure after the war, as victory is during it.

It appears we differ on one or two points, Bun, but that's not a bad thing and really, none of this has anything very much to do with the fun we have, and personally, I'm in favour of more of it.

I'm hoping to get a week-end (mirabile dictum wonderful to hear) in a couple of week's time (too late for your birthday, I'm afraid, but not too late to want to see you). The dates – if uncancelled – I will let you know and I hope you aren't night duty every night.   News from here is at the same time enormous and non-existent, for most of it didn't ought to be talked about, much less wrote about.

I'm now duty four or five nights out of seven (in addition to the normal jobs) and if the present circumstances conspire much further, I shall finish up by running an immoral establishment in Plymouth (of all places!)

The raids are really quite reasonable, although a little one-sided, for we take a good deal more notice of the Huns then they seem to do of us. However, the damage is practically nil despite one quite serious day-light attempt which produced twenty minutes good solid entertainment (I always did have a sneaking preference for the Dress Circle rather than the Stalls). Definitely quiet by comparison with the Home Counties.

Well, à bientôt, Bun dear. Because you're a woman, I should say "Best Wishes" and "I'll see you sometime", but because you're Funny Face, I guess I can say "I'll see you soon".

Take care of yourself, lady. Lots of love from Attie.

Upton
11th October 1940

My Darling Bunny,

Ever so many thanks for your last two letters, the last one arrived yesterday. You people seem to have got quite used to the bombing, must say it is quite impossible for us to picture it, as to the various stable landmarks in the West End and City being hit, it is too vile to think of.

No, we have never received any Edinburgh rock, probably eaten by the censors!! Hope they don't read that one.

Helen's wedding was a great show, and I was lucky in having Essie as chief bridesmaid, so naturally I made a good speech as I could have a crack at her with her T'dad boy friend whom she always says he does not have anything to do with, afterwards there was some necking to report, but after all that's what people will do with fizz!!

Mollie and Julian dined at Upton last night and we played bridge - it was Grannie's 71st birthday too. I gave Mollie your love, they are busy building a new house, his father has retired from their group of estates, and so Julian has moved from Norwood and looks after the family group now, quite a good job I should think.

Mummie has been playing tennis again, but has had some trouble with a sciatica nerve, if she would have out a few teeth all would be well.

Will continue here [new page] as it must be difficult to read on the back.

This business of training entails three nights a week, then exams, and of course practical stuff as well. No Johnnie Mc is not in it, for one thing he hasn't got Cert 'A' and its officers they want, then they are not accepting even C 'A' entries over 30 years old. As far as going to Europe or England, I don't think I would be passed for service in probable trenches in Europe, for with my passed illness with kidneys they would be likely to have effect in cold and wet. This however does not apply in the Carib, at least that's how I got the doctor to pass me here, anyway they want officers so I naturally joined, I still think it unnecessary for untrained men to leave here and go to England. Johnnie Manning has heard that he has passed his medical for the RAF so now waits to see where they will send him.

Darling, I must close now, you will have had a letter from Gran and Mummie, which probably arrived before your birthday, this may be a little late, anyway Darling, Many Happy returns of the day and here's hoping that the next one will be under better conditions. There is a little parcel on its way; goodness knows when you will get it.

With lots of love, Bob

HMS Hyperion
12th October 1940

My Darling Bun,

How very sweet of you to send that cable, of course I should have sent it straight back really! But as it did come in so remarkably useful, all my pay papers having gone down, and red tape being what it is, I hurry on and appreciated it to the full. One day when next we meet, you shall have it all back in a "Gynormous party". Thank you my sweet.

Every now and then you are everything one likes! But only every now and then of course!

Amusing, I had a letter from Father the other day, after he had seen something of you and 'wee Janie'. As you know we have much in common, and I have always been quite definite in my thoughts that you were not so bad. All he would ever say was – "No! No! Tony, just another one of those bloody Wests!" To which I would reply "You're perfectly entitled to your own opinion!" However, whether you were diplomatic or as I suspect, just bloody. He took it, and now the old boy agrees with me.

I am in this job pro tem, while the 1st Lieutenant proper has his guts removed. And I hope I shall stay, as they are a nice lot, and we have taken Hardy's *[HMS Hardy]* place as Leader of the flotilla. Luckily Captain D dislikes my predecessor – so perhaps I shall.

We've had quite a lot of fun lately, as the Fleet has been unenforced. The other day we bombarded some of Graziani's little efforts from about a mile off at night. Caught 'em properly, and after we'd left at speed, we could still see the blaze an hour and a half after! *[Rodolfo Graziani, 1st Marquis of Neghelli an officer in the Italian Army who, during Mussilini's dictatorship, led military expeditions in Africa during the war]*

Today we have just accounted for a destroyer and some torpedo-boats, but Hyperion did not actually take part. However we had the satisfaction of seeing the destroyer blow up – a big bang and smoke belched up to about 6000'.

Sheena's *[Tony's sister and lived well into her 90's]* letters show her in much better heart than when I left England, which is most good – for she was being low when I saw her last poor pet.

You people at home do give us a bit of a kick the way things are coming up to scratch – as one always knew they would – Here goes Air alarm!

Later.

Now that there's more cloud about, the Italians come a bit lower and perhaps there are some Huns amongst 'em! Anyway touch wood the thirty or so bombs they've just dropped all chose the water! And the fleet can now put up quite a decent barrage.

I think the Yanks will be in before February, and possibly before Christmas too. But life down here will liven up considerably now that they're driving for Syria – Honestly these bloody Frogs do give me piles or I should say "haemorrhoids" when speaking to "ma jeune fille"!

No more now Bun, love to them all with you. And "tüsan täks" for your most sweet cable, which I appreciated more than a little – you will have to wait for our party – but it will be a PARTY. S'long m'sweet. Tony

Upton
30th October

My Darling Bunny,

Thanks so much for your letter received last week, London sounds very gay, in spite of no lights!! We have just received an Air Mail letter from the family and they say that the Bowrings are not coming with them in the Costa Rica, a pity; it would have been much nicer to have known some people on board.

Well, I had a lovely time at Bathsheba and got nicely burned, I would liked to have a week of it. Mummie is a little better, although I think she is doing too much, and of course gets very tired. As soon as Gran comes it will be much better as then she won't have so much to do.

Things go on with increasing monotony, and even bridge has gone back on me with my holding terribly bad hands. With the rehearsals I only go to a flick once a week, that being on Saturday – last Sat: was the opening of the Morgan Club. They are in a new place just been built above John's overlooking Rockley Golf Club. They say it is much nicer than the last, I suppose they mean that it has more room for dancing.

Darling there is very little to write about, Oh! By the way don't send me any Xmas presents this year, think it better not to give presents this year.

By the way Sister was very pleased to get your letter which she got last week. Good night my Darling, take care of yourself.

With all my love, Bob.

Newspaper cuttings of the Loss of HMS Hyperion after she struck a mine on the 22nd Dec 1940

DESTROYER LOST

Times 22/1/41

SUNK BY OUR FORCES AFTER BEING DAMAGED

The Board of Admiralty regrets to announce that H.M. destroyer HYPERION (Commander H. St. L. Nicholson, D.S.O., R.N.) has been lost. H.M.S. Hyperion sustained damage by torpedo or mine which rendered her incapable of steaming, and she had subsequently to be sunk by our Forces.

The next of kin of casualties have been informed.

HOW CRIPPLED HYPERION WENT DOWN

Escort Duty in Enemy Waters

SACRIFICES FOR SECRECY

Alexandria, Friday.—The brief Admiralty announcement a few days ago of the loss of H.M.S. Hyperion through an enemy mine or torpedo—the price we have to pay from time to time for the safe passage of our convoys—conveys to the world only the news of the loss of a destroyer in the fulfilment of her duty.

But behind that brief announcement there is a story worthy of the highest traditions of the British Navy—the story of how a small destroyer, protected by one other destroyer, lay crippled in the sea almost under the very guns of the Italians for nearly two hours before the call for assistance was sent out, in order that the operation on which she was employed should not be detected. Finally, responding to the call, three destroyers rushed to the rescue of her crew and, working against time, made good their getaway from under the lee of powerfully-fortified enemy territory.

The destroyer formed part of the light forces which, sweeping the Adriatic as far as Durazzo three nights previously, were detailed to carry out a sweep some miles ahead in order to deal with any E-boats or submarines which might appear.

Our sweep proved uneventful, and eventually turning back for home, almost two hours afterwards we did not know for some two and a quarter hours afterwards that an hour after passing us. The Hyperion, investigating the possible presence of a submarine, had struck a mine and was badly holed aft.

A QUICK DECISION

It was essential, however, that the main forces should proceed unmolested as they were still within easy range of E-boats. One destroyer was detached as protection, and not until these main forces were well clear of any harm was the wireless signal sent out recalling us to her assistance.

While we were going all out to reach the scene of the disaster the protecting destroyer came alongside her crippled companion, transferred the casualties together with some of the officers and crew, and endeavoured to tow her. The effort was at first successful, but unfortunately the tow-rope later parted,

and it was thus we found the Hyperion with cabins and wardroom flooded, motionless on the water, with the attendant destroyer looming a cable's length away.

Our captain had to make a quick decision. His small destroyer force was in a vulnerable position, with only two more hours of darkness in which to get clear. In the circumstances the idea of towing had to be rejected, and, calling the signalman, the captain said: 'Prepare to abandon ship.'

Slowly, in eerie silence, we were skilfully manoeuvred alongside the stricken ship while other destroyers formed a slow-circling screen. Although her after-deck was awash, the smooth sea enabled the men with the utmost calm and discipline to clamber over the sides.

HER GAPING WOUND

We then withdrew a short distance, and the signal was given to one of the circling destroyers to sink her. Nobody spoke a word as we stood on the bridge waiting for the end, together with some of the Hyperion's officers. There followed a flash from the torpedo tubes a few seconds pause, then as torpedo tubes, a few seconds pause, then a deep, muffled explosion.

The shock of the explosion broke off the after funnel, a column of water and smoke shot skywards from amidships, and the Hyperion slowly rolled over. There were no flames or smoke gently she sank, and one of her officers quietly remarked, 'How gracefully she goes down! She was a graceful ship.' It was a moment of great sadness.

As the ship heeled over, her gaping wound could be seen. Then only the keel was visible as she gradually disappeared from view. When we thought she had gone for good, her bows suddenly broke surface and she remained thus perpendicular for some minutes, presumably owing to an air pocket, before the waters finally closed over her.

Again, as was the case in the Adriatic, we were at no time attacked by any enemy from the air or by seacraft, and it seems incredible that, with excellent visibility, the exchange of incredible flashing signals, and the burning of a floating flare, we were allowed to pass close to the enemy coast no less than four times that night.—Press Association.

THE HOME GUARD	GAELIC ON THE RADIO
Every Battalion May Have a	

LOSS OF THE HYPERION

A DUTY FULFILLED

MINE STRUCK IN THE ADRIATIC

The brief Admiralty announcement of the loss of H.M.S. Hyperion through an enemy mine or torpedo—the price we have to pay from time to time for the safe passage of our convoys—conveys to the world only the news of the loss of a destroyer in the fulfilment of her duty (says a Reuter message from Alexandria).

But behind that brief announcement there is the story of how a small destroyer, protected by one other destroyer, lay crippled in the sea almost under the very guns of the Italians for nearly two hours before the call for assistance was sent out, in order that the operation on which she was employed should not be detected.

Finally, responding to the call, three destroyers rushed to the rescue of her crew and, working against time, made good their getaway from under the lee of powerfully fortified enemy territory.

The destroyer formed part of the light forces which, sweeping the Adriatic as far as Durazzo three nights previously, were detailed to carry out a sweep some miles ahead in order to deal with any E-boats or submarines which might appear.

Our sweep proved uneventful (says Reuter's correspondent), and eventually, turning back for home, we did not know that one of the escort had struck a mine half an hour after passing us. The Hyperion, investigating the possible presence of a submarine, had struck a mine and was badly holed aft.

It was essential, however, that the main forces should proceed unmolested, as they were still within easy range of E-boats. One destroyer was detached as protection, and not until these main forces were well clear of any harm was the wireless signal sent out recalling us to her assistance.

TOWING ATTEMPTED

While we were going all out to reach the scene of the disaster the protecting destroyer came alongside her crippled companion, transferred the casualties, together with some of the officers and crew, and endeavoured to tow her. The effort was at first successful, but unfortunately the tow-rope later parted, and it was thus we found the Hyperion, with cabins and wardroom flooded, motionless on the water, with the attendant destroyer looming a cable's length away.

Our captain had to make a quick decision: his small destroyer force was in a vulnerable position, with only two more hours of darkness in which to get clear. In the circumstances the idea of towing had to be rejected, and, calling the signalman, the captain said: 'Send this to Hyperion: "Prepare to abandon ship: I am going to sink you."'

Slowly, in eerie silence, we were skilfully manoeuvred alongside the stricken ship while other destroyers formed a slow circling screen. Although her after-deck was awash, the smooth sea enabled the men with the utmost calm and discipline to clamber over the sides. We then withdrew a short distance, and the signal was given to one of the circling destroyers to sink her. There followed a flash from the torpedo tubes, a few seconds' pause, then a deep, muffled explosion. The shock of the explosion broke off the after funnel, a column of water and smoke shot skywards from amidships, and the Hyperion slowly rolled over. There were no flames or smoke—very gently she sank—and one of her officers quietly remarked, 'How gracefully she goes down! She was a graceful ship.'

Again, as was the case in the Adriatic, we were at no time attacked by any enemy from the air or by sea-craft, and it seems incredible that, with excellent visibility, the exchange of

---

HMS Medway c/o GPO

17th January 1941

My Darling Bun,

Before I start – this will be a bad letter! For I'm in a state of flux – "neither on my – or my elbow" if you get me.

First they said I should be sent home, then to another destroyer out here – and now God knows, and he won't be definite either! At present I am at the base still with the Hyperions – they are all transferring shortly to another boat, which has already got a 1st Lt. and anyway it is the same type of ship so I'm glad I'm not going. I insisted on ten days leave this time, and spent a very pleasant time with the Pagets. They live on top of a golf course, so I took it up seriously – at last. And I'm quite keen for the moment – and probably will continue to be. For it's essentially a game for the middle-aged – and 'pon my soul Bun, I'm nearly there.

It's regrettable, but every now and then I get very angry with those of my companions with whom I don't exactly agree. Perhaps it is that since the Hostile when I had some very good friends, I have lived very much on the surface in the Hyperion. And altho' very pleasant chaps I've never really felt I was one of them.

Well – things have never yet failed to turn out for the best – so I "maun bide a wee" in what little patience I can.

I've just received yours of 10/10 and 5/11. Yes. You were wise to go into nursing, I find "madschën in uniform" are all very well but – and it's a fairly large but.

22nd June, 1941 Germany attacks the Soviet Union. 7th December, 1941 USA enter World War II after the attack on Pearl Harbor. Britain declares war on Japan. No Wimbledon.

I'm afraid Mary has gone off recently she completely lacks charm of manner, actually I think her home life has done that in. Altho', I can never remember her having had much. Far too material. Of course I know you are just as material really Bun – but you hide it so cleverly m'dear!!

Funny you thought you had a cold, for a fiver of I'd come home in Aug. The fact is I'm going broody! And obtain little amusement in gadding about with any Jill nowadays – I suppose it's as it should be, but I've met so dammed few I'd feel like "teaming-up" with. But then of course I've not met many widows!!

Thanks again for your cheque (in the letter of 10/10) Yes the Admiralty do pay – but when? I've not received a brass farthing on my Sept. claims yet! Oh, and I nearly forgot "the Lady with the lamp" she is sweet, and adored by me until I'm sunk next time.

Well my letter started with a moan, so I'd better finish with some better line. Sorry can't think of any.

Best love to you Bun and a drop for Wee Janie and the Wicked.

Tony

In early 1941 Tony was posted to HMS Nile, the naval headquarters in Alexandria, Egypt.

The Clydesdale Hotel, Lanark
[Undated]

My Darling Bun,

Well at last I have managed to put pen to paper to write and thank you most awfully darling for the cigars I smoked the last one tonight – they were excellent.

There is a firm who I know make our brooches, so I will write and ask them what I can obtain one for, as soon as I can find their address.

Well as you see we are back here again – we moved from Haddington about a month ago back here and now we are awaiting our orders for the land of goodness knows where ?!

As you seem to have heard of my movements lately I can only say that I am very happy and enjoying life as much as one can in this B-awful war. Muriel only lives 30 miles away so I am able to see quite a lot of her.

Last fortnight I went on a cooking course near Edinburgh and stayed at the Caledonian Hotel. Muriel stayed with her mother and we had two marvellous evenings. Tomorrow I am going over to see her she has been in bed with flu this last week.

The week after next I am going on leave for five days. I hope she is coming to Lanton. *[Lanton Tower home to Frank and Lil Fasson's, Jim and Tony's parents.]*

Old Tony must have 7 lives. I wish he would come home as I should like to see him before we go off.

Do write to me as I love getting your letters even though it takes me two months to reply.

The farm is not in too healthy a state just now. I am trying to get a manager for it as it is too much for Dad now with all his other work.

I hope you are not being too hard worked and are able to have a party occasionally.

No more just now, with my very best darling. Jim.

Written on a scrap of paper

Dated April 3rd 1941

My Darling Bun, Here I am on my way to the sunny climes where your grandfather used to live. *[Bombay – James Blair was a banker in Bombay]* This letter will be short as it is only to give you my address so that you can write to me. Capt. J. C. H. Fasson, 155th(LY) Field Regiment RA, c/o Army Post Office No 990. At the moment of writing this we are just getting to the hot weather and we are about to make our first call.

I will write again next week and tell you all the news. I must get this posted now as if I don't I will not get one from you for ages unless I do, as it will take about 3 months – but may be quicker by air mail.

I have found out that you can get a silver broach quite nice ... for a very small sum from Wilson and Sharp. Jewellers Princes Street Edinburgh:

No more darling just now. Look after yourself. I will write soon. With my very best love. Jim.

Captain James Fasson

Upton 21st June 1941
posted to Mare Cottage, forwarded on to Thorpeness
and then Green Park Hotel, Pitlochry

My Darling Bunny,

What a hectic couple of weeks I've had!! Afraid I've been guilty of lots of necking, you see an old flame of mine arrived up with the tennis team and so the trouble started. She is an awfully nice person and as the team knew our past affairs they soon began by giving us hell. It was suggested by a friend of mine in a speech for the men of the T'dad team that they thought I would be making a speech to announce intentions of keeping their lady champion up here. I had to deny my engagement several times in the next few days. Anyway, she is safely back in T'dad now and I'm living a very quiet life.

We of course lost the tennis they had a very good side, and we lost Mrs Douglas in the first match with a torn muscle, bad luck as she and Dr Sheet would obviously have won their matches.

Johnnie Mc captained the side and played grand tennis. He of course takes it all too seriously with all the organising and has been in bed ever since they left with flu. We gave him hell about a girl that came up, supposed to be keen on their captain, but who ended up been very attached to Johnnie.

Thanks awfully for your letter, Mummie begs to thank you for hers, she will be writing soon. Hope you have quite got over your bad throat. What about moving suppose you will have moved from the north, any way you should have by now. The news one gets is all so muddling and depressing. The Americans seem to get so much more bad information than anywhere else.

There are a few good flicks coming, I haven't been to one for over three weeks. Mummie has gone to one with Doll tonight.

The Old Man has been made to stay upstairs for a month or so, not his old trouble, it's his heart this time. Apparently if he doesn't keep quiet and let whatever it is (Aorta) go back to normal size he will get one of these heart diseases. Don't think even Grannie knows this so don't say anything except that he is being made to rest for his heart.

Can't think of any more news, should get a letter from you soon haven't heard for ages, suppose you have been gadding around with the naval friend!!

With lots of love, Yours Bob

Lanton Tower, Jedburgh, Roxburghshire
Jedburgh 116
Friday – no date no year?

Did I not thank you for your quite excellent book?

Bun Dear,

How are you my sweet? Well here we are again. Very much the same – but no thinner! I'm waiting for the Admiralty's reply to the announcement of return. This should come tomorrow or Monday. After that we will make plans. I hope to get about three weeks leave before my next job.

All are well here – especially the Pet who flourishes despite her patient. Wasn't it amazing luck meeting James at the Cape? Most efficient and military the old man was too.

He'll have a damn good time in India. Polo and what not. I feared they might be directed to Iraq – which will not be a picnic.

Some love not much to spare after ten days in Durban. I'll write you again. Tony

Bunny's mother moved up to Scotland to be close to her daughter Lilias as Thorpeness was evacuated for army training. The Mare Cottage in Bovingdon was rented out to very old family friends, the Langton family, and Bunny lived there with them, while her father lived at The Dolphin, Suffolk as he was managing the Thorpeness Estate, having retired from Bull and Bull Solicitors.

Pine Trees Hotel, Pitlochry
Monday 28th July 1941

My Belovedest,

Got your letter this afternoon. I am so sorry you are worried and a bit depressed love over this affair. A bit of lightening touch about it. Quite romantic as Tony would say. Don't put him off entirely darling. You never know he may be your fate, very sudden and unexpected (like your Ma's Irish lad) but as to marriage ah ner-no-naught away. You must know him longer and also he is on a terribly dangerous job. Bunny dear, one must admire the lad and he is probably very, very nice. You must not push everyone away from you. I didn't think you would ever really be happy with Bob, what you have told me of him or would you live far from London and be happy. I think you should put him more in the background or he is going to spoil you for some fine lad over here. If he is at all like Attie in nature, he is a fine chap, but must have the finest guts remember to be what he is. I only wish I could talk to this lad. You must marry a he man too to carry you away but not till you know John a wee bit better. Where is his own home, what his prospects are etc. I live romance myself and got a real man (Charlie) against everyone, but didn't look for an ideal man and miss the mark. There never was a perfect man Bunny. You have to take all the good points against the few bad ones. So, this lad more or less a gentleman nice manners hands etc. For of course he must have lively steady blue eyes!!!

Attie is right about you. Someone must overcome you. I once told Attie this myself. Break down your reserve my sweetest!! Still I don't want you to miss the best man or marry the wrong one. How tall is this lad? I'd love to hear it all and will keep quiet. It would be lovely to have a diamond flying broach darling and join on his DFC! Anyway, don't ye laugh! I fear Thorpe did get it, as I had a wire last night saying "We are all well writing". I fear those Huns are coming over again. I do think Lily will now remain, anyway until end of September. That bloke James won't write when she wants him to about schools and Lily has had a splendid letter from the line school. Patricia only was at Nairn the weekend as they hated the place and came back here on Monday. June is never in now! Malansky turned up at 9.30 Saturday night and they danced. Then he slept on the sofa in the kitchen after 4o'c! They went off bathing and lunch picnic yesterday. I helped them away while Auntie was at Church, she lunched with Ada and came to dinner with me. Auntie liked Malansky very much. He really is .... I wish Lily could marry him!!! He adores Jill. I've been to tea round there, they were going to a film tonight, Tom Browns School Days. June and Jill too. Mrs Adams has also had a mail from Barbados and Trinidad, very happy though.

I do hope "John" back proves to be the last straw perhaps. What an escape darling. Your photo may have brought him luck. Isn't it a queer world my darling and things go so fast now. All my love sweetest. I wish I could help you. Send me a photo of John. Your loving and understanding Mum.

Your patients must be like bombs in the night! Lily has a tea party tomorrow – I'm coming.

Your Jam will be lovely. Frank has sent off for more butter. Very good.

Unfranked letter card ? 25th September 1941
Thursday

My Darling, only just a line to say I hope you have good news of John from Iceland. He and you have been so much in my thoughts. I'm in bed since Saturday evening. When I ought to have gone down to dinner I felt awful so lumbered into bed when I found I had a temp 100. Rang for Dr Newton. I ached all over to my finger tips so had to give up. Do you remember on the phone I was croaky. A germ there I think. I have still a heavy chest and feel very weak and shaky. Temp down to 99 this morning but it goes up at night. Old Newton is kind and comes in each evening to see how I am and even asked if I would like a nurse in first to wash me down. Not I! This is a brighter day so I'll be better presently so don't worry only I just have no energy to write or even to read. All love my sweetest. Mum

2 ladies most kind and get me anything.

I ... so don't worry love.

Beloved, I'm not very fit, some streptococcus germ got me. Temp keeps around 100. I'm very weak I accept just can't get up nasty cough and pain down my side (not lungs Newton says). He has just been in and says he must get the nurse in to tidy me up tomorrow morning and evening. His partner is coming to call, one Dr Hayes, as he has to get his teeth seen to in Edinburgh. If I am not better tomorrow he says he must see if you could get off for a week or 2. He was going to phone Dad I said don't yet till I'm better. Can't eat a thing, drink gallons! Hope to hear of John's safe arrival home. So sorry to worry you. Had ... but I have been very ill last 2 days. All love. Mum

Only two days after writing this card Bunny's mother dies on Thursday 2nd October 1941, at The Pine Trees Hotel, Pitlochry, Scotland. Bunny and her father had to take a train to Pitlochry.

Royal Naval Engineering College
"Manadon" Crownhill, Plymouth,
Telephone Plymouth 71783
Saturday (4th October)

Bun dear,

With people who mean as much to me as you do, I'm not a conventional person. There isn't any need to tell you that really, but believe it especially when I tell you how sad I was at receiving the news of your Mother's death.

I am sorry because it was Ma West to me and it is your Mother – really sorry. But there must be a lot of people to tell you that and, for all I know, to feel it far more intensely than I. For that, all I can say is that I find real sorrow or real joy a little hard to feel these days, but I know them the better for that.

There is another something special to me however, which I feel you might like to know.

Before this war made chaos of the hopes and plans of this world, there was a fortnight at Thorpe. Of course, I had a good time, but I've had other 'good times'. Then too, you were there, which meant something special. But there was more to it than that. The essential thing about it was a sort of unity, a centre composed of the three of you as a body, not so much as individuals, and really quite independent of circumstances within or without. I was given something special that none of you may have appreciated, and not least by Ma West. It has become for me a reality, a sort of picture which I don't suppose anyone but an 'outsider' could see, and I was made to feel it as well.

In all the instability and uncertainty of today, that picture remains as a guide to ideals, hopes of what can be. It would not be there but for Ma West.

Bun, I'm finding it very hard to explain in black and white. You know that I'm sorry for your sorrow, but what I did want you to know also, was something that is personal to me, and that there is a reality which remains for me.

It probably sounds terrible. I hope not, Bun, but if it does, just think that your Mother helped to give me something that will influence me all my life.   Attie

HMS King Alfred
(Naval Establishments, Lancing)
Shoreham-by Sea, Sussex.

6th October, 1941

My Darling Bun,

Poor "wee Janie" the dear thing. I will not give vent to a lot of sentimental rot – but I shall miss her a lot, more than a lot. But after all – if we believe in what we preferred to believe in, she is even now much happier than ever before. And we shall all meet again – sooner than anyone can tell maybe.

Now my sweet – do you not think it might not be a bad plan to go up to Lanton for a week? It's so different and peaceful there and I know they'd love to have you for as long as you'd care. I do think perhaps a complete change of atmosphere at this psychological moment will help you unbelievably.

My prayers will be towards "strength for the Bun" bless her heart. Good luck and God bless my sweet. To.

I could come up and see you October 25th if it would help.

Reedlands, Thorpeness, Suffolk
Aldeburgh 290

21st October 1941 *[Bunny's birthday]*

My Darling Rat,

Must send you just a small personal reply to your letter. Have written a formal one to my two daughters. Nothing to bother about with the codicil. We will sort it all out somehow and as long as we all feel we are carrying out Mum's wishes nothing else matters. Its beastly having to deal with anything in a business way but that must be done and thank God we four are all of the same mind.

Thank you my dearest for what you say. I fear you and I are both a little bit oyster like but we do know each other and what we are both going through. The whole world seems so completely empty now but we have each other and that will mean such a lot. At present I simply can't pull myself together but I go about and see people and try to get away from thinking all the time. At times I just feel that I cannot stand it and then I think of you and the other two.

It's you I am so dreadfully sorry for Rat as at present you are so utterly alone. But you must not think, as you say, that you have only got me. You have many good friends who love you. That and time will help you old lady with your own good pluck.

Don't think anymore than you can possibly help about the "episode". It was nothing more. Just a very nasty piece of dirt you came up against but will have no lasting mark. I fear you are blaming yourself. There is no need of that my dear. Times are not normal and we are not normal ourselves. When you found out the true position you behaved with the good sense, the courage and sense of humour even that I know I can always look for in you. Forget it and try and look forward to the happiness which will come to you one day soon. It shan't be my fault if it doesn't.

Bless you Bunny now and always.

Your very loving Pop.

I may telephone you and probably shall not. There is really nothing to say except that I love you and that you know.

'John' turned out to be very questionable, a wartime military imposter. I think this is what is being referred to as 'the episode'.

A letter from the nurse who was with Bunny's mother when she died.

14 Tomcroy Terrace
Pitlochry
4th December

Dear Miss West,

I am so sorry to be so long in writing to thank you for the very nice gift which you sent. It was very kind of you and I will find it so very useful. Blue is my favourite colour.

I was waiting until I had time to write properly and tell you about your mother's illness and time seemed just to fly as I have been very busy. I am quite sure your mother had no idea she was so ill. In fact, she really wasn't at all bad until the last day. I shall try and tell you well as I can what happened.

On Tuesday evening Dr Newton asked me if I would go along and give her a sponge down and make her bed. Well. She appeared then just to have a chill and feverish cold and was quite apologetic for asking me. She had had a little fish for dinner and she asked me to have a cup of coffee with her. On Wednesday morning she said she'd had a not bad night and although perhaps not quite so well she appeared pretty comfortable, after I had finished with her, she had a cup of tea. She said at first not to come back at night and then she asked if I would mind. She said it would just ensure she would be settled for the night. (She never dreamt that there was anything seriously the matter with her.) When I went at night she appeared much worse though she really didn't realise it, only she had just grapefruit for dinner and felt pretty fagged.

I phoned Doctor when I got home (I didn't tell her I was going to) and he went over to see her. She was worse then and he felt she shouldn't be left alone in an hotel, so I said I'd stay. When Dr Newton took me over she was so anxious about whether I would be comfortable and made them bring in a divan into the room. I didn't use it but it made her more satisfied to think I had somewhere to lie down. She had no pain but was very, very thirsty and whenever she wakened she asked for a drink. Then after a time she wasn't even thirsty. The last thing she said to me was "I'm really very comfortable; I think you should go to bed". It was not long after that that she went into the coma and I'm afraid she didn't regain consciousness.

I asked if she had any friends in Pitlochry that she would like to know, but, she said Oh! No they'd only worry me and I'm not as ill as that. She told me of you all. She was very proud of you all and only wished she had been able to be more use herself. She spoke of you having leave and hoped you would come through Pitlochry to see her in fact she meant to write and ask you. She showed me your photograph and your sister and brother. I know she was as happy in The Pine Trees as she could have been anywhere away from home.

She seemed very fond of the maids and the porter was most obliging. I think she would have been very surprised if we'd suggested sending for any of you and I really feel you should not worry too much about not being there because I think she got a letter from you just that morning and she said it was just the next best thing to having you with her. She said you wrote such nice letters. I think she was longing to see your brother. She said "you know 2 years is a long time but I'm so pleased he is well". She also said she was lucky to have had her married daughter to live here with her and she mustn't be greedy as her first duty was to her husband but most of all I think she was looking forward to seeing Mr West at the end of October.

I think that is all I can tell you about your mother. I wish I had more. I was so sorry things turned out as they did. It was a pleasure for me to nurse Mrs West and I only wish I could have done more.

Thanking you again, very much for the beautiful gift.

Yours sincerely, Dorothy Stewart

HMS King Alfred
(Naval Establishments, Lancing)
Shoreham-by Sea, Sussex.
Monday 15th December 1941

Bun dear,

Despite your lady like reluctance to reveal the price of those tickets – I hereby enclose a cheque, which I trust you will be good enough to cash. Also in memory of a "local encounter" – "the siege of pleasure" might amuse you. Tho' I fear it's a trifle sordid!

The news from James's part is bad, I do hope the old lad comes thro'. But as I said, he may well have marched the apex of his present existence – in which case there is nothing to get fussed over. Well I only hope I shall have the chance of revenge, and that I am good enough to take it, when it appears.

Actually I am most pleased to leave here, for I have been out of the war altogether too long. Exactly a year since Hyperion went down – and what have I done in that year? Spent a lot of "time" and thought I was enjoying myself. But in reality I wasn't. So there is only one way to be happy and content. To live an unselfish life – and that I have not done.

I shall let you know as soon as I hear where I'm off to. My relief arrives today – a man at best as senior as Hugh McLean, and a 6 bottle man to whit.

Bye Bye Bun, and I hope you enjoyed the party despite my refusal to dance!

Best Love,
Tony

SPIRIT OF THE AGE.

Tony was posted to HMS Petard as First Lieutenant in early March 1942

The St. Enoch Hotel, Glasgow
Central 7033-8
17th March

Bun m'dear,

At great personal inconvenience! I rushed over to see Miss Goodenough D.D. WRNS at 8pm last night. The dear girl was in conference until that late hour. But "expanded" visibly when once I got mi hands on her.

She promises nothing, but will gladly see you, if you let her know in advance when you will next be in town. I explained your situation in not being available for some months and merely wishing to get firsthand knowledge of the openings. Lillian of course will say – you get that in your present job. But then the dear thing has a mind nearly as low as him!

But seriously Bun, I think it would be well worth your while seeing Ma Goodenough within the month or so. Address: Sanctuary Building, Great Smith Street, Westminster, Formal title Deputy Director Woman's Royal Naval Service. A driver would be your best job. I think – but what about a Signal Lady? She said they're starting a new branch shortly. Always good to get in on the ground floor.

Well, I've just collected my gear and am off to Edinburgh for the night – then on to Newcastle tomorrow – Spring has got as far North as this and it is most pleasant. Thank you and Lillian more than a little for looking after me so well when I took you by surprise. Have you any petrol left after those numerous but entirely nerve-wracking "racing changes" yesterday morning. I thought I should collapse, after running up those steps with my "couldn't be heavier" suitcase.

Let me know the results of your "fireside-chat" with the Dame. She is quite charming and had, I regret to say, no difficulty in seeing what I was after! "So you think I look kind hearted and sympathetic do you"!

Love. Tony

8 Mann House Road, Jesmond, Newcastle
Undated letter but postmarked 8th April 1942
Monday

Bun dear,

I'm writing this because you seemed a bit low in your last – cheer up my sweet – sentiment or not, you've had a lousy six months. And I do wish I could help you a bit – It's easy to say as I did – "that there's no

room for it" until one loses something, or one might say, "anything", one loves dearly. Then unless one is entirely inhuman, you cannot but be hurt terribly.

But Darling Bun, you must just push on with a heavy heart, and refuse to be got down by it all. And as sure as anything is worthwhile in this world – you're effort will be, and it will, lead you out of the drain but one must have faith. I'm no "bible thumper" but I do know this, Prayer, if sincere, is unbelievably helpful.

I do hope something may come of your talk with Dame Goodenough. Unless I am a very bad judge – she is a most charming and worldly wise lady. And if she does give you any advice – it will be 100% sound. Please give her my regards, and say I didn't think she only looked soft-hearted, but perhaps you'd better not, or she might take it in the wrong way!

Talking of blondes – I think you must realise that when eventually I might meet "the real thing" it's not a thing I shall talk about so "the primitive" must fall into the catalogue of very swift but no more.

Tony on HMS Petard

Ran into James Currie [Bunny's brother in law, married to Lilias] the other evening! What fun we had. A bit alcoholic but a suitable reunion – we toasted "the good old days" once or twice.

Well a little distressed, "Sam Beattie" of the Campbell Town was our CO to be in Petard. A very good type, but they say he's PofW.

God bless Bun, Best love, Tony

Army and Navy Club
Pall Mall, SW1
Monday a/n (no date or envelope)

My Dear Bun,

I got the readdressed telegram. Thanks a lot. – but no London I'm afraid – so our party will have to wait two years; and by that time you'll probably have to wash the "spawn" at party time! However, I'll think of it all to come. Possibly it will help me to bear the sun, the mad dogs and the horse faced women!

I enjoyed the visit, altho' at first in a vile mood, which the weather and general depression did not help – much.

Well "stay sweet as you are", apart from getting married and the things that go with it, so that when I return "lean and war worn" we can have our party.

Yours Tony

HMS Petard
c/o GPO
15th July 1942

Bun darling,

I've been fair barmy and have only written about three letters since leaving N'castle six weeks ago. But now at last one can see daylight – my, my, I've never known what work was until this job hotted up.

That's damnable about the CNR – surely some friend of the "wicked's" could pull some strings, worth going the whole hog of posterior licking I feel.

We've got a very fine lot in the wardroom, not least of whom is a young two-striper who among other things is a member of the Magic Circle – and produces almost anything from the most embarrassing positions of his victim.

I hope to get home for a day before we finally go elsewhere within the next ten days or so – but there's no hope of getting South I'm afraid. You will have heard that the Pet's affair has come to an end. Apparently David has become impossible quite, after his crash and subsequent invalidity from the FAH. Perhaps it's just as well – but he wasn't a bad type of chap.

I enclose a letter from Peter Medd, which will interest you – I'm sure a letter from you would be much appreciated.

They say one may write to James now. We may see him one of these days. How I long for some decent weather – it has drizzled off and on for a month up here. Sheena is with Mary Conan at Forrest Row and reports tropical weather.

Talking of my bank account I suppose I've only spent £1 apart from my mess bill since leaving the yard six weeks ago. So I'm building up for a colossal letdown one of these days.

Best love. Tony

Upton
July 29th 1942

Bunny Darling,

Its ages since I wrote and I have the idea that you haven't been writing so often either. In my case I have been very much bewildered. The truth is that I've fallen rather badly, and of course the girl doesn't seem to really care very much. Apart from that we have gone into production again, so that means rehearsals and lots of learning at home, anyway it keeps me at home in the evenings! I've suddenly realised that all my male friends are married and that here I am, anyway who knows how it will turn out. I seem fated, as when other people are in love with me I can't make up my mind, and now it turned on me.

Life goes on much the same here, we can't go far on bicycles, but we save up gas and get out every now and then. The "Morgan" is the main place for night life, and they are often crowded out, especially on Saturdays.

We have a "good will" cricket tournament on now – T'dad and B'dos. We have closed for the half day so I'm writing this at the B'Town Club before going down. This place is always full of T'dadians and naval people on leave, they pick here to get good bathing and good Rum!!

Grannie has been having some trouble with her eye she is starting cataracts on one of them, I wish they would go up to The Crane for a few weeks, staying at Lorne all the time is not very exciting and they miss their change.

Now please be nice and write soon, remember when you were toying with the idea of your RAF boy I still wrote, as it looks now this girl will not be likely to fall for me.

With lots of love,
Bob.

HMS Petard
c/o GPO
9th August 1942

Bun darling,

Thanks for your letter actually arrived some time ago, but I'm still "fair tremendous with work" as "The Maan" would say. However, one begins to see faint glimmers of light – which incidentally is as well.

Put on my "rescue uniform" yesterday, and sweating hot it is too! Rather amusing we put in at a neutral Port the other day, and lay alongside a jetty under construction by a German firm! C'est la guerre je suppose, mais il est une monde vraiment fone! *[It is the war I suppose, but it is a really funny old world]* "The burst of gutturals" all due to a vin d'honuer of no small dimensions onboard a Neutral destroyer also in Port – quantities of port and maderia were drunk – as their officer of the guard had boarded from a pulling boat. Not to be outdone, the officers inclined our whaler and pulled over to them. Now when it came to pull back "quel dommage"! I was Cox'n and apparently (for here my memory is not good) my orders to the crew consisted of numerous exhortations to them in which the word Bastardos and Bolsheviki featured a good deal. However, breeding will out and I made a perfect come alongside to a faint cheer from one's ship's company. Lining the side, before falling over the tiller, when, I gather, I paused for breath before mounting the gangway as stiff as if reporting to the Admiral!

Chzurtooida! Sheena's well out of her swamp – I learnt a good deal about David and decided it must stop – and so altho' the Pet was very down for a bit, she's a great hearted lass, and with Mary Cowan's assistance seems well on the way to recovery by now.

I'm indeed sorry to hear of the wicked *[Bunny's father]* being so poorly. Poor Old Boy I do hope the summer will help him over. Give my love to him. And yourself my sweet, I do so hope you'll manage the WRNS. Yes – father is a quite remarkable man – at times he could not be kinder. I always feel that if he had married the right woman "for him" he might have done great things.

Did I ever tell you of Paul of Dunbar? Perhaps it's as well that Miss Beryl and I are just friends!   Must stop now. Best love Bun dear.
Tony

Bunny Darling,

Many thanks for your last two letters the last one came in record time – 7 days- Bunny how like you to be sweet and helpful. I don't know how it all happened, I didn't think of falling in love, it just came as rather a shock – she is really very sweet and quite attractive, a little extravagant, so now I will have to be the one to watch the spending, rather funny for me!! We will be announcing our engagement soon, probably about the 19th and hope to get married early next year. Lu and Plunks have been transferred to St Lucia, he will be head there so I have arranged to take over his house, $50°° a month – it's a new one on Pine Hill, you know up there above Belle Ville, you get to it by going right on top of Bishops Court Hill, or past GH from the other side. With the high prices now we will have to live a bit quieter than I do now, of course we are lucky to get all our ground provisions free. Oh! I suddenly realised that you asked if it was Betty Gearwood, yes indeed.

You said you hoped to be out of nursing soon. How are you getting on, I think you should get the family to see what they can do for you, as you are obviously very tired of it. Since your letter about laying up the car, we hear they have stopped all green line buses and cheap day returns - that will be a snag when you get your day off. I do hope Rhoda will have heard from Hugh by now, Mummie is knitting some socks for him and will be getting them over soon we hope – by that opportunity we will try and get off a parcel for you – no more cakes I'm afraid, anyway whatever it is we will send it.

We have been working almost every day, Sundays included, on the new show "Tony draws a Horse". It is on, on the 16-18th – very soon now!

Theo has the German measles, there have been quite a few cases here and there, Johnnie's wife's people have sold their house in T'dad and have come up here to live.

Bunny my dear, I must close now, please write occasionally and I do feel that I have been responsible for making you very unhappy from time to time – it makes me feel very low really. All the very best and I do wish you more than that.

With love, Bob

From Gwen King

I do hope the censors do not open this as I, as a local censor, would curse the fine writing and there is absolutely nothing in it, as I know better than to write anything.

My Darling little girl,

I do not know how I start writing this letter there is so much to say and my feelings are so mixed. Bob told me about Betty last Thursday night and honestly for days I felt perfectly ill -he bowled me so completely over. I knew he was friendly with Betty but he has always been such a butterfly I did not know he was serious this time. Also I suppose I always hoped it would be you, and you know my feelings on the subject. Darling what worries me for one thing is that he is hurting you. I asked him at once if he had told you anything and he said yes. I try to comfort myself that I do not honestly believe you would have like to have lived out here for always, away from your people, and Grannie feels that too. I think what hurt me so terribly was that he had given me no inkling, but Bob does not realise one fraction how often he has hurt me. I suppose I am a fool for being so sensitive and sentimental. Now please do not misunderstand me because as I say my feelings are so mixed. As it is not to be you, I have quite made up my mind to be as nice to her as I possibly can and as I wrote to tell her I hope she and I will be much more to each other than just in-laws. And I shall do my part. She is a very nice child I believe but so young not yet 20. That is what makes me afraid for them. What men can she have known and seen in that time. Unfortunately Bob has not even brought her here at any time but as he says this petrol rationing has really interfered a lot. Anyway I hope soon to get to know her and love her dearly. She lost her Mother nearly 3 years ago now and has had to run her Father's house, so she is very capable and I think has her head screwed on the right way. She is very sweet looking and if she really feels as she wrote to me I know she and I will soon be great friends. As you know I have always wanted Bob to get married but naturally at first, although I am very pleased, it was a bit of a shock and from my selfish point of view it will make such a big difference in my life here, with just the old people, especially with the petrol ration and not being able to get out. Anyhow that is neither here nor there as every Mother has to expect this sooner or later. Of course Bob says none of the present day young people are sentimental, it is old fashioned, anyway Betty wrote me a very sweet letter indeed. As you know he likes to do things in a rush. Lou and Plunks have a very nice house just below the Pine, you turn off by Bishop Court (you remember the top of the hill from town after you turn out of Belle Ville) just 5 mins from there. They are being transferred to St Lucia and before everything was definitely freed up Bob heard this he asked for the refusal. As I tell him it is too large and too big to rent to start with and it means he will have to pay Mary Morte's rent before they are married. Anyway Bob says he rather go the other way as he can use a bike to town from there and it is a nice position except for the soots during the crop. I beg him not to rush things as it is during ones engagement you start to get to know each other. They have not announced it yet, Bob says after the play next week. Molly is supposed to be having a party on 19th and I think they will announce at that. I shall have to try and get a small gee on after he is married otherwise I shall be very dead up. Her people are very old friends of my husband and his family – it is rather funny eh? Anyway, I hope they will be very very happy and that I will still get a daughter who can be spoilt.

And lastly I am nearly finished Hugh's socks in fact I had finished but found I had made one shorter in the foot than the other so I am putting that right now. I shall have to send them c/o you as I do not know Rhoda's address. I do hope she has heard something of him now. Fancy after all these months people we know have just heard from their son in Hong Kong. He is a Dr. there and his wife (a scotch woman) was a trained nurse so refused to be evacuated. He does not even know if one is dead or alive. Bob has been terribly busy rehearsing for this play 'Tony Draws a Horse' to be produced next week. This time they had afternoon rehearsals on account of the petrol ration. We heard over the wireless yesterday even 'Green line Buses' and cheap day tickets were to be stopped. A number of girls were supposed to be shortly going from here to do war work. Some had even given up their jobs and now they were told yesterday none were to go until they were qualified for some special job. Poor old Prince, it has been terrible to see him the last few days. He got his tongue very badly cut and could not lap. It was pitiful to see him look at the water then look up to me in a pleading way. Anyway he is all right again. Then a few weeks ago Tinker for some unknown reason developed hysteria. Anyway the vet gave him some Vit. B tables and I hope he has got over it. We have gone back to normal time again, I must say I did like the long afternoon although at the end the mornings were terribly dark.

Well darling, this is a wretched letter and I should not have inflicted you with all of this, but you know I can always "chat" to you as if you were my own age. I am longing to tell Doll and chat to her. Many thanks for my share in Grannie's and my letter. There is a mannequin parade at the Marine for War Funds on Saturday night I am trying to arrange to go with Hilda Challenor even if we have to hire. Very best love Darling, Yours as always, Gwen. M. King

Bunny Darling,

I was so sorry afterwards that I had written you such a miserable letter. It was very selfish of me, but I was so completely knocked out at first I did feel like that. I was so thankful I knew of it a few weeks before it was announced, as it gave one time to collect myself. I did not sound at all pleased, but it was not that a bit, I was feeling it from my selfish point of view what my life here will be without him. I really am very very pleased and the more I see of her the more I like her and she is so sweet to me. So do forgive me dear, yet my heart does ache when I think of you. Anyway this is your birthday letter, not to be a miserable one. This may get there in pretty good time and I am enclosing Pam's and asking you to forward it to her for me. Her birthday is on 17th. Very very many happy returns of 21st and we will be thinking of you. It is almost impossible to send anything now but later I hope we may be able to send some jam. Well! The next excitement is that I have bought a little 2nd hand Morris 8. I had not intended to get it until Bob was married but this was going now and with practically new tyres so we thought it best to get it at once. It is shabby so I am going to have it put in thorough order at once. It was a necessity after he was married, because with my cash we can go nowhere and I would not have been able to get my work at all. I see in today's paper no taxis after 5 pm so it is just as well I got it at once, as if he is not coming home to dinner and I am in town I used to take a taxi. Oh! I am sitting writing at my table with very few clothes on (I have just come up from tea) and I am bathed in perspiration. Do you remember Sam Lords Castle, above The Crane? It has been turned into a very modern up to date hotel. As a very special treat, Bob, Betty and I spent last week there. It is a marvellous spot, every comfort you can imagine. It is expensive but you get what you pay for. I would love Mother and Daddy to go there for a change but you know how conservative Mother is. As I tell them we go to England and spend 1000s of £s so they could quite well go there a bit, but No!! We are all going to the Old Crane on 6th November for a week. Mother is looking terrible and as I told the Old Man if she did not get a change one would have a breakdown. I had hoped she would go for 2 weeks, but must be thankful for small mercies. 'Tony draws a Horse' was a great success, they certainly did it splendidly, and Mr. Wood knows how to get the best out of them. When you write, or send it by Pam, please tell me exactly how to address Hugh's parcel as I do not want Rhoda to pay duty and if it is addressed to him c/o her I think it is duty free. There are 2 pairs of socks and Grannie's scarf. Do you remember Esmée Archer? Her brother has got the DFC. Johnnie is returning to England at the end of the month so Audrie will be coming back here as she can't get over with him. I suppose you heard over the wireless that we had the War at our doors. More I cannot say. It gives one a peculiar feeling in this quiet peaceful spot, not fear I can't explain it. We went to see Pinocchio the other afternoon; I liked it better than Snow White. We are going to see Green was my Valley tonight. Grannie is writing too. Darling please do not call me Mrs King, it sounds to formal. I had always hoped it would be Mum one day, but as it can't be that please call me Gwen or anything you fancy.

Very fond love and every good wish for 21st.
Yours as ever, Gwen.

My dearest Bunny,

I am sending a few lines to wish you very many happy returns of the 21st and I wish I could have sent you a parcel but all the things we used to send are now forbidden, in fact we haven't got them, but I am going to send you some jelly or marmalade, as soon as I get some boiled. We can send anything we make and sugar (only 2lbs) but nothing else. Things are getting scarce here now; there is nothing to bring them down of course. The mails to England are very few and far between, and of course we don't know (some people do tho') when they are going, so just take a chance. Well, my dear, I wonder if you were surprised at Bob's news. I saw it coming, but his Mother told me, it lurched her all of a heap. I told her I didn't know where her eyes were, but I think she had so made up her mind it was to be you, that that was the reason. The Old Man and I had both set our hearts on you, but I saw it was not to be, so I was not surprised, but my dear, you will always be the same to us, I don't care who you marry. Somehow I don't think you would have ever cared for the life out here, or I try to console myself with that, but other English women come out and settle down and are very happy. However, Betty seems a very nice girl, and certainly very capable, so I trust and sincerely hope they may be very happy. Her mother died very suddenly a little over two years ago, and she has had to run her Father's house ever since, she hadn't even left school when her Mother died. We are having a good share of heat this year, even now, it is intense and makes one feel worn out. We haven't had a great deal of rain so far and that is the reason. For the last few days we have had very threatening clouds, but no rain. I have been living in dread ? terror of a thunderstorm like we had last year. This three successive years of hot weather, without been able to get away has taken it out of me. Well, I have lost flesh very well, but I feel quite well but don't say anything about this in any of your letters, as the family only fusses. I have had a lot of trouble with my eyes, missing their trip to England and at present am in Dr Gibbon's hands. I am getting a cataract on the left eye, but still can see out of it quite fairly well. Then the right eye got infected somehow and the duct is all wrong and Gibbons would very much like to remove it, but I am not going to do that. The sight in that eye is quite good, but I have to put drops in it all the time. Then last, but by no means least, the servants have been making me see the devil again. Remember that good parlour maid I told you about, well that brute Reece all but succeeded in putting her off her head. I dismissed Reece at once, but the damage was done, and the other woman had to go too, she wasn't able to carry on. Such a pity as she was an excellent servant, feeble minded, but one of the best I have had here for some time. I have got one, but she is very slow and not at all interested in her work and not very willing. They are a sickening lot and get worse and worse all the time. We hope to go off to The Crane for a few days in November; I don't like leaving home in these stormy months. Pam has gone to the Bart's training school at Northwood, for six weeks, so she won't go to the hospital proper before Nov. That forestry work did her lots of good and she enjoyed it too I think, it was such healthy work. My little (as I call her) Elizabeth is terribly busy this term working for her school cert in Dec. I do hope she will do well; she has worked the whole holidays for it and deserves to do well. Kitty is still up to her eyes in work, everyone is trying to make money for all the different war funds, and believe me, one wonders where the money comes from. Now my dear, I must stop, as it's nearly bedtime.

With heaps of love and every good wish from the Old Man and myself.

I am ever your loving Grannie (as was to you)

Lanton

Sunday Evening 1st November 1942

Bunny Darling,

I hate to have to send you more bad news but this evening we were rung up by the Police Station with a message from The Admiralty to say that our beloved has been killed in action. I feel I must tell you before anyone else, but I don't know where you are – so I had better send it to Cara, and she can find out and re-address it. I know how dreadfully you will feel this awful loss to us all darling. We had several air mails, photos and a letter lately, and one long cheery one from Durban – so like his happy old nonsense. We think he was in the Med again as he expected to see Paddy soon – Budgie's husband. He was told that he would get his own Command in about 2 months time – he'd have got it poor darling boy. My head is well nigh bursting. Good night darling-one.

From your Auntie Lil

Do tell one how Gilly is when you write, and where you are, and your address. There are so few to write to now-a-days and I like to hear what you are doing and to keep in touch. I hope you like your work if you have started it.

Lieutenant Francis Anthony Blair Fasson RN GC

Dead Narvik hero wins George Cross

George Crosses have been awarded posthumously to Lieutenant Anthony B. Fasson, R.N., of Lanton Tower, Jedburgh, who was mentioned in despatches for his services at Narvik, and Able Seaman Colin Grazier.

Lieutenant Fasson's father said last night: "We know about the action which won our son the George Cross, but we are not at liberty to tell you about it."

LIEUT. F. A. B. FASSON, G.C., R.N.
The George Cross, posthumously awarded to Lieut. Fasson, was recently received by his parents at an Investiture held by H.M. the King at Buckingham Palace. Lieut. Fasson's exploit has not yet been made public, as he died while carrying out secret duties. He had been in the Royal Navy for sixteen years.

Lt Anthony Fasson RN killed in action

I imagine only a month or two after receiving the letters from Barbados, and having lost her mother exactly a year before, to receive the news that on the Friday 30th October 1942 her beloved cousin, Tony, had been killed in action must have been absolutely devastating. It was learnt much later that his ship, HMS Petard, had sailed from Port Said and joined a submarine search operation about 70 miles north of the Nile Delta. There was a 10-hour attack dropping depth charges as the German U-boat 559 was known to be in the vicinity having been spotted by a RAF Wellesley aircraft of 47 Squadron. When the U-boat crew abandoned ship, a boat was launched with a boarding party and Tony and Able Seaman Grazier swam naked to the U-boat and retrieved papers and two vital code books from the captain's cabin. These were passed to Tommy Brown, a NAAFI canteen assistant, holding onto the conning tower. They went back to try and extract equipment and the enigma machine but, tragically, the U-boat went down suddenly with Tony and Able Seaman Grazier still on board. They were both postumously awarded the George Cross for conspicuous gallantry.

I have tried to acquire images of the actual two vital code books obtained from U-559, the Kurzignalheft, the Short Signal Book and the Wetterkurzschlusse, the Short Weather Cypher but I have checked with Bletchley Park, GCHQ, National Archives, Imperial War Museum, Edinburgh Castle and others and no trace of them can be found. GCHQ are of the opinion that the collection "...was ruthlessly pruned at the end of the war - only those that had value as cryptanalytic training material were retained. I'm afraid they no longer exist in our collection and suspect they have been destroyed." They were

Frank, Lil and Sheena collecting Tony's George Cross

printed with red ink on blotting paper so that should an attack be imminent they were to have been thrown in a bucket of water and therefore rendered useless. Having scuttled the submarine the Germans probably were not expecting derring-do sailors to jump in through the conning tower and retrieve them. The images below are very similar to those that Tony would have picked up.

Although German Intelligence remained convinced that Enigma was unbreakable, Bletchley Park had managed to break the code with a Werftschlussel providing a crib for Alan Turing's Bombes. A German Admiral was suspicious that submarine results were poor and a new 4 rotor enigma machine was introduced with new code books in February 1942. Bletchley immediately lost their ability to read submarine signals and remained unable to decrypt any traffic until the arrival of the code books from U-559. They arrived via Palestine at Bletchley Park (Hut 8) on 24th November, and this enabled enemy encrypted signal traffic to be read from mid-December, allowing code breakers back into Shark, the German submarine coded messages. As a result, Allied convoy traffic could be diverted away from known U-Boat activity during the sea battles in the Atlantic during 1943 saving the lives of thousands of seamen.

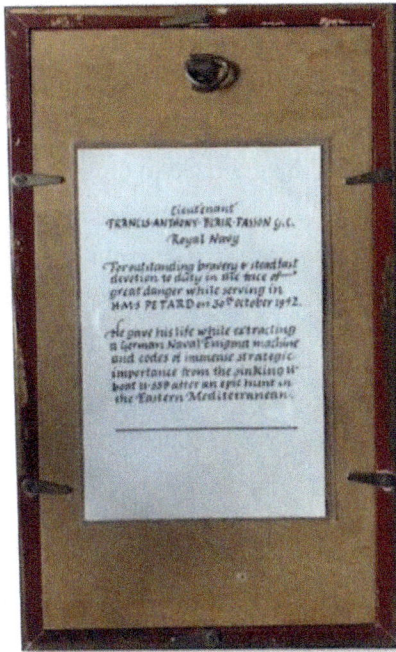

© Roderick d'Anyers Willis

Kurzignalheft, Short Signal Book

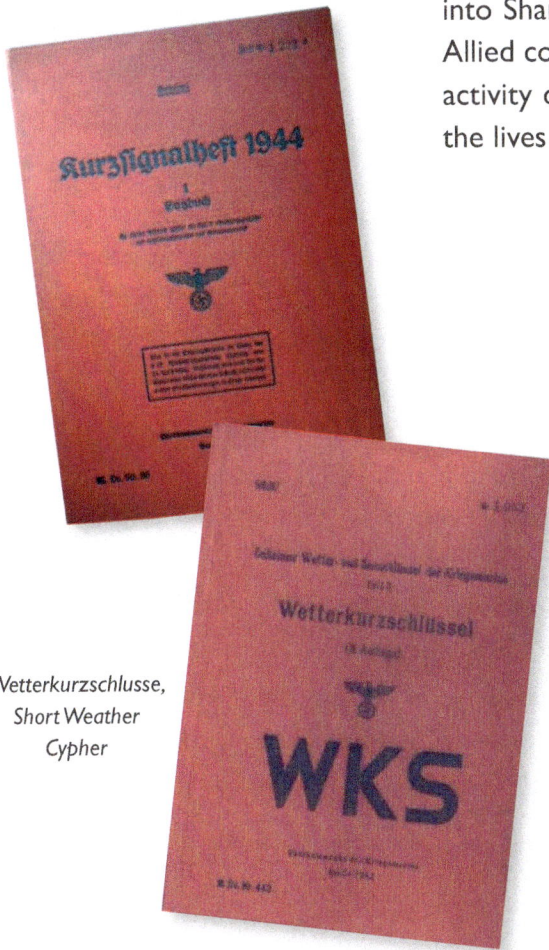

Wetterkurzschlusse, Short Weather Cypher

© Used by kind permission of Cipher Machines and Cryptology

A four-rotor enigma machine similar to that on U559 which was not recovered.
By LukaszKatlewa - Own work, CC BY-SA 3.0, https://commons.wikimedia.org/w/index. php?curid=64805658

In a letter to Sheena Fasson, copied to Bunny, Ralph Erskine wrote:-

"… No similar captures were made by any of the Allied navies until U505, by the US Navy in June 1944. It is therefore impossible to overemphasise the impact of the bravery shown by your brother, Colin Grazier and Tommy Brown. Their efforts almost certainly shortened the war by at least one year. All the countries involved in the war, on both sides, therefore owe them an immeasurable debt". In a note that Erskine sent to Tony's George Cross file in the Imperial War Museum he said "…If Shark had not been penetrated, the Allies would almost certainly not have established naval supremacy in the Atlantic until the second half of 1943 at the earliest – so delaying the invasion of Europe until 1945. Few acts of courage by three individuals can ever have had so far-reaching consequences. …".

There is a whole room (when I visited several years ago) dedicated to Tony at Bletchley Park.

This tragic event was depicted in The Hornet comic in 1969, somehow breaking the code of silence that surrounded the total secrecy of Bletchley Park. Bunny had faithfully kept a copy. More recently there have been a number of films and books describing the Enigma story.

Sub Lieutenant Gordon Connell, the Petard's 25-year-old Gunnery Control Officer, (see "Fighting Destroyers" GG Connell 1976) wrote in his book that he was about to attempt boarding the U-boat when Tony appeared, already stripping off his clothing and boots, and ordered the GCO aft to complete the task of lowering the whaler while he and Colin Grazier dived naked into the sea, so saving the life of the GCO, a married man.

Nearly 70 years later, in 2008, Gordon Connell's grandson, Dan Davies, was discussing his family with his then girlfriend. He recounted the whole story, and how his grandfather decided to write his first book after his chance discovery of Tony's memorial in Jedburgh. What Dan did not know was that he was telling this story to Tony's great niece, (his sister's granddaughter), who already knew it. It was hardly surprising that this was the moment that Iona d'Anyers Willis, my cousin Roderick's daughter, felt that fate and destiny had hit her in one fell swoop; she and Dan married in 2012 and now have three children.

Tony's midshipman journals dated 1930-33 (when he first joined the Navy at the age of 17) have only recently surfaced in a box sold by house clearance at auction in March 2022. No one seems to know where they came from. I managed to contact the buyer who allowed me to see the journals along with an early 1900s photo album and some family papers. My Scottish cousins are immensely grateful to him for the family papers – a good swap with some port was arranged! My thanks to Philip and Stephen Luff for allowing me to publish some of the artworks.

The journals contain a daily record of Tony's activities onboard the various ships he served in, numerous technical sketches, cartoons and very competent artwork, some of which are reproduced throughout this book. It was an immense tragedy to lose him so early in a life which was so full of promise.

CONTINUED FROM FRONT PAGE

Depth charges probed the sea

The submarine was forced to the surface and the guns opened up.

A HIT! WE'VE HOLED HIM!

The German crew was taken off and H.M.S. Petard came alongside the doomed submarine.

IT'S A CHANCE IN A MILLION TO GRAB ITS SECRET PAPERS AND DOCUMENTS. THE ADMIRALTY WOULD BE TICKLED PINK. BUT THE U-BOAT IS ALREADY SINKING.

I'LL GO AND GRAB WHAT I CAN, SIR. TWO OF US WILL BE ENOUGH IF I CAN GET A VOLUNTEER.

Lieutenant Tony Fasson found his volunteer in Able Seaman Colin Grazier.

DON'T STAY DOWN TOO LONG, TONY, SHE'S SHIPPING WATER FAST.

AYE, AYE, SIR.

GRAB WHAT INSTRUMENTS YOU CAN, I'LL FIND THE CAPTAIN'S CABIN. THE IMPORTANT PAPERS WILL BE THERE.

HERE, TAKE THESE UP AND HAND THEM OVER, THEN COME BACK FOR MORE. THEY HAVEN'T DESTROYED A THING.

RIGHT, SIR. GOSH, THIS WATER'S RISING FAST NOW.

THE SKIPPER SAYS TO WATCH IT, SIR!

I KNOW, BUT THIS PLACE IS A GOLDMINE OF SECRET DOCUMENTS. WE'VE JUST GOT TO GET THEM OUT.

Now the U-boat was lying very low in the water.

TONY, TIME'S RUNNING OUT.

JUST ONCE MORE, SIR. THEN WE'LL HAVE GOT THE LOT.

But one more time was once too many!

SIR! YOU'VE GOT TO GET OUT, IT'S SINKING FAST!

QUICK! HIT THE LADDER...

They were just too late. The sea wolf had given up many secrets, but it had cost the lives of two brave men. In September 1943, posthumous George Crosses were awarded to Lieutenant Fasson and A.B. Grazier for their heroism.

THEY'VE GONE. TWO OF MY BEST MEN, MEN WHO JUST WOULDN'T GIVE UP, NO MATTER WHAT THE DANGER WAS.

NEXT WEEK—The thrilling story of the front-line hero who didn't fight!

Printed and Published in Great Britain by D. C. THOMSON & Co., Ltd., 12 Fetter Lane, Fleet Street, London, E.C.4.
© D. C. THOMSON & CO., LTD., 1969.

Two months after Tony's death, Bunny joined the WRNS on 2nd December 1942 as a Wren Trainee Motor Transport (MT) Driver at HMS Pembroke. On 24th December she was posted to HMS Armadillo, Ardentinny, Argyll & Bute, on the western shore of Loch Long, Scotland. In the blackout she had to take a train up to Scotland on New Year's Eve.

Glenfinart House was requisitioned during the war and designated HMS Armadillo.

Bunny on Loch Long wearing Jim Fasson's regimental brooch

Bunny second left

1943

January: Bob King and Betty Yearwood were married.

September: Although they had not met at this stage, my father, who was a prisoner of war in Fontanellato Italy, was let out of the prison, when Mussolini was deposed, and spent 2 months on the run before being captured by the Germans and sent by rail to Moravia, Germany.

1944

Bunny was awarded 3 War service chevrons March 1944 and mentioned in despatches for bravery during a fire at Ardentinny (ammunitions went off in the boat) when she helped save and nurse victims of the fire throughout the night.

She was later transferred to Submarine HQ in London and, as an MT driver, drove the Admirals involved in the sinking of the German battleship Tirpitz (sister ship to the Bismarck) to report back to Submarine HQ and The Admiralty. During this time Bunny shared a flat with Sheena Fasson at Northfield Flats in Swiss Cottage.

Bunny's Father, Gilbert West, dies. He had been ill for some time and had moved into Wood Cottage with his brother Temple, and two sisters Mary and Laura who had previously run a small prep school together where Temple taught, Mary catered and Laura was matron. There are no letters kept from this period.

1943 16-17 May Dambusters Raid - 617 Squadron drop Barnes Wallis's bouncing bombs to breach Ruhr Valley dams. July/September Allied invasion of Sicily then Italy starts. December Colossus computer at Dollis Hill completed to assist cryptanalysis at Bletchley Park.

1944 6th June D-Day landings: Western Allies land on the beaches of Normandy in Northern France. Battle of the Bulge begins. Germans develop the V2 missile. Establishment of United Nations proposed.

3rd January 1945 - 27th September appointed to HMS Pembroke.

Life took a turn for the better in 1945. Bunny was introduced to Clifford Charles (Bill) Bass by Tommy Langton. Tommy was an old family friend of the West family and knew Bill through rowing. They met at drinks with Bud and Cherry Mitchell at 15 Stanhope Gardens.

Clifford Charles Bass M.C. T.D. joined The Rifle Brigade, The Royal Green Jackets Regiment, as a TA Volunteer in June 1939. He was captured in the Western Desert at Acca Agedabia, Libya on 3rd April 1941 and taken to Italy as a Prisoner of War. He spent time in Sulmona, Montalbo and 6 months in Fontanellato.

On 8th September 1943, after the Italian Armistice, the camp of some 600 men 'walked out' of the Fontanellato camp through the wire behind the building. He was hidden in a hut by a wonderful family in the village of Spiaggere, in the hills above Parma, with Larry Holroyd. They were re-captured in November 1943 and transported to Oflag VIII F, Moravia and then transferred in May 1944 to Oflag 79 Brunswick, Germany. He was eventually liberated by the Americans on the 12th April 1945 after 4 years as a prisoner of war and returned home. In 1949 he went back to Spiaggere with Bunny to thank Luigi Franchi and his family for looking after them.

1945 CCB shortly after release from POW

1949 CCB outside the hut in Spiaggere

1945 Churchill, Roosevelt and Stalin plan the final defeat of Germany. 12th April Roosevelt dies and Harry S. Truman becomes president. 30th April Hitler commits suicide. 8th May VE Day Victory in Europe – formal acceptance of German surrender. UN is established. 6th and 9th August Atomic bombings of Hiroshima and Nagasaki; 15th August Japan surrendered. 2nd September World War II officially ends. The Holocaust – under the Nazi regime the systematic extermination of 11-17 million (including Jews, Poles, Russians, prisoners of war, those disabled, gay etc). Benjamin Britten's Peter Grimes premieres in London, seen as the rebirth of British opera.

As I said previously, Bunny kept everything! Even the note that CCB had phoned for the first time.

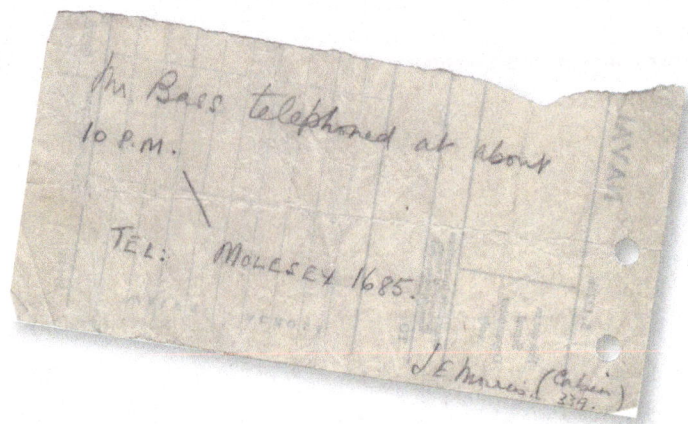

The Yews
Church Street Hampton
Middx Molesey 1685
23rd May 1945

Joanna My Dear,

I doubt whether it will be worthwhile writing to you from Roughs Fort, so am doing so before I leave. I shall be back on Monday next and will phone you. If you can manage to get Tuesday off, would you care to meet me, this time I will try and be a little better organised as to booking tables etc.

I failed to get to the Langton's on Sunday or Monday as I lost my petrol Coupons. Have since found them lurking under the front seat of the car - but had a word with Uncle Leslie *[Langton, Tom's father]* who asked after you. I reported fully on you and stated I had great difficulty on keeping you to the straight and narrow, but was doing my best, must finish now as Dad is asking too many questions. So, till next Tuesday I hope.

Be good, Best love, Clifford.

The Yews
Church Street Hampton
Middx Molesey 1685
City 30th

Joanna Dear,

The forms for the insurance of your car. If you let me have the particulars, I can get you a cover note at once. I will phone tomorrow as promised so have your logbook handy.

My sweet, you should be slapped for giving me those most expensive cigarettes, they are lovely, Dad wants to know where you got them! I had another surprise early this morning, when I got home, another present from the Old Man – a very pleasant sized cheame *[I think he must mean a chamois - spelling was never his strong point!]*

After three hours in bed am still feeling grand. Love Clifford

p.s. later. Licence forms. Definite relapse setting in. Love C xxx

In the first months of freedom CCB's main job was to bring back into service Bunny's beloved Sunbeam Talbot (named Anna) which had been in mothballs during the War.

My Very Own Darlingest,

It seems fairly clear that I shall be through by Wed evening. I have given the flat address to make sure I shall finish at Olympia – I do hope Mrs Seaman doesn't mind.

This is a complete waste of two days, so far have had a form filled up, and a mild medical, the whole taking about an hour. Tomorrow, we have a parade to allow the Col. to say a few well chosen words to us. This place is so bloody cold and misé. I cannot get away soon enough.

The big day will be fairly long we start for York at 0715 and should finish in London by 1800 hrs so expect me fairly soon after that. Laden of course with masses of the best civvy kit. So until then my very own be good and love me lots.

Yours C

Would like to pop down to the Old Bell for an egg sandwich but there is NO TRANSPORT

Wed Night

My Very Own Poppet,

As I am not very sleepy at the moment so I thought I would just write a short note to wish you a happy holiday.

I enclose also £1 to settle my just debts as per att. a/c and my addresses just in case you have a moment just to send one line to let me know "how much" = I will send you a long xx at 2300 every night, so spare me a thought then. Darlingist, do have a lovely time, enjoy yourself and take care of yourself,
All my love, yours ever, Clifford

In account with Miss Joanna West,
Wren also the VOSPP of CCB

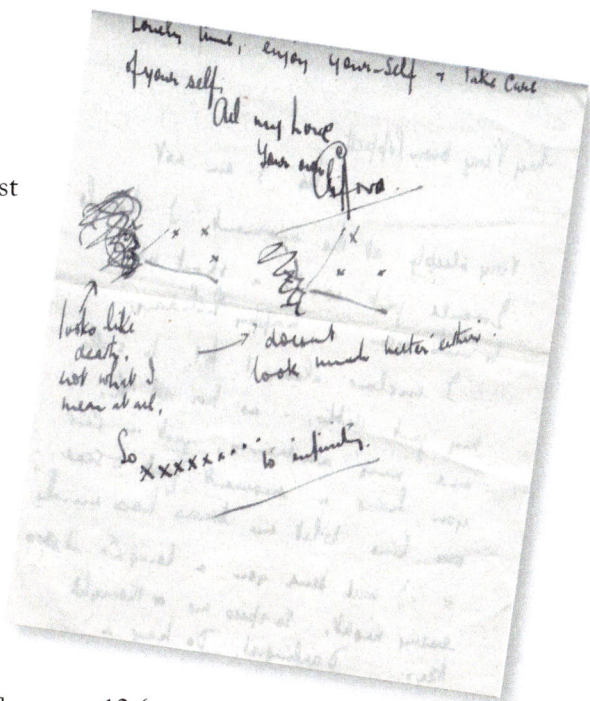

Dr	100 Churchman supplied to Aunt M [Mildred Langton]	12.6
Dr	Untold quantities of soap and other [..?]	4.6
Dr	2 Toffee apples to be supplied to as present	.3
	Unknown miners at R.H.Bay [Robin Hood Bay, Yorks]	
Dr	In case Telegram's are sent	2.6
Dr	To be spent separately only in case of urgent necessity …	.3
		20/-

My very own Darling Poppet,

Have just spoken to Mike Edwards and have arranged to go to Retford on Tuesday for lunch – stopping about two days. So will be leaving fairly early in the morning.   Anna *[Bunny's sunbeam alpine]* is panting to leave as soon as possible, but I told her she must be patient as she has to have clean rompers and a clean face before she sees you.

Spent a very busy afternoon yesterday with Dad, seeking and buying furniture, so hope by the time you return the little room will be ready for use.

I went to bed last night at 9.30 full of white pills; most effective, I slept for about 10 hours!!   My Darling, I do hope the journey wasn't too lousy and now you are having a lovely time. Do take care of yourself and if it's a bit chilly don't rely on locknit, but use woollens – good thick jobs!! I know what those winds are like off the moors they simply get everywhere.

Please convey my good wishes to the most accommodating Sister; have you given my two new nieces the toffee apples yet! And to you Darlingist a very tight hug (a 5 min job) and all my love, yours C

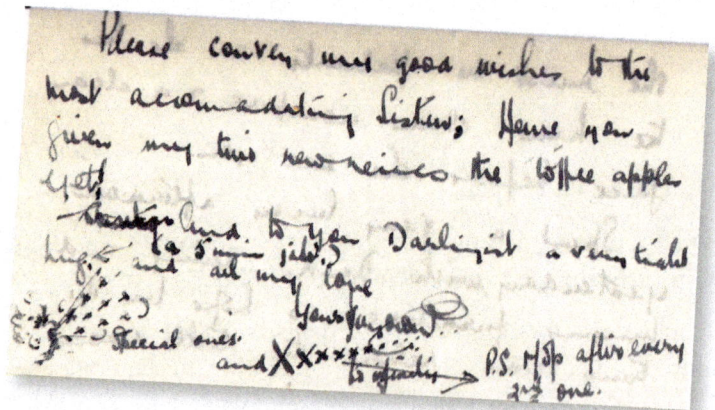

Friday 2300 hrs
In bed

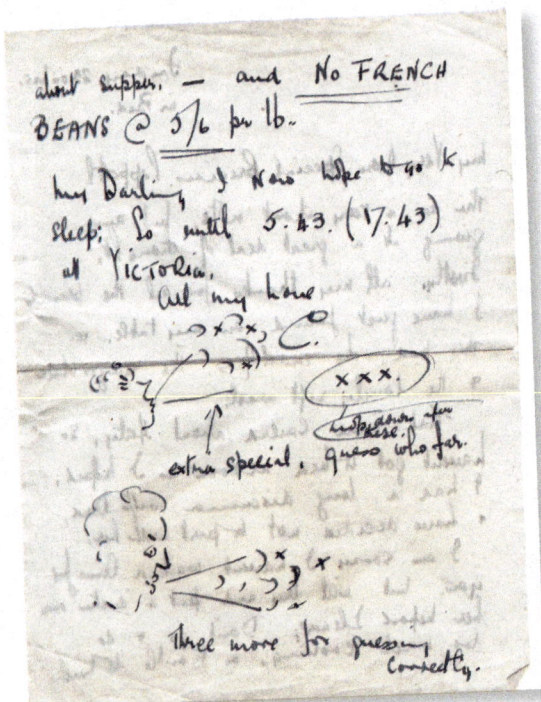

My Very Own Special Precious Poppet!!

This is a very short note, just am giving it a great deal of thought. Firstly, all my thanks for all the presents I have just found on my table. i.e. this pad, the envelopes, the razor blade and the lovely soft wool.

That man called about Hetty, so haven't got to bed as soon as I hoped. I had a long discussion with Dad, and have decided not to part with her.

I am sorry I haven't washed Anna for you but will try and put a duster over her before I leave; Don't go and do too much cooking, or trouble too much about supper – and NO FRENCH BEANS @ 5/6 per lb.

My Darling I now hope to go to sleep; so until 5.43 (1743) at Victoria. All my love. C

Taken in the Warwick Road flat CCB just demobbed and got engaged

The Yews, Church Street,
Hampton, Middx
Molesey 1685

Monday D3

My Very Own Precious Poppet,

No letter/not even a telegram!! What have you been up too? I took Anna round to the garage this morning to be prepared, and when I told her she positively snorted. Hetty overheard, and refused to start. So had to have her towed again; I missed you.

Am in rather poor way this morning. I played squash yesterday with Mick, I stubbed my toe, - also Mick drove the ball as hard as he could straight into my ear; now the size of a very large cabbage and I am so stiff I can hardly walk.

However, tomorrow morning very early being D4 (it being four long days since I have seen you) little Anna and I will start the trek north until there is not that much "ll" between us; so until then Darlingest, All my love Yours C

Bill and Larry Holroyd were asked up to Scotland to join Derek d'Anyers Willis and his family for a weeks shooting (post-war recouperation) at Druminnor, north east of Aberdeen, Scotland.   Derek and Larry were CCB's best friends from POW – Derek's Brother Guy then met and married Sheena Fasson, Bunny's first cousin.

Druminnor
Wednesday 22nd (August)

My Very Own Darling Poppet,

Firstly, as ever I love you. 2nd I arrived quite safely after not too bad a journey. I, of course, failed to get out at the right station, not entirely my fault, as the bit of the train I was in didn't pull into the station, so passed

191

gaily through waving madly to Derek who was there to meet me. However, I tumbled out at the next station where D soon arrived, and all was well.

The house we are staying in is very pleasant, and the party good fun. D's mother and father (step-mother - aunts young and good looking) and young step-sister, and Larry Holroyd.

Directly after lunch we rallied forth to the moor and walked miles, my poor "old plates" thought I had gone quite mad. However, I managed to break my duck fairly early, and finished the day with a brace and one rabbit; the total bag for the 3 of us was 2 brace, 3 hares and 3 rabbits. So didn't let your Pop's gun down. It was a lovely thing to handle Darling, I cannot thank you enough. It has now been cleaned and kissed goodnight - till tomorrow when I hope we can keep up the same standard with driven birds which I feel will be rather a different cup of tea.

My sweet, I do wish you were here with me because I miss you so already and I know you would love it so, it is the most lovely country - the first thing I did was to pick you some heather which I shall enclose with this, must finish now, more tomorrow. So goodnight Darlingist, all my love xxx xxx xxx

Druminnor
Rhynie
23rd

My V.O.S.P,

Last night's note was written in bed by candle light. Please excuse. Further news nil, except Derek knows of a flat which might interest us. 1. At 20 Albion Street (area Marble Arch) – consists of 6 rooms (on three floors) 2 bathrooms. 1 kitchen and 1 Lav: 3 years lease £675.

D considers that is possible to sub let Top rooms, but the snag is only having one lav: however would you care to ring Derek's sister who would give you full particulars. Name and address as follows: Mrs WATTS, c/o Romney Court, Shepherds Bush, W12. Phone Park 9636 any evening. Derek is letting his sister know that you will be phoning.

We are just off to see the local Tweed Factory. Will collect patterns and details in case we require anything. Cannot buy as came with no coupons and no cheque book. Will be shooting again after lunch.

Hope you are well, happy and love me, How much?

All my love to you my sweet, Yours only Bill

Druminnor
Wed. Thursday @ 0004

My Very Own Darlingest,

I am rather late going to bed tonight, so you must excuse this being rather short. D and I went down to the village this evening, and had a drink with the local Dr. Two strong ales, made us rather talkative on our return so have only just got to bed.

Your two long letters arrived this morning, thank you my Poppet. I'm very sorry that charming little house is almost sold – so cheap too! – perhaps it is as well that you didn't increase the bid to get it. Ref my return on Saturday, much as I should love to see you at Kings X, I won't expect you. I hope Mary [West] will be able to cope when I turn up.

I will phone directly I reach London. I have written to Dad, telling him to expect me Saturday or Sunday and I will phone details when I arrive. So make what arrangements you like for sat: - we can talk it over anyway: it will only take the odd 5 mins, so perhaps I had better be prepared to spend the night.

When you arrive at the flat don't be surprised to find me in bed – as I leave here on the 3.10 and sleepers are off. I didn't produce your card – which was lovely – all over the breakfast table – I've had letters from you before.

Darlingest, I can't think of anything else except that in two days it will be Sat. And I shall see you, and will hold you so tight you will really know I am back. So, till then my sweet all my love, and simply masses and masses. Yours B

reams of these   (kisses)

P.S. what would you like me to bring you from Scotland?
Will think of a surprise

P.P.S I have thought of it, I hope I can get it. In case I don't please don't be disappointed.
Also tell Smudge, I don't think she has a nice mind.

Druminnor
Thursday night

My Very Own Darlingist,

As my candle is burning brightly I thought I would spend a moment writing a few words to you, perhaps two letters in one day is a little much, but I doubt if this will be posted before Sat - I don't think it will matter. We drove into Inch this morning and spent most of the time in The Tweed Shop, (Russells).

Thank God I had no coupons and no cheque book, but I managed to collect some patterns which I hope you will like; aided by the Willis family who were most helpful. In the afternoon we tried for some duck, without success. But managed to retrieve the day by getting 7 pigeon in the evening as I got 4 of them. You can take it the gun is doing well without much help from me; so it had an extra rub, and a double ration of oil for dinner.

I forgot to mention I bought a 7lb bag of oatmeal for you this morning!

Are you very lonely my sweet with no one to take care of you. I seem to have been away ages already and there are still 4 more days before I shall see you again. All my love Poppet, take care of yourself.
Lots of kisses, all round the clock, so goodnight
Bill xxxx

Druminnor

Friday night

My Very Own Darlingist,

I am writing this from bed as am just about out, and simply bulging with food – I surprise myself the amount I eat.

Your letter arrived this morning, my sweet, it did sound rather misé. How I wish you had come with me and how much I wish you were here. Heaven knows what would happen if you were here, as I am so bursting with rude health – eggs are not in it.

We had a driving day today, but with a gale of wind, the few birds that did come over, passed by like V1s or jet propelled jobs, however I managed to get the only Blackcock, and the odd hare, plus a great deal of excerrize exercise – I do wish I could spell. There is a Golf Match on Sunday – Derek is teaching me to play in the spare few minutes we have, am doing quite well, at present, mainly I think, as I haven't been allowed a ball yet. I think it will be quite funny. Bed calls, lonely as it is. Darling all my love, Tons of xxxx mop and repeat.

Yours ever,

Bill

Druminnor

Saturday night (25th)

My Very Own Darlingist,

Your delightfully long letter, written Thursday received today. Am rather glad you have missed me a little as I have missed you so much. Your letter made me ever more homesick, lovesick, than ever, and I can assure you not at all due to the two hard boiled eggs I had for lunch.

We had another fairly hard day to day, without much success, the gale still continued making the shooting too difficult anyway for me, added to this it was very cold waiting in the butts for something to happen, which, more often than not, didn't.

I find the news in the paper to-day rather dreary, especially with reference to petrol; It doesn't look as though there is going to be much future in that direction for some time to come; I shall see Fred B as soon as I get back in the hopes he might find me something to do; and at least see what he thinks about things.

I hope you are going to be free at least part of next weekend you will find me in the flat Saturday morning if I don't find you there; I failed to get a sleeper for the return journey. The local Dr here is going to see what he can do for me, but the situation looks ugly. I could face a cattle truck again as long as you will be there at the end, so don't care a lot.

Must finish now as I can hardly keep my eyes open. Be good and take great care of yourself my Poppet, because who's very special Poppet are you?

Darling, all my love, Yours ever, B.

My Very Own Darlingist,

I have just written a note to Ron, would you please check for spelling mistakes etc and please forward. I hope it will do – what does one say on these occasions? It cost me about most of the pad, and 10 cigs, till I got bored and just dashed something off.

We went over to Ballater today for lunch and played Golf, a most shaky performance. Derek and I played D's step-mum and Larry – need I mention we lost. They were all so kind the way they looked for the balls – when I managed to connect. We took the dog who was a great help; it was all good clean fun, but don't think it is a game I shall take up unless I have to!

Only a week to next Saturday, 7 days – 168 hours, they won't tick round quick enough. I shall not go through this again unless it is vital. How much my sweet? I do wish you were here; then you could tell me, Darling all my love, the tightest of hugs and (kisses) and so on for hours. Take care of yourself, until I can look after you. Yours B

Quite possibly they were virtually engaged just before CCB went up to Scotland – as Bunny's parents had both died, CCB must have been writing to eldest Brother Ronny for her hand in marriage.

My Very Own Poppet,

Very little to tell since my letter of last night – I hope you realize that I have written every day, even if two days mail has gone in one envelope.

We had a very good day today, much less wind, and quite hot, not many birds about, but those that were a little easier to shoot at.

Had my best bag so far 1 ½ brace 3 hares and another Blackcock; the latter was a younger bird than the first as rather lacking in tail feathers.

Am eating like two horses here, masses of milk buttered "eggs" – eggs for breakfast and HB for lunch today, so expect to spend a restless night – added to which I've just had a large glass of milk – so I'm pretty certain I shall.

I do hope you are having some successful house and or flat hunting expeditions. Have you been in touch with Derek's sister yet?

I've had a letter from Mike Edwards this morning saying he has passed on my requirements to the right sourgs [sic] sauces No. I cannot spell it, so guess.   [?source]

Must finish now as I can hardly keep my eyes open. In four days time I shall be on my way home and when I wake tomorrow morning, in 4 days time I shall hope to be with you. It seems such ages ago since I said goodbye, just a week, it might be a year – it won't be long now as the B said to the A.

All my love Darlingist, thousands of (kisses) yours B

My Darling Poppet,

This is in the nature of a P.S. as I am suffering from a cigarette crisis. Derek has kindly lent me 100 as they are impossible to get here, could you be an sweet and when you pass through Grosvenor St next send Derek a 100 cigarettes for me. I do hope you are keeping a careful check of what you are spending for me:-

I know 34/- + 5

We went out after pigeon after tea and got wet through again. Larry has gone to bed early with a chill.

The evenings seem very long here, the nights seem longer, with you so far away. It is 3 ½ days now before I shall see you. Till then all my love to you my sweet.
Yours B

p.p.s. Derek is D d' A Willis Esq., c/o Mrs Grant, Druminnor, Rhynie etc

Druminnor
Wed Afternoon

My Own Darlingist,

We have just returned home after a rather wet morning. The first wet day we have had so far; rather misty on the moor and very little to shoot: we seemed to hit most of what there was.

Am now taking it rather steady in front of the fire, as usual have eaten too much lunch, so can hardly keep my eyes open, which no doubt accounts for this page of rather smudgy writing. Which reminds me, I never thanked Smudge for the ½ bottle of gin, will you please convey my apologies for the remission [sic] – can you? Or is she still away. What have you been up too? I haven't heard a word from you since last Thursday, which is 5 days ago. I hope you haven't been getting into mischief.

I think I must finish this and relax. So goodbye my Poppet, until tomorrow, only three more days, and then I shall be on my way home.

All my love, from here to China and back again, two or three times.
Yours B (kisses)

Bunny remained working as a Wren until 28th Sept - Unpaid leave until 9th Nov 1945 and was released finally on 25 January 1946.

My Very Own Darlingist Poppet,

As I have only just arrived the worst is only rumour? Or at least unofficial but I gather that I shall not be back until Wednesday or Thursday.   We leave here Wednesday morning 0715 hours for YORK - death of course. I understand after that we sign bumf etc, and then leave for London, collect bowler hat, and all is such. So prepare to see me Wednesday night - suggest you book table for dinner at The Berkley, if 0600 hrs feels like it, may I stay the night.

Please phone Dad to let him know I shall be home about Thursday. Three days before I see a Girl!! What a frightful time we are having.

All my love, be good, give Boil stick. More and more love. I love you so.

Yours C (kisses)

P.S. Have no more news to add but you might ring Archie if you have a moment (H.B. Nisbet & Co.) and see if he has any news of the contract.

I will come straight to the flat when I am through.   Will also send telegram from York when I leave. All my love and tons and tons of it. How much? Yours C

Clifford Charles Bass (Bill) and Helen Joan West (Bunny) were married on 15th November 1945 at St Michael's Chester Square, reception at 23 Knightsbridge. Bunny left her bouquet behind. With no parents, Aunt Cara West was hostess. The first night of their honeymoon was at The Berkley and then at The Spread Eagle Hotel at Midhurst. Their first home together was The Holt, Wargrave, Henley. The lawn ran down to the river which was a plus, but a minus when it flooded. They had to row down to the lock to collect the furniture that had floated out of the garage. About 9 months after I was born we moved to St John's House, Grange Road, Cambridge now the main house of St John's Choir School.

Clifford Charles Bass born 29th May 1911 died 21st September 1971. My Father was a keen oarsman, rowed for the London Rowing Club, won at Henley in the LRC Eight in1935 and became a member of Leander Club. He then coached Clare and Jesus Cambridge crews in the late '40s and early '50s. He shot and fished regularly, always making his own flies. Pre-war he worked with Bowings Insurance, post war for Regent Oil Co. and then Texaco and was Managing Director of the East of England area when he died aged 60.

Bob King born 13th January 1914 died on 11th June 2002. In 1947 he became Managing Director of the family firm Alleyne Arthur, an import/export company which among other things had the franchise for bottling Coco Cola. In an appreciation of his life Jill Hamilton wrote "… he made his contribution towards bringing corporate Barbados into the modern world of business …" He was always keen on amateur dramatics and an avid orchid grower. He lost his wife Betty in 1997 exactly three weeks before his beloved daughter Sandie also died.

Helen Joan Bass (nee West) born 21st October 1916 died 9th November 2007. My parents just managed to get in their 25th wedding anniversary before my father died. My mother had an enduring love of tennis and everything stopped for Wimbledon. She was a brilliant gardener and cook, always trying something new and interesting.

Sheena Margaret Fasson Sheena Margaret Fasson (born 1917 died aged 99 in September 2016) sister to James and Anthony Fasson. She was both a VAD (Voluntary Aid Detachment) nursing wounded at the Military Hospital in Edinburgh Castle and then a Mobile Red Cross Nurse. She later joined the WRNS and became a Leading Wren MT (Motor Transport) driver to Rear-Admiral Lachlan Mackintosh of Mackintosh. She would have happily married Peter Medd (see letters on page 9 & 10) had he not tragically been killed when his plane crashed in 1944. She later married Guy d'Anyers Willis in December 1947 and they had three children.

Sheena Fasson with Rear Admiral Mackintosh during WWII

ADMIRAL SIR FRANCIS TURNER

Admiral Sir (Arthur) Francis "Attie" Turner, KCB, DSC, a former Chief of Fleet Support, died on October 26 aged 79. He was born on June 23, 1912.

"ATTIE" Turner's most valuable legacy to the Royal Navy was his introduction of planned maintenance for the fleet. Instead of ships simply being repaired when they broke down, components were routinely replaced at pre-planned intervals. By improving the reliability of warships, the system (first applied to naval aircraft) increased the navy's operational capability.

The idea behind it was not Turner's own. But it seemed revolutionary to naval traditionalists at the time and it needed a man of his force and determination to enact it. He also left his mark on naval dockyards by appointing to each a naval base commander. He thus unified the disparate civilian workforce under one authority and strengthened its relationship with the fleet.

Turner's strength lay not so much in his considerable ability as an engineer but in his shrewd judgment and abundant commonsense. The machine he knew best was perhaps that which drove Whitehall. This explains his steady advancement past contemporaries who were technically more brilliant, culminating in his promotion to admiral in 1970.

He thus became the first officer from outside the elitist seaman's branch to reach four star rank, although the way had been clear for one to do so for 14 years following the introduction of the general list in 1956. Admiral of the Fleet Lord Louis Mountbatten, under whom he had served in the Mediterranean, was among those who wrote to congratulate him on his historic achievement.

"Attie" Turner (he did not know himself where the nickname came from) was born in Scotland, the son of an engineer rear-admiral who had fought at Jutland, and was taught at Stoneyhurst College and at Keyham, Devonport, which was where the navy's school of engineering was then based. He was captain of cricket at Keyham and later played for the navy's first XI.

Commissioned in 1931, he began his career as a marine engineer but later switched to aeronautics with the development of the Fleet Air Arm and became one of the navy's first specialists in the field. He later lectured on aeronautical engineering at the Royal Naval Engineering College, Manadon.

During the last two years of the war he served in HMS *Indomitable*, the flagship of the Pacific fleet's carrier task group, and took part in the Okinawa operation. Though desperately short of spare parts and maintenance staff he kept his Avenger and Hellcat aircraft flying and was rewarded by being twice mentioned in dispatches and by winning the Distinguished Service Cross. The citation for his 1945 DSC paid tribute to his "gallantry, skill and great devotion to duty".

After the war he was seconded to Australia to help plan the Australian navy's own fleet air arm. He served in the cruiser *Glasgow* in the Mediterranean, then began a sequence of increasingly senior staff jobs. He was director of aircraft maintenance and planning in the late 1950s, returned to the Mediterranean as chief staff officer (technical) in the early 1960s, and in 1964 found himself back in Britain as director-general of aircraft (naval).

He was in this post from 1964 until 1967, throughout the period of Denis Healey's defence review which in 1966 announced the phasing out of aircraft carriers. Britain would henceforth have a small-ship navy with only helicopters at sea, relying for fixed-wing support on shore-based aircraft. Perhaps fortunately for Turner he moved on next year, before the problems

posed by the government's decision loomed large, and was made chief of naval supplies and transport — a post which was expanded in 1968 into that of chief of fleet support with a seat on the naval board. When he retired in 1971 his fellow members of the board transported him down river in an admiral's barge for a farewell dinner at Greenwich.

"Attie" Turner could be brusque and somewhat formidable to deal with and his humour tended to be on the dry side. But he was also kind and considerate to subordinates and worked well with civilian officials in Whitehall. He was a devout and lifelong Roman Catholic.

He is survived by his wife, Elizabeth, whom he married in 1963, and by their two sons.

Lt. Col. James Fasson became the CO of the 155th Lanarkshire Yeomanry after the Colonel of the regiment was killed in action following the fall of Singapore. He was a POW, held at Kinkaseki and Shirakawa before being sent to Japan and then to Manchuria in 1945. He was later 'Mentioned in Despatches' for his leadership and example during the POW years. Post war he farmed near Kelso in the Borders and was Master of the Field of the Buccleuch Hunt. Born October 1909 died May 1985.

UNSUNG HEROES OF THE BORDERS

TONY FASSON

TONY FASSON (1913-1942)

A descendant of one of Nelsons captains, and truly an unsung hero, Tony Fasson (Jedburgh) helped break the U-Boat stranglehold on Britain in 1942. He did this by capturing information relating to the German Enigma coding machine, whose messages Britain was unable to decode.

Fasson's ship, HMS Petard depth-charged a U-Boat carrying vital information on Enigma, and when the Germans abandoned ship, he did not wait until a boat could be lowered, but led others in

swimming to the U-Boat. They made 3 trips below, retrieving key documents about Enigma, but a further trip proved fatal for Fasson and another shipmate, Grazier, when the submarine sank, costing them their lives.

The subsequent ability of the Allies to crack the code, led to a reversal of the Atlantic war, but to prevent the Germans suspecting the code was broken, Fasson and Grazier were awarded the civilian George Cross instead of the Victoria Cross.

Printed in Great Britain
by Amazon